THE VANISHING NEST EGG

A Twentieth Century Fund Paper

The Vanishing Nest Egg:

Reflections on Saving in America

by
B. Douglas Bernheim

P
P Priority Press Publications/New York/1991

The Twentieth Century Fund is a research foundation undertaking timely analyses of economic, political, and social issues.
Not-for-profit and nonpartisan, the Fund was founded in 1919
and endowed by Edward A. Filene.

Library of Congress Cataloging-in-Publication Data

Bernheim, B. Douglas.
   The vanishing nest egg: reflections on saving in America /
by B. Douglas Bernheim
   p. cm.
   Includes bibliographical references and index.
   ISBN 0-87078-313-0 : $9.95
   1. Saving and investment—United States. 2. Budget deficits—
United States. 3. United States—Economic conditions—1981–
4. United States—Economic policy—1981– I. Title
HC110.S3B47   1991
332'.0415—dc20   91-25273
                                                         CIP

Foreword

Many Americans are uneasy about their country's prospects for economic growth. The sharp increase in public and private debt accumulated during the last decade and the somewhat longer period of relatively slow productivity growth seem to be a weak foundation for optimism about the future.

In the 1950s and 1960s, the median family enjoyed after-tax income growth that averaged about $450 per year (in 1984 dollars). After 1969, median family income growth slowed down. After 1973, it reversed. From 1973 until 1984, real family income fell by about $150 a year. In the late 1980s, the median family recovered most of the ground lost after 1973, but only because more and more family members joined the labor force. Average real weekly earnings (in the nonagricultural private sector) did not recover. They continued to decline in the late 1980s, as they had since 1973. By 1989, an average worker was earning less than in any year since 1961.

While opinion is divided about the proper policy mix to reverse these trends, there is a reasonable but not universal consensus that any solution will include an increase in the national saving rate. Such superficially diverse issues as cutting Social Security taxes and extending the school year essentially involve arguments about the level of saving and investment. The Twentieth Century Fund commissioned B. Douglas Bernheim to write about what is basically the threshold question in this area: What, in fact, has happened to saving rates in the United States?

The result of that effort, this paper, should become the benchmark for analysis of this critical issue. Bernheim marshals his evidence impressively and makes a powerful case for his conclusion: the real decline in national saving has had negative consequences for the nation's economy. He builds upon his experience as an economist to explain many of the forces that shape the current consumption and expenditure practices of institutions and individuals. And, he is willing to step beyond economics to discuss the cultural and other factors that so influence the personal choices involved in forgoing current satisfaction in order to plan for and invest in the future. Policymakers who read and understand the implications of Bernheim's work must take the lead when it comes to this central issue of national growth.

Those who choose to lead, however, will not find the road easy. In America, the media seem to insist that the measure of prosperity is consumer spending. Government expenditures, by contrast, have a rather bad press; they are often described as economically unhealthy alternatives to private purchases. The mass media normally see corporate investment as a local story, as in "XYZ corporation to build new plant." And saving, well, saving is simply not good copy (I mean it just sits there!). Small wonder that our politics produces policies that reflect a preference for consumption.

The first step in solving a problem is recognizing that you have one. Bernheim's paper makes a real contribution to this awareness. We at the Fund thank him for his efforts. His paper exemplifies the kind of contribution to the understanding and discussion of public policy in the United States that the Fund has sought to make for over seventy years.

Richard C. Leone, DIRECTOR
The Twentieth Century Fund
April 1991

Contents

To my grandparents

Acknowledgments

In preparing this manuscript, I relied heavily on the research of many prominent economists. Conversations with Michael Boskin, Laurence Kotlikoff, John Shoven, and Lawrence Summers were particularly helpful. I am especially grateful to Edwin Mills, James Poterba, James Tobin, and staff members of the Twentieth Century Fund for their detailed comments on an earlier draft. I am indebted to Fumio Hayashi, who was kind enough to share some important data based upon his own painstaking calculations. Finally, I would like to thank Adam Wantz and Cheryl Ebben for providing invaluable research assistance.

Introduction

The United States has become a nation of consumers. During the last decade, Americans maintained high standards of living in part by neglecting the need to provide for their collective future. This cannot continue forever. Inadequate rates of saving have begun to threaten the very foundations of economic prosperity. Before the final bill comes due, Congress and the president must take decisive steps to limit excessive national consumption.

This paper provides an overview of saving in America. I sort through a multitude of confusing and even contradictory assertions, as well as the causes and effects, of secular changes in the level of saving with the ultimate objective of formulating a coherent policy response.

The paper begins with a review of the official government figures on saving in the United States. These statistics show that rates of saving have declined precipitously during the 1980s, and are currently much lower than in any other comparable period of our history. The United States also has saved a much smaller fraction of its national income than other industrialized countries throughout the postwar period. Despite clamor over federal budget deficits, low rates of national saving are primarily attributable to behavior in the private sector.

Several revisionist views of U.S. saving are the next subject examined. While some economists argue that the official data are not comparable across countries, others insist that arbitrary accounting conventions result in the exclusion or mismeasurement

1

of certain forms of saving. I defend the relevance of the official statistics by arguing that they measure several important components of saving (broadly defined) reasonably well. Moreover, even if one credits the critics, appropriately measured rates of saving are still very low, both by historical and international standards, and the analysis must still attribute most of the decline in saving to private-sector behavior.

The next chapter explores the consequences of low saving. Here, I argue that most individuals are not currently saving enough to provide themselves with adequate financial security. In addition, low rates of saving depress investment, thereby depriving the economy of new plant and equipment that are necessary for continued growth and prosperity. At the same time, inadequate saving raises both the likelihood and expected severity of a recession by rendering the economy more vulnerable to external shocks. Finally, our obsession with consumption has contributed to the deteriorating competitiveness of American industry, and has driven us to sell a rising fraction of the American capital stock to foreign investors.

The third chapter examines several alternative explanations for low rates of saving. In it, I argue that traditional economic factors do not account for the decline of saving during the 1980s. Rather, the most plausible explanations emphasize the importance of psychological factors. Specifically, the fraction of wealth held by individuals born during or before the depression era has declined dramatically. Younger generations have not experienced widespread hardship, and have therefore been less inclined to exercise financial self-discipline. At the same time, the longest peacetime expansion on record has promoted a false sense of economic security and stability, reducing the perceived need for saving. In addition, the composition of income and wealth has changed in ways that increase the temptation to consume. These compositional changes are in large part attributable to increases in corporate leverage. Likewise, standard economic theories do not explain why the Japanese are so much more frugal than Americans. Nor are the differences between Japan and the United States attributable to the immutable influences of culture. Rather, the Japanese government has actively and systematically promoted saving by creating an environment in which the seeds of financial self-discipline are more likely to take root.

The final chapter evaluates a variety of policy options. I argue that a national saving strategy should promote both public and private saving. Clearly, it is important to bring federal deficits under control. Unfortunately, political considerations make this an extremely difficult undertaking. Moreover, even if we could eliminate budget deficits instantaneously, the rate of national saving would still fall far short of its historical average. Consequently, the federal government must take significant steps to stimulate private saving.

Five specific steps designed to exploit both psychological and economic motives for saving are set forth. First, we should establish a variety of special, tax-favored savings accounts. Each type of account should be dedicated to a specific, readily identifiable purpose, such as retirement, college, or purchase of a home. Incremental contributions to these accounts should be eligible for favorable tax treatment only if the taxpayer's total saving exceeds some fraction of his income. Limits on contributions should either be extremely high or nonexistent. Considerable public fanfare should accompany the introduction of these accounts. Second, we should modify tax provisions and institutions that promote personal borrowing. Subsidies for borrowing in any given context should be converted to subsidies for saving. Third, we must protect the tax-preferred status of employee pensions, and in addition we should specifically encourage the growth of defined contribution plans for both primary and secondary coverage. Fourth, we should eliminate the tax advantages of corporate leverage while preserving both investment incentives and the level of corporate tax revenues. This would require limitations on the tax deductibility of interest, an acceleration of depreciation allowances, and a reinstatement of the investment tax credit. Finally, the U.S. government must institute a high-profile, public campaign designed to promote more frugal behavior. Following the example of Japan, we should combine economic incentives with effective marketing.

Chapter 1
U.S. Saving Rates in Perspective

Rates of saving in the United States fell precipitously during the 1980s and are currently much lower than in any comparable period of our history. Although this disturbing phenomenon was not by any means confined to the United States, America has had the dubious distinction of leading the way. We currently save a much smaller fraction of national income than the rest of the industrialized world, and have done so throughout the postwar period.

Despite the journalistic clamor and political furor concerning federal budget deficits, the decline of national saving is primarily attributable to changing patterns of consumption and investment in the *private* sector. This observation does not diminish the importance of fiscal responsibility on the part of the government, nor does it absolve lawmakers of responsibility for our current predicament. However, it does augur limited success for remedial policies that fail to address the causes of languishing saving among households and corporations.

Which Rate of Saving?

National accounts usually provide detailed information on gross saving, net saving, private saving, personal saving, corporate saving, public saving, and national saving. Sadly, there is no such thing as a single, official rate of saving.

Data on gross saving measure the total flow of resources that are available to finance some specified class of investments. Part

5

of this simply compensates for the depreciation of existing plant and equipment. Net saving is intended to measure real increments to the capital stock, and is equal to the difference between gross saving and depreciation allowances.

For most purposes, it is preferable to net out depreciation when measuring saving. If the proprietor of a business fails to maintain or replace deteriorating equipment, he is in effect reducing the value of his operation in order to obtain higher net cash inflow. The concept of net saving would reveal this fact, while the concept of gross saving would not. The same reasoning applies to an individual investor, a corporation, or a country.

Even so, there are good reasons to examine the data on gross saving as well. For one thing, depreciation is not directly observable. For the United States, the Commerce Department estimates it through a series of complex calculations. The accuracy of these estimates is open to question. Conceivably, the procedure for calculating depreciation could skew estimates of net saving in a particular direction, perhaps producing spurious "trends."

A second consideration is that new capital investments may embody recent technological advances. When old machines break down, they are in some cases replaced by new machines that are more productive to begin with. Official measures of net saving usually do not reflect these productivity gains. Data on gross saving may therefore provide a better measure of the rate at which new technologies are assimilated into the capital stock.

Statistics on national saving describe the total flow of domestic resources, either net or gross, available to finance new investments in reproducible physical capital. In practice, investors use some of these resources to purchase foreign assets, including the securities of foreign governments, and some domestic capital formation is financed with resources from abroad. As a result, national saving affects domestic investment, interest rates, exchange rates, net foreign investment, and the balance of payments (all of which will be discussed at greater length in Chapter 2). The rate of net national saving is therefore a natural yardstick for evaluating economic performance.

National saving consists of two components: private saving and public saving. Private saving takes place in the personal and corporate sectors of the economy. Public saving is the sum of budget surpluses (deficits) for federal, state, and local governments. For the United States, the National Income and Product Accounts (NIPA), published by the Commerce Department, provide extensive data on each of these sectors.

Most economists believe that it is possible to obtain a better understanding of the national saving rate by decomposing it into these various pieces. For example, low rates of national saving might be attributed to household behavior (high propensities to consume out of disposable income), corporate behavior (a reluctance to retain earnings), or government behavior (a tendency to run large budget deficits). An examination of these pieces may therefore facilitate the diagnosis of an economic malady.

Nevertheless, some economists contend that this decomposition of national saving rates is meaningless. They point out that all economic assets and liabilities ultimately belong to households. Consequently, saving is saving, regardless of where it occurs. If this is correct, then the allocation of national saving among sectors is merely an exercise in accounting and has no behavioral significance.

This argument has been used to dispute the validity of decomposing private saving into personal and corporate components. Individuals own corporations. Owners have proprietary rights to corporate earnings, and, moreover, corporations save on behalf of their owners. The allocation of saving between the personal and corporate sectors also creates artificial distinctions between the treatment of incorporated and unincorporated enterprises. Conceptually, it is difficult to justify the practice of treating profits differently, depending upon whether they are retained by an unincorporated partnership or by an otherwise identical corporation.

Some economists have taken this line of argument a step further, applying it to the public/private distinction as well. They point out that the government must repay budget deficits at some point in the future, and that future taxes are liabilities for the private sector. By reducing the net wealth of the private sector, the government dissaves on behalf of taxpayers. Likewise, when the government runs a surplus, it reduces future private-sector liabilities, thereby saving on behalf of taxpayers. To put it another way, individuals "own" the government in the sense that they are ultimately accountable for financing its activities.

These issues are of great practical importance. If one accepts the premise that the allocation of saving across sectors is meaningless, then many policies designed to increase national saving, such as steps toward reducing the federal deficit, are in fact completely impotent (these arguments will be addressed at greater length later). The available evidence leads me to conclude that the sectoral composition of saving is extremely important. Changes in corporate or government behavior can in principle help to explain low rates of saving. Likewise, it is possible to stimulate national saving by adopting policies that target the corporate or government sector.

The Official Story

As illustrated in Figure 1.1, official U.S. government statistics on saving paint a rather grim picture of the most recent de-

Figure 1.1: Net National Saving for the U.S.

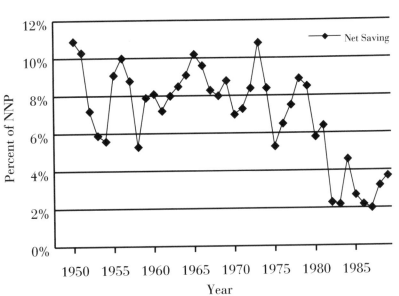

Source: U.S. Department of Commerce, *The National Income and Product Accounts of the United States, 1929-1982*, and *Survey of Current Business*, various issues.

cade.[1] The rate of net national saving (expressed as a fraction of net national product, or NNP)[2] remained relatively constant during the 1950s and 1960s. The preliminary indications of trouble appeared during the mid-1970s. Saving peaked at 10.8 percent of NNP in 1973, but then fell abruptly, matching its postwar low of 5.3 percent only two years later. Yet nascent concerns were short-lived, as saving rebounded to just under 8 percent of NNP—roughly its postwar average—in the last two years of that decade.

Unfortunately, national saving began to diminish once again in 1980. Two years later, the bottom fell out. Despite minor rallies in 1984 and 1989, the rate of net national saving has in every year since 1982 remained well below its previous postwar low. Overall, this rate plummeted from an average of 7.9 percent in the 1970s to a paltry 2.7 percent during the late 1980s.

To obtain a better understanding of this phenomenon, it is necessary to study the data in some detail. For those who are interested, the most telling statistics on saving appear in the Appendix. For those less inclined to pour over quantitative materials, the major points are briefly summarized on the next few pages.

Although net saving is the generally preferred concept, measures of gross saving should also play a role in national policy debates. Unfortunately, official statistics on gross national saving provide little comfort. The rate of gross national saving (expressed as a percentage of GNP) fell from an average of 16.7 percent in the 1970s to 13.0 percent during the second half of the 1980s. At the same time, depreciation on existing plant and equipment rose by a full percentage point relative to GNP. Both factors depressed the rate of net saving. Yet, of the two, the first was clearly more important, as it accounted for roughly 80 percent of the concurrent decline in the rate of net saving.

Widespread clamor over record-breaking federal deficits has created the impression that the government's lack of fiscal restraint is primarily responsible for the low rates of national saving—net and gross—witnessed during the 1980s. This is an exaggeration. Changing patterns of consumption and investment in the private sector have been quantitatively more important than public deficits. As noted earlier, the rate of net national saving fell by a staggering 5.2 percentage points between the 1970s and late 1980s. Roughly 3.3 percentage points, or nearly two-thirds of the total change, was attributable to declining rates of private saving (that is, the ratio of private saving to NNP). Of that amount, 2.7 percentage points—more than half of the total change—reflected plunging rates of personal saving. Even with skyrocketing federal deficits, government saving fell by only 1.8 percentage points. This breakdown attributes little more than one-third of the total decline in national saving to the public sector.

The fact that Americans save less than in previous decades means that our consumption of final goods and services has risen. Public consumption has actually changed little during the last few decades. Instead, private consumption has risen dramatically. This observation does not necessarily absolve lawmakers of responsibility for our current predicament. In particular, federal deficits have allowed the government to keep taxes low (relative to spending) and have therefore raised disposable income. Naturally, most people tend to spend more when their take-home pay rises.

Yet in practice, public deficits cannot account for most of the evident increase in private consumption. When an individual receives an additional dollar of disposable income, he usually spends some and saves some. Consequently, higher levels of disposable income should boost both private consumption and private saving as fractions of NNP. Yet private saving has fallen.

It is very difficult to explain the simultaneous decline of private saving and rise of private disposable income. Yet this issue is of paramount importance. Assuming that the propensity to save out of private income had not declined between the 1970s and 1980s, then national saving would have averaged about 6.2 percent of NNP during the late 1980s, rather than 2.7 percent. In contrast, the total elimination of all public deficits through increased taxes probably would not have raised the rate of national saving much beyond 3.7 percent.[3] Clearly, neither skyrocketing federal budget deficits nor rising government consumption is primarily responsible for our current troubles. Surprisingly,

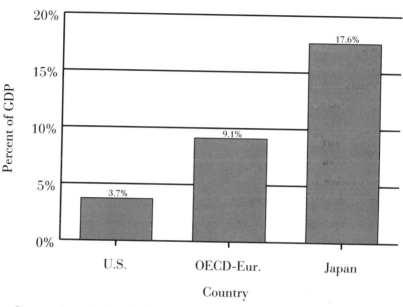

Figure 1.2: An International Comparison of
Net National Saving 1980-1987

Source: Organization for Economic Cooperation and Development, *Economic
Outlook, Historical Statistics*, 1988

the behavior of private individuals and businesses emerges as
the principal cause of declining saving.

Since most countries keep detailed national income accounts,
official data are readily available for the purpose of making international comparisons of saving rates. Unfortunately, accounting
conventions differ from country to country, and these differences
can in principle render comparisons meaningless. Several international organizations, including the United Nations, the International Monetary Fund (IMF), and the Organization for Economic Cooperation and Development (OECD), collect extensive
data on worldwide economic activity and compile national accounts based upon standardized accounting conventions. These
efforts at standardization are not perfect, and therefore some
problems of comparability remain.

Figure 1.2, which is based upon OECD data, depicts rates of
net national saving as percentages of gross domestic product[4]

(GDP) for the United States, Japan, and a collection of European countries.[5] One conclusion is inescapable: the United States saves very little relative to other developed countries. Specifically, the European economies save roughly two and a half times as much as the United States (relative to output), and Japan saves nearly five times as much. Additional data presented in the Appendix reveal that this is not a recent development: the United States has saved a significantly smaller fraction of output than the rest of the developed world throughout the postwar period.

The current U.S. saving rate also pales in comparison to those of rapidly developing countries. In 1986, gross saving amounted to 46 percent of GDP for Singapore, 37 percent for Taiwan, 33 percent for South Korea, and 25 percent for Hong Kong (compared with roughly 13 percent for the United States). Remarkably, none of these countries has a long history of high saving. In 1960, Singapore saved essentially nothing, and Hong Kong set aside a mere 2 percent of GDP.[6] As late as the 1970s, the low rate of saving in Korea was the subject of considerable study.[7]

Conversely, it is important to realize that thrifty habits have not always been so unfashionable in the United States. Indeed, during a period of roughly seventy years prior to World War II, the United States had an extremely high ratio of gross capital formation to GNP. Among the set of developed countries for which data are available, only Canada invested a larger fraction of output during this period, and the United States was a close second. Moreover, while Japan is widely thought of as a frugal nation, this is a relatively recent development. Prior to World War II, the United States invested roughly 50 percent more than Japan as a percentage of GNP.[8]

Those who point to federal deficits as the primary cause of low saving in the United States would do well to consider the statistical record in greater detail. A comparison of the components of national saving across countries reveals once again that patterns of consumption and investment in the private sector are primarily responsible for our low rate of saving. During the last decade, many developed countries—including Japan—battled enormous budget deficits comparable to those observed in the

United States. Nevertheless, American households were much less inclined to save than their European and Japanese counterparts (see the Appendix for more details).

The private sector is also responsible for the phenomenal increase in the saving rates of many developing countries. Household saving led the way in Taiwan, rising from a mere 1.9 percent of GDP in 1952 to 17.8 percent in 1986. At the same time, corporate saving jumped from 7 percent of GDP in the 1950s to 15.7 percent in 1986. While government saving posted moderate gains in the 1970s, these gains were eroded during the 1980s. Progress in Korea was almost entirely attributable to the household sector, which put away 18 percent of GDP in 1986, in comparison to a paltry 2.4 percent for 1965. During this period, corporate saving in Korea remained relatively constant.[9]

In summary, the official data clearly indicate that the United States saves very little, both by historical and international standards. Moreover, the behavior of the private sector—particularly the household sector—is primarily responsible for the steep decline in U.S. saving, as well as for the large differentials between the saving rates of the United States and other countries.

The Unofficial Story

A number of economists are skeptical about the validity of the official data on saving. Some contend that international comparability remains a severe problem, despite efforts by the OECD and other organizations to standardize national accounts. Others argue that arbitrary accounting conventions result in the exclusion or mismeasurement of certain forms of saving. Some analysts have even gone so far as to suggest that, once one adjusts the official figures appropriately, "saving rates in the middle 1980s are generally higher than the rates during the 1950–65 period and only slightly below the averages for the entire 1950–85 period."[10]

One must evaluate these criticisms with care. Saving is an ambiguous and elusive concept. Disagreement over how to measure it is spawned by controversy over how to define it. To take one example, some economists have argued that expenditures on education should be classified as saving, while others maintain that these outlays are more akin to consumption. Fortunately, there is no real need to resolve these definitional squabbles. Individuals provide for the future through a variety of different activities, and most of these activities serve different economic functions. As a result, no single statistic can adequately summarize the overall intensity of saving. While measures of aggregate saving have their uses, public policymakers ought to focus their attention on the individual components of saving. Official government statistics (for example, those in the U.S. National Income and Product Accounts) measure some important components reasonably well, and therefore provide appropriate yardsticks for evaluating economic performance.

Even if one is inclined to credit the critics, it is important to emphasize that this would not significantly alter any of the qualitative conclusions discussed so far. No matter how you slice it, rates of saving in the United States are very low, both by historical and international standards. Moreover, this state of affairs is in large part attributable to meager levels of private saving.

Comparability across Countries

Comparisons between the United States and Japan are currently in vogue. Yet the enormous and well-publicized gap between the official rates of national saving for these two countries is almost certainly overstated. There are at least two differences between the national income accounting practices of the United States and Japan that turn out to be quantitatively important.[11]

First, the Japanese calculate depreciation on physical plant and equipment using each asset's historical cost. In contrast, the U.S. Department of Commerce estimates depreciation on the basis of replacement costs. During periods of high inflation, replacement costs substantially exceed historical costs. As a result, the Japanese accounting convention understates economic depreciation and overstates net saving. According to some estimates, this consideration implies that net national saving rates for Japan should be revised downward by as much as 6 percentage points during certain periods.

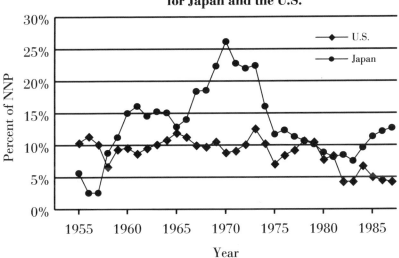

Figure 1.3: Rates of National Saving for Japan and the U.S.

Note: The statistics on national saving for Japan have been adjusted to enhance comparability with U.S. data

Source: Fumio Hayashi, private communication

Second, the Japanese national accounts treat government purchases of physical plant and equipment as both saving and investment. Moreover, this has been a large component of Japanese saving. According to the official figures, investment by the Japanese government averaged 5.7 percent of GNP between 1970 and 1987. In contrast, the United States counts these outlays as current consumption rather than as saving or investment. (The appropriateness of including government investment as a part of national saving is discussed below. For now, the reader should simply note that these accounting conventions may cause the official figures to overstate the differences between the United States and Japan.)

Figure 1.3 displays national saving as a percentage of NNP for the United States and Japan. The series for Japan differs in two respects from the one that appears in the official national accounts. First, depreciation is valued at replacement cost rather than historical cost. Second, government investment is treated

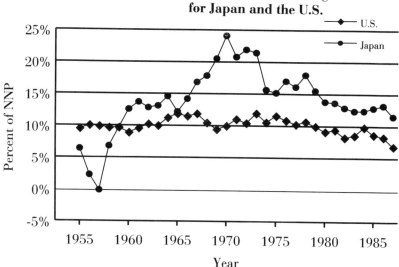

Figure 1.4: Rates of Private Saving
for Japan and the U.S.

Note: The statistics on national saving for Japan have been adjusted to
enhance comparability with U.S. data

Source: Fumio Hayashi, private communication

as current consumption. These adjustments eliminate the two major differences between the accounting conventions of the United States and Japan.

Generally speaking, even the adjusted data indicate that net national saving has historically been much higher in Japan than in America. The discrepancy between rates of saving peaked during the mid-1970s. Surprisingly, these rates converged rapidly during the late 1970s, and for a short period were roughly equal. Nevertheless, a substantial gap—roughly 8 percentage points— has reappeared during the 1980s.

Figure 1.4 tracks private saving rates for the United States and Japan, once again incorporating the necessary adjustments to assure comparability. Although the gap between these rates narrowed somewhat after 1970, it has remained both substantial (roughly 5 percentage points) and relatively stable in recent years. The temporary coincidence of national saving rates in the late 1970s clearly did not result from changes in private-sector behavior. Rather, during this period the Japanese government incurred enormous budget deficits that just offset the private saving rate differential.

While the official figures overstate the difference between the United States and Japan, the adjusted data probably understate it. For one thing, government investment is probably a legitimate component of saving. We should therefore add it to U.S. saving rather than delete it from Japanese saving. As it turns out, the Japanese government invests much more as a fraction of national output than does the U.S. government. Even when one adjusts the official figures to incorporate appropriate depreciation allowances, investment by the Japanese government averaged 3.6 percent of GNP between 1970 and 1987, far more than the corresponding figure for the United States.

Moreover, the adjustments considered above may actually overstate depreciation for Japan. Unfortunately, given the available data, it is necessary to estimate replacement cost depreciation through a rather indirect procedure. The estimates imply that depreciation amounted to as much as one-third of GNP for certain years during the 1950s—a figure that should evoke considerable skepticism. While estimated depreciation settled down to a more reasonable range during the 1960s, 1970s, and 1980s, the possibility remains that the adjustments are too large in these periods as well.

Yet regardless of whether one credits the official data or the adjusted data, certain conclusions are inescapable. First, the gap between saving rates for the United States and Japan has almost always been extremely large. Second, differences between rates of private saving account for a substantial portion of this gap.

A number of other studies have suggested that official statistics may also overstate the true differences between saving rates for the United States and Europe. For example, the Deutsche Bundesbank has compared household saving rates for the United States and four European countries. It concluded that somewhat more than half of the difference between the United States and Europe results from dissimilar methods of calculating saving.[12] Yet even if one accepts the premises of that study, there is still a substantial gap between the true rate of household saving for the United States and the true rates for European countries.

Alternative Forms of Saving

The U.S. National Income and Product Accounts (NIPA) classify each purchase of goods and services as either current consumption or investment. Critics argue that certain expenditures categories are misclassified. Three specific items have received a great deal of attention: consumer durables, education, and research and development.[13] Each of these is treated as current consumption, even though many economists think of them as forms of investment. Indeed, in the 1989 *Economic Report of the President*, the Council of Economic Advisers embraced the view that these items should be added to official measures of capital formation.

The logic of this criticism is most compelling for the case of consumer durables. When an individual purchases a car, he acquires a physical asset that will produce transportation services over a substantial period of time. Since he consumes only a small fraction of these services during the year of purchase, the acquisition primarily provides for his future needs. But that is the very the essence of saving.

Regardless of whether or not one agrees with this argument, it is very difficult to rationalize current national income accounting practices. When someone purchases a new car for his own use, the Commerce Department records this as consumption. But if instead a business acquires the car and leases it to the same individual, then the purchase is recorded as an investment. It is hard to imagine a justification for treating these two transactions differently.

Although the National Income and Product Accounts generally classify consumer purchases of durable goods as current consumption, there is one notable exception: housing. This is far and away the most significant category of durable goods. By value, dwellings account for just under 30 percent of all physical capital in the United States, nearly three times as much as all other consumer durable goods combined. To be consistent, the Commerce Department should count new housing as investment only when it is built for business purposes (that is, for lease or rental). In practice, the construction of owner-occupied housing is also treated as investment instead of consumption. If this practice makes sense for housing, one might well argue that it should be used for automobiles as well. And what goes for housing and automobiles also goes for televisions, stereos, furniture, appliances, and so forth.

Similar considerations suggest that expenditures on education and research and development should also be treated as investments. Education is the process through which we accumulate human capital, while research and development provides informational capital. Like physical capital, both human and informational capital have lasting effects on productivity. Indeed, college tuition is often referred to as an investment in a student's future. Similarly, companies that invest heavily in research and development are typically thought of as more forward-looking.

Consumers in the United States are reputed to have strong tastes for durable goods. Traditionally, Americans have placed a great deal of emphasis on education. Likewise, many U.S. companies invest heavily in research and development. It is therefore conceivable that, in some broad sense, the United States saves as much as other developed countries.

Unfortunately, the facts do not support this kind of speculation. Table 1.1 displays various measures of gross capital formation as a percentage of GDP, averaged over a fourteen-year period (1970–84). Statistics for the United States and a sample of eleven other countries appear separately. According to the official figures, the gap between the rates of gross capital accumulation for the United States and these other countries averaged 5.4 percentage points. If purchases of consumer durables are counted as gross saving, the gap closes to 4.5 percentage points. The addition of educational expenditures results in a slight further reduction, to 4.4 points. Finally, when research and development are also included, the gap falls to 3.8 points.[14]

As expected, the use of a broad-based measure of capital formation reduces the apparent difference between the United States and other countries. However, roughly 75 percent of the origi-

Table 1.1
Gross Capital Formation as a Percentage of GDP, 1970–84

	U.S.	Average for 11* Other Countries	Difference
Official figure	18.1	23.5	5.4
With adjustments for:			
Consumer durables	23.1	27.6	4.5
Plus education	28.4	32.8	4.4
Plus R & D	30.1	33.9	3.8

* The countries are Canada, Japan, Austria, Denmark, Finland, France, Italy, Netherlands, Norway, Sweden, and the U.K. The final line is based on only ten countries.

Source: Robert E. Lipsey and Irving B. Kravis, "Is the U.S. a Spendthrift Nation?" National Bureau of Economic Research, Working paper no. 2274, Cambridge, Mass., June 1987.

nal gap remains. As a result, these adjustments do not overturn the conclusion that the United States saves significantly less than other developed countries.

All of the statistics in Table 1.1 concern gross expenditures. As mentioned earlier, for most purposes it is preferable to net out depreciation when measuring saving. Certainly, both human and informational capital depreciate. Workers age and die, skills become rusty, and information grows obsolete. Unfortunately, depreciation of this kind is impossible to measure. Consequently, there are no reliable estimates of net saving that include education and research and development.

On the other hand, it is possible to estimate depreciation on the stock of consumer durable goods. Table 1.2 presents official rates of net national saving for the United States, as well as rates that are adjusted to reflect net investment in consumer durables. The inclusion of durables raises the net national saving rate substantially. However, the impact of this adjustment is greatest during the 1960s. It declines somewhat in the 1970s, and drops still further in the 1980s. Far from reversing the historical pattern exhibited by the official data, the inclusion of con-

Table 1.2
Net Saving with Adjustment for Consumer Durable Goods

Measure of U.S. Net National Saving as a % of NNP

Period	Official Statistic	Adjusted Statistic	Difference
1952–61	7.50	9.55	2.05
1962–71	8.48	11.14	2.66
1972–81	7.64	10.08	2.44
1982–85	3.11	5.38	2.27

Source: Patric H. Hendershott and Joe Peek, "Private Saving in the United States: 1950–85," National Bureau of Economic Research, Working Paper no. 2294, Cambridge, Mass., June 1987.

sumer durables accentuates the decline of net saving during the 1970s and 1980s.

So far, I have said nothing in defense of NIPA accounting practices. In a sense, this is not really necessary—the preceding statistical presentation demonstrates that the proposed adjustments do not significantly alter any of the qualitative patterns just discussed. Even if these adjustments had made a significant difference, the official figures would still be alarming.

In principle, broad-based measures of saving indicate the total extent to which a nation provides for its future. But in practice, the composition of saving matters at least as much as the total. As will be shown below, adequate investment in physical plant and equipment is a vital ingredient for economic success. The United States is not likely to achieve high growth of output, income, and wages without substantial conventional capital accumulation. Training and information also contribute to productivity, but there are limits on the extent to which they can substitute for concrete, steel, and silicon. Likewise, if the nation's factories were somehow suddenly converted into piles of VCRs and stereos, it would be small comfort to know that we could look forward to an abundant service flow of movies and music.

The case for treating educational expenditures on a par with investments in physical capital is particularly tenuous. In recent years, it has become increasingly apparent that these expenditures do not necessarily translate into human capital accumulation. Despite the fact that the United States spends a relatively high fraction of national income on education, its schools are notoriously unsuccessful. Research has shown that an alarming number of Americans lack basic analytical skills. For example, in one study only 44 percent of whites, 20 percent of Hispanics, and 8 percent of blacks between the ages of twenty-one and twenty-five could correctly determine the change they were due from the purchase of a two-item restaurant meal.[15] It is therefore arguable that educational expenditures often represent spending on child-care services rather than investments in human capital.

If one is nevertheless inclined to ignore important differences between these various activities and to construct a single, all-encompassing measure of saving, then it is difficult to know where to stop. How, for example, should one treat expenditures on food? Eating practically defines consumption. Yet one could argue that good nutrition enhances human capital by promoting good health. Indeed, the body actually "saves" certain nutrients by storing them in fat cells.

Fortunately, these definitional squabbles are of little practical relevance. The adequacy of capital formation, education, research and development, transportation services, nutrition, and so forth is a vital concern, but each one is also a separate concern. Since the official rate of net national saving measures the flow of resources available for financing conventional investments, it provides an appropriate yardstick for evaluating one critical aspect of economic performance. Other yardsticks exist for measuring other dimensions of performance. If these measures are treated independently, relatively little is learned from adding them up.

Stocks versus Flows

Most economists define wealth as control over resources that can be converted into consumption. Saving refers to the accumulation of wealth. There are two fundamentally different ways to measure this accumulation. One is based on flows of resources. NIPA provide an example of this approach. The Commerce Department constructs a measure of income generated from the production of goods and services (output), and estimates the volume of current output devoted to consumption. Since income must either be consumed or added to wealth (saved), the difference between these two numbers represents saving.

The second approach is based on stocks of resources. Specifically, if one can measure wealth at two distinct points in time, then it is easy to compute the change in wealth that occurred during the intervening period. This change offers an alternative measure of wealth accumulation, or saving.

In general, one would not expect these two approaches to yield similar estimates of saving. Yet despite their obvious differences, they are easily reconciled. Wealth changes for only two reasons: either new assets are accumulated or the market revalues existing assets. The Commerce Department does not count net asset revaluations (capital gains and losses) as part of income. As a result, it also excludes revaluations from its measure of saving.

Many economists insist that this exclusion is inappropriate. Moreover, they suggest that this could potentially explain the low conventionally measured rates of saving observed in recent years. Specifically, rising land prices and a bullish stock market may have provided investors with adequate asset accumulation, thereby reducing the need to channel other current income into saving.

To illustrate the logic of this argument, consider two investors, each of whom owns ten shares of corporate stock worth $10 per share. The first investor receives a dividend of $1 per share, but no capital gains (the share price does not change). He uses his dividends to buy an additional share of stock. At the end of the year, he owns eleven shares of stock, worth a total of $110. The second investor receives no dividends, but experiences a capital gain of $1 per share (the share price rises to $11). At the end of the year, he owns ten shares of stock, also worth a total of $110. Both investors find themselves $10 richer at the end of the year. But according to NIPA accounting practices, the first investor has saved $10, while the second investor has saved nothing.[16]

If one broadened the official definition of income to include capital gains and losses, then stock- and flow-based measures would coincide, at least conceptually. In practice, reliable data on unrealized capital gains and losses are unavailable. As a result, the only practical way to include asset revaluations in measures of saving is to compute changes in the stock of wealth.

Some economists also argue that stock-based measures of saving are more reliable than flow-based measures. Recall that the Commerce Department calculates saving as the difference between income and consumption. Both of these flows are much larger than saving. As a result, even when income and consumption are measured with relatively little error, estimated rates of saving may be very imprecise.[17] While the same point applies with a vengeance to stock-based estimates of saving,[18] errors in measuring wealth are no more likely to produce a high estimate than a low estimate. In contrast, there is reason to believe that flow-based measures systematically misstate the rate of saving. Specifically, the Commerce Department fails to count substantial fractions of national income and consumption. Unless these fractions happen to coincide, official figures will tend to either chronically overstate or chronically understate the rate of saving (depending upon whether underreporting is more severe for income or consumption). By some estimates, the "underground economy" now accounts for roughly 40 percent of GNP. It is also alleged that there was relatively little unreported income during the 1950s and 1960s.[19] Conceivably, the observed decline in the official rate of saving could therefore be nothing more than a statistical illusion caused by the growing importance of the underground economy.

The Board of Governors of the Federal Reserve System publishes national balance sheets that contain extensive information on national wealth.[20] In principle, they include data on the current value of all assets, including land, owner-occupied housing, consumer durables, U.S. gold and special drawing rights (SDRs), and certain financial claims against foreigners. Several economists

Table 1.3
Measures of Saving Based on Changes in Net Worth

Period	Private Saving (% of GNP)	Public Saving (% of GNP)	National Saving (% of GNP)
1950–59	12.1	0.5	12.6
1960–69	9.5	0.0	9.4
1970–79	12.8	0.0	12.8
1980–84	5.0	-2.3	2.7
1985–87	7.9	-3.6	4.3

Source: Michael J. Boskin, "Issues in the Measurement and Interpretation of Saving and Wealth," National Bureau of Economic Research, Working Paper no. 2633, Cambridge, Mass., June 1988.

have used these data to calculate stock-based estimates of saving.[21]

Since the market values of existing assets often change dramatically over relatively short periods of time, stock-based measures of the savings rate exhibit much greater variation from year to year than do flow-based measures. Nevertheless, when one averages these data over a number of years, certain long-run trends become evident. One set of estimates appears in Table 1.3, which reveals several striking patterns. First, the rate of national saving declined precipitously between the 1970s and 1980s. In contrast to the official figures, it recovered a bit in the late 1980s, but still remained well below the levels achieved in previous decades. Thus, contrary to the assertions of some economists, the low conventionally measured rates of saving of recent years are not attributable to the existence of unusually large capital gains. Second, the private sector led the decline of national saving. The public sector accounted for roughly 25 percent of the drop between the 1970s and early 1980s, and just over 40 percent of the drop between the 1970s and late 1980s.

It is also possible to make some limited international comparisons by using the available data on national wealth for Japan. Between 1970 and 1984, the ratio of net saving (including asset revaluations) to NNP for Japan was approximately three times the corresponding ratio for the United States. Much of this difference reflected skyrocketing Japanese land prices.[22]

There are a number of acknowledged problems with national balance sheet data for the United States. For one thing, it is extremely difficult to measure the market values of some items, such as land. Other items are not even carried at market value. Tangible capital owned by businesses is valued at replacement cost,[23] and bonds are carried at par. The treatment of the government sector is particularly simplistic, since it does not include the value of any physical assets owned by federal, state, or local entities. Nevertheless, the available evidence indicates that these problems do not account for any of the patterns noted above.[24] Overall, analyses of stock- and flow-based measures of saving lead to very similar conclusions.

So far, nothing has been said that would question the appropriateness of treating asset revaluations as a component of saving. In fact, it is *not* always appropriate. One important practical problem is that it is very difficult to assemble a comprehensive account of all assets and liabilities. In many cases, one party's asset is another's liability (for example, a bond is both an asset and a liability). Revaluations of such assets certainly alter the distribution of wealth, but do not change total wealth (saving by the first party just offsets dissaving by the second). Unfortunately, there are some situations in which it is easy to measure gains or losses for one party but difficult to measure them for the other. If, for example, Congress passes legislation reducing corporate tax rates for a period of five years, then the stock market will rise, and the investors will receive capital gains. However, there is an offsetting loss to the government—future tax revenues decline. Clearly, the nation as a whole is no better off. Any analyst must therefore draw a distinction between this scenario and one in which rising stock prices reflect greater productivity. To do this requires measurements of changes in the present discounted value of future government revenues. No such measure is currently available, either in the national balance sheets or elsewhere. Moreover, any attempt to estimate these kinds of gains and losses would be highly speculative at best.

A related point concerns the treatment of gains and losses induced by changes in relative prices. In most cases, it is not appropriate to count these revaluations as saving. Suppose that I own a bunch of objects, which I will call "widgets." If the price of widgets goes up, am I better off or worse off? If I plan to sell my widgets, I am better off. But if I plan to buy still more widgets, I am worse off. Loosely speaking, an increase in the price of widgets creates gains for those who intend to sell and losses for those who intend to buy. If accounting procedures simply add up all the gains on existing widgets (as in the national balance sheets), they are in essence assuming that everyone intends to sell all of their widgets, and that no one plans to buy widgets. This position is clearly untenable.

Several examples help to clarify this point. First, suppose that an investor purchases a bond that pays $1 per year, in perpetuity. If nominal interest rates rise but inflation remains unchanged (so that real rates rise as well) subsequent to his acquisition of the bond, then the market value of the bond falls and the investor experiences a capital loss. Should this loss be subtracted from his other saving in order to measure the extent to which he provides for the future? Probably not. This "loss" does not change the investor's command over future resources—using the proceeds from the bond, he can still purchase $1 worth of goods and services in each subsequent year. Unless he plans to sell the bond immediately and consume the proceeds, he is no worse off.

Second, suppose that the proprietor of a business purchases a personal computer for $3000. One month later, a new processing chip appears on the market. The new chip is no more powerful than its predecessor but is much less costly to produce. As a result, the market value of the old computer tumbles to a mere $500. Although the proprietor has taken a capital loss of $2500, this should not be netted against his other saving. The appearance of the new chip has not reduced the productivity of his old machine, nor does it induce him to scrap his old machine (although the new machine is cheaper, it does not offer more power). The proprietor is certainly no worse off than he would have been if the chip had not been introduced.

Third, when the price of land rises, homeowners experience capital gains (recorded in the national balance sheets). However, they also find it more difficult to upgrade their residences. If a homeowner plans to move to a larger house, an increase in the relative price of land actually reduces his command over economic resources, despite his apparent capital gain. Individuals with plans to buy their first home also lose out when housing prices rise. Yet the national balance sheets do not tally these losses.

These three examples share a common feature: the revaluation of an asset occurs because of a change in the relative prices of goods and services.[25] As a result, capital gains do not necessarily increase one's command over economic resources, and capital losses do not necessarily reduce it. By way of contrast, consider a fourth example in which the price of a corporation's stock rises to reflect substantial retained earnings. In this case, the resulting capital gain definitely reflects an increase in the shareholders' command over economic resources. Since it does not occur because of changes in the relative prices of any goods or services, it should be counted as saving.

Unfortunately, national balance sheet data do not allow us to identify gains and losses that result from changes in relative prices. Yet even if it were possible to exclude this class of revaluations, one might still regard flow-based figures as more relevant. As argued in the previous section, all-encompassing measures of saving are of little value, since the individual components of saving matter at least as much as the total. One important component of saving is the flow of resources into the formation of new physical capital. When capital gains arise from revaluations of existing physical assets, the associated "saving" is locked into the old asset and is not used to purchase new plant and equipment. On the other hand, when the retention of earnings raises the price of a corporation's stock (as in the fourth example discussed above), the resulting capital gains do reflect a flow of resources into new capital formation. Moreover, that flow is already included (as undistributed corporate profits) in the Commerce Department's measure of saving. Consequently, the flow-based official statistics provide a better yardstick for evaluating one key component of economic performance than the stock-based national balance sheets. While capital gains and losses are certainly important, it makes better sense to evaluate them separately.

The Government Sector

Unlike most other developed countries, the United States fails to keep explicit capital accounts for the government. Both the Department of Commerce and the Federal Reserve equate public saving with net lending, and count all governmental outlays as current consumption.[26] This simplistic treatment of the government sector makes no allowance for the fact that federal, state, and local entities own complex portfolios of assets and liabilities.

Many economists contend that the accumulation of physical assets by the government should qualify as public saving. A simple example serves to illustrate the logic of this position. Suppose that a local government requires a new school building. It considers two different methods of acquiring the building. One alternative (method A) is to borrow the necessary funds and engage the services of a private construction company. The other possibility (method B) is to find a private investor who is willing to fund the construction of the building and then lease it to the government.

Suppose for the sake of argument that the interest payments associated with method A would equal the lease payments for method B, and that in either case, the government would cover this yearly expense by increasing taxes. Then these two transactions would entail the same real activity (construction of the same building), and would result in identical cash flows between the public and private sectors. Nevertheless, method A produces a budget deficit in the first year, followed by balanced budgets in every subsequent year, while method B yields a balanced budget in every year. As a result, official measures of both government saving and national saving would be lower in the first year under method A, and equivalent in all subsequent years.

Table 1.4
Net Government Investments as a Percentage of GNP

Level of Government	Period			
	1951–60	1961–70	1971–80	1981–85
Federal	1.4	0.4	0.5	0.9
State and local	1.4	1.7	1.0	0.5
Consolidated	2.9	2.1	1.5	1.4

Source: Michael J. Boskin, Marc S. Robinson, and Alan M. Huber, "Government Saving, Capital Formation, and Wealth in the United States, 1947–1985," NBER Working Paper no. 2352, Cambridge, Mass., August 1987.

This peculiar result reflects the fact that the Commerce Department treats construction of a building as current consumption under method A but counts it as investment under method B. If instead it consistently treated physical capital formation as investment even in the public sector, then the puzzle would not arise: under method A, the government would acquire an offsetting asset and liability in the first period, so that its net saving would be unaffected.

While this argument has merit, the reader would do well to recall an overarching theme of this chapter: the composition of saving matters at least as much as total saving. If some public investments are motivated by politics rather than profits, then they may be less productive than private investments. Moreover, in many cases, public and private investments serve different needs. Even when public investments are highly productive, they often do not reduce the need for private investments. Certainly, most of us would not be willing to swap all of the nation's factories for tanks, bombs, and missiles, regardless of how effective these weapons might be. It therefore makes little sense to treat all government capital formation—particularly military capital formation—on a par with private investment. Instead, one should evaluate the adequacy of public and private investment separately.

Various economists have attempted to measure net government capital formation. One set of estimates appears in Table 1.4. While net investment for the consolidated government sector has declined steadily as a fraction of GNP since the 1950s, there was relatively little change between the 1970s and 1980s. But the consolidated figures mask some important trends. Capital formation by state and local entities peaked during the 1960s, and has since declined precipitously. Government investment would have fallen by almost a third between the 1970s and 1980s, had it not been for a near doubling of federal investment. Moreover, the lion's share of the increase on the federal level has taken the form of investment in military equipment and facilities. Public, nonmilitary capital formation, such as the construction of highways and educational facilities, has continued to fall dramatically.

Government entities in the United States also invest much less than their Japanese counterparts. As noted earlier, public investment averaged at least 3.6 percent of GNP in Japan between 1970 and 1984. That is roughly two and a half times the rate of public investment for the United States during the same period.

If one believes that measures of national saving should reflect capital gains and losses on private assets, then it is also appropriate to include revaluations of public assets. One important category of federal assets is oil and gas rights. In 1980, the value of these rights totaled $493 billion (in 1985 dollars). It rose by $142 billion in 1980, and by another $126 billion in 1981—these changes actually exceeded the growth of net federal debt for both years. Of course, revaluations can cut both ways. Indeed, the value of federal oil and gas rights declined in every year from 1982 to 1986, plummeting a total of $280 billion. Federal, state, and local entities also own a tremendous amount of land. But the value of this land declined from $957 billion in 1981 to $812 billion in 1985.[27]

Clearly, the inclusion of capital gains and losses on public assets would do little to overturn any of the conclusions that are based on official data. If anything, saving in the 1980s would appear to have fallen a bit further, and the public sector would be responsible for a somewhat larger share of the decline. One should bear in mind, however, that the gains and losses mentioned in the preceding paragraph largely reflect changes in relative prices that are not related to productivity. For reasons already discussed, the case for treating these kinds of revaluations as saving is not at all compelling.

The liability side of the government balance sheet is also surprisingly complex. In particular, the public sector has substantial implicit debts that are not recognized in any official accounts. The most important of these are retirement programs and various financial guarantees.

According to the most reliable estimates, the net deficit for the retirement and disability portion of Social Security should amount to $0.5 trillion over the next seventy-five years. The hospital insurance portion (Medicare) adds another $2.5 trillion. In addition, the unfunded liabilities of the federal civil service and military retirement systems totaled roughly $1 trillion in 1980.[28]

The federal government also has substantial contingent liabilities arising from financial guarantees. The expected payments that are associated with these guarantees do not show up anywhere in official accounts. Deposit insurance is probably the most well publicized financial guarantee. The recent savings and loan debacle demonstrated in dramatic fashion that these hypothetical liabilities can quickly become very real. Yet, incredibly, Congress has still contrived to keep a significant fraction of the bailout costs—now estimated by many to exceed $200 billion—off-budget.[29] Other guarantee programs, though less publicized, are equally important. By some estimates, implicit federal liabilities include $30 billion in support of direct loans, $80 billion in support of loan guarantees, and $50 billion in support of federally sponsored enterprise debt (for example, the Federal National Mortgage Association, or FNMA).[30]

Some economists have argued in favor of adjusting measures of both private and public saving to reflect changes in the value of implicit government liabilities. It is important to realize that this kind of adjustment would not affect the amount of national saving, only its composition—recognizing the accrual of an implicit debt to the private sector would reduce public saving and increase private saving by offsetting amounts.

Unfortunately, changes in implicit liabilities are extremely hard to measure. For the case of Social Security, a few economists have argued that payroll taxes should be treated as private saving (with associated public liabilities), on the grounds that these taxes are actually contributions to a retirement system. This view implies that private saving has actually fallen very little since the 1970s, and that the public sector is almost entirely responsible for the decline of national saving.[31] I am, however, inclined to challenge the premise of this argument, since each taxpayer's "contributions" are only weakly tied to his eventual benefits.

More generally, one should regard estimates of implicit liabilities as budgetary projections, rather than as contractual debt. When liabilities are substantial, this simply means that the government must change the rules of the game. That is exactly what occurred in 1983, when Congress reduced the projected deficit of the Social Security system by some $1.6 trillion just by enacting new legislation. Even now, the Social Security Administration's optimistic assumptions imply that the system will run a $3.4 trillion surplus over the next seventy-five years, while pessimistic assumptions point to a $2.6 trillion deficit.[32] To put this uncertainty in perspective, the disparity between optimistic and pessimistic deficit projections is roughly three times the current federal debt total. Depending upon which scenario materializes, the government will presumably redress the imbalance by changing the law.

Rather than adjust saving rates to reflect highly speculative estimates of changes in implicit government liabilities, it is far better to stick with more conventional measures of saving. At the same time, it may be possible to explain a portion of the decline of private and national saving by examining the effects of programs such as Social Security. (I will return to this possibility in a later chapter.)

If one believes that measures of public saving should reflect capital gains and losses on assets owned by the government, then it is also important to include revaluations of outstanding liabilities. The government incurs capital gains and losses on all liabilities, including conventional debt instruments.

The market value of conventional debt changes for two reasons. First, inflation erodes the real value of outstanding debt.

Table 1.5
Federal Deficits as a Percentage of NNP

Period	Official Deficit	With Adjustment for Inflation	With Adjustments for Inflation and Interest Rates
1953–59	-0.4	0.8	1.2
1960–69	-0.3	0.6	0.6
1970–79	-1.9	-0.4	-0.4
1980–84	-4.2	-2.8	-3.1
1985–87	-4.9	-3.8	-4.2

Source: Robert Eisner, private communication.

If total debt rises in current dollars but falls in constant dollars, it makes little sense to say that the government runs a deficit. Rather, a reduction in real, constant-dollar net liabilities implies that public saving is positive. Second, the market value of conventional liabilities fluctuates with interest rates. When rates rise, bond prices fall, and vice versa.

The arguments in favor of adjusting measures of deficits for inflation seem compelling. On the other hand, the case for interest rate adjustments is more tenuous. Interest rates measure the price of future consumption relative to current consumption. As noted earlier, capital gains and losses resulting from changes in the relative prices of goods and services should not, in general, be counted as saving.

It is fairly easy to adjust the official statistics on government deficits so that they reflect revaluations of conventional liabilities. For example, Table 1.5 reports official and revised deficits for the federal government as percentages of NNP. The first revised series nets out changes in the value of outstanding debt resulting from inflation, while the second adjusts for both inflation and interest rate fluctuations. Generally, the adjustments imply that deficits have been somewhat smaller than the official figures would suggest. However, the total decline in government saving between the 1970s and late 1980s is somewhat larger for the adjusted series (3.4 percentage points for the first series, 3.8 for the second) than it is for the official series (3.0 percentage points).

When there is a change in the market value of federal liabilities, there is also an offsetting change in the value of private assets. As a result, the adjustments discussed above do not alter the level of national saving—they merely affect its composition. For example, the data in Table 1.5 would result in a larger fraction of the decline of national saving being attributed to the public sector; yet even adjusted for inflation, the private sector still accounts for 60 percent of the decline in national saving.[33]

Overall, the qualitative patterns exhibited by the official data emerge intact from a detailed examination of government assets and liabilities. After adjusting liabilities for inflation, and after accounting for reduced public-sector investment, the government emerges with a somewhat larger share of the blame for the dramatic decline in national saving. Nevertheless, an impressive portion of this decline is still attributable to behavior in the private sector.

Chapter 2
The Consequences of Low Saving

When an individual fails to save, he jeopardizes his own economic security. Following retirement, serious illness, or involuntary job loss, he may well find that his resources are insufficient to maintain his accustomed standard of living, and at times he may experience significant hardship. Even if his luck holds out during his own lifetime, he will contribute little to the enrichment of his family line.

When a society fails to save, its members must ultimately pay the price for collective profligacy. For a time, a strong demand for consumer goods may buoy the economy, but robust economic performance simply masks the symptoms of a serious malady. Sooner or later, stagnation must displace prosperity as performance deteriorates.

Most individuals are not currently saving enough to provide themselves with adequate financial security. In addition, low rates of saving depress investment, thereby depriving the economy of new plant and equipment that are necessary for continued growth and prosperity. At the same time, inadequate saving renders the economy more vulnerable to external shocks, thereby raising the likelihood of a severe recession. Finally, our obsession with consumption has contributed to the deteriorating competitiveness of American industry, and has driven us to sell a rising fraction of the American capital stock to foreign investors. Although I believe that the significance of this last effect has been overstated, it is nevertheless regarded by many as a serious national concern.

The Social Consequences of Low Saving

Saving by Americans provides funds for new investments both at home and abroad. Similarly, a portion of foreign saving ultimately finances purchases of new plant and equipment in the United States. Total investment in the United States is therefore equal to domestic saving plus net inflows of capital from abroad. This simple observation has far-reaching implications. Specifically, lower rates of domestic saving must, of necessity, either depress domestic investment or boost net inflows of foreign capital. The relative importance of these two effects depends upon certain key features of the domestic and global economies.

To understand the link between saving and other macroeconomic aggregates, it is necessary to think in terms of the supply and demand for financial capital.[1] When an individual saves, or when a foreign investor diverts resources to the American market, additional financial capital becomes available. In other words, the supply of new financial capital consists of domestic saving plus net inflows of foreign capital. When a business undertakes new investments in plant and equipment, it attempts to raise the necessary funds either internally or externally. Accordingly, the demand for new financial capital reflects the profitable investment opportunities of domestic businesses. As in other markets, the price of financial capital adjusts to bring supply and demand into balance.

At first, it may seem odd to think in terms of a price for financial capital. After all, a price is the monetary compensation that one receives in exchange for a good. If the good in question is money, how does one measure a price? Doesn't each dollar cost exactly one dollar? To resolve this puzzle, it is necessary to distinguish current dollars from future dollars. The supplier of financial capital receives dollars tomorrow in exchange for dollars today. The amount received tomorrow for each dollar provided today defines the price of financial capital. This price is more commonly known as the rate of interest.

A decline in domestic saving at prevailing rates of interest reduces the supply of financial capital relative to demand. When demand exceeds supply, many businesses find themselves unable to raise funds for profitable investment opportunities. Some of these businesses are usually willing to bid for scarce funds by offering higher rates of return to potential investors. Thus, the price of financial capital, or rate of interest, rises in response to a supply shortage. Higher rates of interest provide more generous rewards to those who supply financial capital and consequently tend to stimulate supply. Rising interest rates also increase the cost of financial capital for domestic businesses, thereby reducing the number of potentially profitable investments. These two effects bring supply and demand back into balance at some higher price. If the supply of financial capital is very responsive to interest rates, then a small increase in these rates will restore balance, leaving investment largely unaffected. On the other hand, if supply is relatively unresponsive, then interest rates will have to rise substantially, producing a more pronounced decline of investment.

The weight of the available evidence indicates that domestic saving is rather unresponsive to interest rates (see Chapter 4). If foreigners were unable to invest in the United States, a sharp drop in the rate of saving would therefore produce significantly higher interest rates and lower investment. In practice, U.S. capital markets are open to foreign investors. As interest rates begin to rise in the United States, foreigners divert funds from projects in their own countries to more profitable American opportunities. If foreigners are sufficiently responsive to rates of return in the United States, then declining rates of domestic saving should have very little impact on either interest rates or investment. However, larger net inflows of foreign capital would then result in greater foreign ownership of American assets.

Unfortunately, economists disagree sharply about the extent to which higher domestic rates of interest attract greater inflows of foreign capital. According to one school of thought, political, cultural, and legal barriers impede the free flow of financial capital across national borders.[2] If this is correct, then domestic saving must be the primary determinant of domestic investment. The proponents of this view point out that, for most industrialized countries, differences between domestic saving and domestic investment have rarely been large; net inflows of capital from abroad are typically quite small.

At one time, there were significant barriers to international capital mobility. However, over the last decade, liberalization programs have largely eliminated these barriers. As a result, financial markets have become increasingly well integrated. The consequences of financial integration are evident: both American investment abroad and foreign investment in the United States have risen dramatically. Even when net inflows of foreign capital are small relative to GNP, gross flows are usually enormous. For example, in 1982 U.S. net foreign investment amounted to a mere -$4.6 billion. Yet American investors acquired some $118 billion worth of foreign assets in the same year.[3] Net flows of capital were small simply because the gross flows largely offset each other. More recently, even net flows have surpassed $100 billion.

Many analysts believe that the progressive integration of international capital markets has severed the link between domestic saving and investment.[4] They argue that if financial capital is always attracted to the highest available rate of return, regardless of geographic location, then domestic investment should be determined by the worldwide supply of financial capital rather than the domestic supply. A decline of domestic saving should then simply increase net inflows of foreign capital, leaving investment largely unaffected.

It is important to realize that evidence of financial integration does not justify such an extreme conclusion.[5] Even when capital markets function perfectly, an investor may choose a domestic investment over an equivalent foreign alternative for perfectly good reasons. When U.S. saving declines, foreign investors are indeed attracted by higher rates of return. However, they are not willing to take on unlimited amounts of exchange rate risk. Moreover, they may also begin to anticipate real depreciation of the dollar.[6] Since they are ultimately interested in repatriating their earnings, this makes American investments much less attractive. As a result, interest rates must rise noticeably before foreign investors are willing to make up the shortfall between saving and investment. With perfect integration of capital markets, lower saving therefore produces *both* lower investment *and* greater foreign ownership of American assets.

Several other factors reinforce the relationship between domestic saving and investment. First of all, investors do not and should not regard foreign and domestic ventures as perfect substitutes. Despite progress toward economic globalization, the profitability of most American businesses remains more closely tied to the macroeconomic performance of the United States than to that of, say, Japan or Germany. Although there is some tendency for the stock market indices of the major industrialized countries to move in tandem, these indices often respond very differently to particular world or national events. In other words, American investments contain uniquely American risks, and foreigners do not have an unlimited tolerance for these risks. As they invest increasing fractions of their portfolios in American assets, foreigners become progressively more reluctant to commit further resources to the U.S. market. In addition, as they come to own a greater share of the U.S. capital stock, they may begin to fear a political backlash that would expose their U.S. holdings to either explicit or implicit expropriation.[7] To counter these concerns, American businesses must compensate foreign investors by offering higher rates of return. The resulting increase in the cost of financial capital chokes off investment.

Finally, as a practical matter, governments abhor large net inflows of foreign capital.[8] Substantial net outflows of domestic capital are also politically unpopular.[9] As a result, many governments have in the past attempted to achieve external balance through domestic fiscal policies.[10] During the past few years, however, we have witnessed a dramatic departure from this norm. While it is certainly possible that economic globalization has permanently altered national objectives, political rhetoric still emphasizes the importance of balanced trade and symmetric capital flows. If recent experience is an aberration,

then for political reasons domestic saving will ultimately constrain domestic investment.

Recent research reveals that the link between domestic saving
and investment remains strong, despite the development of international financial markets. According to some estimates, if national saving declined permanently by one percentage point relative to GDP, then domestic investment would drop by a quarter
point within one year, and by half a point within three years.[11]
Net inflows of foreign capital would rise sharply at first but would
then decline gradually over time. This is hardly surprising in light
of the preceding discussion.

Aside from depressing domestic investment and promoting foreign ownership of American assets, inadequate saving also yields
deteriorating current account balances. Indeed, these phenomena
are two sides of the same coin. As a matter of national income
accounting, the current account deficit is necessarily identical
to the total net inflow of foreign capital.[12] Since low saving
stimulates foreign investment in the United States, it must therefore also contribute to the deterioration of the current account
balance. Mechanically, this occurs as follows: When saving
declines, the supply of financial capital falls short of demand,
and interest rates start to rise. Higher returns attract foreign investors, who attempt to acquire dollars in order to purchase assets from American owners. This produces an increase in the
relative demand for dollars and drives the real value of the dollar up relative to foreign currencies. Since foreign goods become
relatively cheap for American consumers, the demand for imports rises. Likewise, the demand for exports declines as American goods become more expensive for foreign consumers. This
imbalance contributes to the trade and current account deficits.

The current account is closely related to the better-known concept of the trade deficit. In particular, the current account deficit
equals the trade deficit plus net outflows of capital income. The
popular press has focused national attention on recent current
account and trade imbalances, and has frequently interpreted
these statistics as barometers for the international competitiveness of American industry. The preceding paragraph suggests

that this interpretation is valid in only a very limited sense. A current account deficit arises when domestic saving falls short of domestic investment. This gap does not reflect a deterioration of the potential for our industry to compete at any given exchange rate. It does not measure productivity differentials, or the quality of productive inputs. Rather, the "loss of competitiveness" is exclusively attributable to appreciation of the dollar, which makes American goods relatively more expensive. Of course, the shortfall of saving may also depress investment, which would eventually affect the ability of American industry to compete at whatever rate of exchange ultimately prevailed. But that effect is not measured in any way by the current account balance.

Finally, inadequate saving renders the economy vulnerable to adverse events, and may as a result increase both the likelihood and expected severity of a recession. As has been noted, low rates of saving foster heavy dependence on foreign financial capital. A sharp decline in investment brought about by an interruption of the flow of capital from abroad would disrupt the U.S. macroeconomy in the short run and severely test the Federal Reserve's abilities to fine-tune aggregate performance. If the pace of economic activity slows sufficiently, many individuals and corporations are currently so highly leveraged that they might well find themselves unable to cover the carrying costs of accumulated debt. The repercussions from snowballing loan defaults and bankruptcies could produce a significant contraction of output and employment.

Interest Rates and Investment

In theory, low saving creates a gap between the supply and demand for financial capital, and the resulting competition for scarce funds drives up interest rates. Yet during the late 1980s, these rates have been roughly comparable to those observed in the 1970s. Since saving has fallen dramatically as a percentage of GNP, this appears to contradict economic theory. There is, however, a simple explanation.

Interest rates consist of two components: a real return to capital and compensation for the erosion of the value of principal

that occurs with inflation. Economists often refer to the first component as the "real" rate of interest. Technically, it is equal to
the difference between the so-called nominal, or market, interest
rate and the expected rate of inflation. The 1970s were characterized by relatively high inflation, and real interest rates averaged close to zero. In contrast, we experienced very little inflation during the late 1980s, and real rates jumped to roughly 4
or 5 percent. To put this in perspective, real rates remained substantially below their current levels in every one of the last six
recoveries. There can be little doubt that the recent increase in
real interest rates is attributable to the decline of national saving.

The cost of financial capital depends primarily upon the real
rate of interest, not the nominal rate.[13] The relationship between these variables is complex and depends in part on features of the corporate and personal tax systems. Several recent
studies have calculated cost of capital figures for the United States,
making appropriate allowances for these factors.[14] This research
clearly demonstrates that rising real interest rates have spurred
a steep increase in the cost of capital during the 1980s.

As financial capital becomes more expensive, investment
declines. Table 2.1 contains average rates of U.S. domestic investment for the last four decades. Gross investment has fallen
only slightly since its peak during the 1970s, and indeed was lower
in the 1960s than in the 1980s. However, as discussed earlier,
net investment is, for most purposes, a more appropriate measure of capital accumulation. This measure declined steadily between the 1950s and the 1970s, plummeted during the early 1980s,
and then recovered slightly during the late 1980s.[15]

As expected, these changes were somewhat smaller than the observed movements of the national saving rate. Between the 1970s
and early 1980s, national saving fell by 3.3 percentage points
relative to GNP, compared to 2.4 points for net investment. Net
inflows of foreign capital offset only slightly more than one-fifth
of the decline in the rate of saving (as indicated in Table 2.1,
the ratio of net foreign investment to GNP fell by 0.7 percentage
points). This stands in contrast with more recent experience. Between the 1970s and late 1980s, net saving has fallen by a total

Table 2.1
U.S. Investment and International Transactions

	Period				
	1950–59	1960-69	1970-79	1980-84	1985-88/89[a]
Gross investment/GNP	16.2%	15.5%	16.4%	15.9%	15.8%
Net investment/GNP	7.5	7.1	6.8	4.4	5.2
Net foreign investment/GNP[b]	0.1	0.6	0.2	-0.5	-3.0
Current account surplus/GNP[c]	0.1	0.5	0.0	-0.8	-2.9

[a] For current account surplus, 1985–88; for all others, 1985–89.

[b] In theory, net foreign investment should be equal to the difference between gross saving and gross investment. After referring back to Table 1.1, the astute reader may notice that this condition is not always satisfied exactly. This reflects the fact that the Commerce Department derives data on saving and investment from different sources. The National Income and Product Accounts record this as a "statistical discrepancy."

[c] In theory, net foreign investment should equal the current account surplus. However, official data on net foreign investment are drawn from NIPA, while the current account surplus is recorded in the Balance of Payment Accounts (BPA). NIPA and BPA accounting practices differ in their treatment of items such as gold and capital gains — hence the discrepancy.

Sources: Department of Commerce, *The National Income and Product Accounts of the United States 1929-1982*, and *Survey of Current Business*, various issues.

of 4.6 percentage points relative to GNP. Investment has dropped only 1.6 points, while net foreign investment has fallen by a whopping 3.2 percentage points relative to GNP.[16] In the last few years, foreign capital has therefore made up for slightly less than two-thirds of the decline of saving. Even so, lower saving has depressed the rate of net investment by nearly 25 percent (1.6 percentage points out of an original 6.8 points relative to GNP).

It is important to emphasize that inflows of foreign capital have only provided the U.S. economy with a temporary reprieve. In Europe and on both sides of the Pacific, many national leaders regard persistent capital and current account imbalances as severe international problems. In the coming years, we will undoubtedly witness renewed efforts to redress these imbalances through direct and indirect government interventions. In addition, foreign investors may soon reach a point of satiation with American assets, particularly as the political climate becomes increasingly hostile. There is already some evidence that they are becoming skittish. For example, when the Reagan administration blocked Fujitsu's bid for Fairchild Semiconductor in March 1987 (ostensibly for national security reasons), foreign investors became jittery and U.S. interest rates rose sharply. A shift toward a less accommodating national posture could well persuade foreigners that they have already overcommitted to the U.S. market. If foreign funds dry up before the United States succeeds in restoring acceptable rates of saving, domestic investment could plummet by as much as 50 percent.[17]

Low rates of domestic investment severely depress economic performance, particularly in the longer run. Capital accumulation is an important determinant of economic growth. Additions to the capital stock lead to the creation of new, higher-paying jobs and boost productivity by bringing new technology to the workplace. Higher levels of investment are certainly necessary to prepare U.S. businesses for new challenges in the 1990s, including vigorous international competition and efforts to restore the health of the global environment.

How much would Americans need to save in order to sustain an adequate level of investment? The answer to this question depends in part on personal preferences concerning the desirability of trading off consumption today for greater wealth in the future. For an economist, it is easier to spell out the terms of this trade-off than it is to prescribe an optimal policy target. If net investment averages 7 percent of GNP, then within twenty to thirty years national income per capita should be roughly 10 percent higher, and per capita consumption 7 to 8 percent higher, than if the current rate of investment (roughly 5 percent) persists.[18] The potential social benefits from additional saving are therefore substantial.

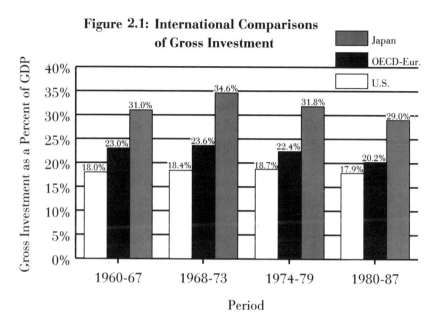

Figure 2.1: International Comparisons of Gross Investment

Source: Organization for Economic Cooperation and Development, *Economic Outlook, Historical Statistics*, 1988

In establishing a policy target for domestic investment, the United States should rely in part on the experiences of other countries. Figure 2.1 compares rates of gross investment for the United States, Japan, and OECD Europe (unfortunately, data on net investment are not available). While the differences between these rates have declined, the United States still invests substantially less relative to GDP than does the rest of the industrialized world. To eliminate this gap, it would be necessary to raise our rate of investment by several percentage points.

To justify a more specific policy target, one must rely on economic models and simulations. According to one set of calculations, the ideal rate of net investment lies somewhere between 11 and 14 percent.[19] If indeed domestic investment is ultimately constrained by domestic saving, then the United States would need to quadruple its current rate of saving in order to achieve this target, a goal that we are not likely to achieve given the need for politically acceptable policies. A more modest objective would simply be to restore the rates of saving that prevailed during the 1960s and 1970s. This alternative should be regarded as a bare minimum. Congress and the administration should therefore be urged to establish a national goal of raising the rates of net saving and net investment to at least 8 percent of NNP within the next five years.

Foreign Ownership of American Assets

During the last decade, foreign nationals have demonstrated a phenomenal appetite for assets in the United States. As shown in Table 2.1, America was a net supplier of capital to the rest of the world in the 1950s, 1960s, and 1970s. But net outflows of capital were reversed in the early 1980s, and the foreign inflow shot up to 3 percent of GNP in the late 1980s. At the end of 1988, the Commerce Department estimated that foreigners had accumulated nearly $1.8 trillion worth of assets in the United States. This number exceeds the value of American-owned foreign assets by more than $0.5 trillion.[20]

At one point in time, most foreign investors expressed a clear preference for financial assets. Indeed, even today roughly 80 percent of foreign-owned assets (including approximately one-sixth of the national debt) are financial. However, this is changing rapidly. Foreign direct investments grew by 23 percent in 1987, and by 21 percent in 1988, reaching $329 billion by the end of that year. About two-thirds of this is attributable to European countries. British investors have acquired the largest block of American assets. At year's end in 1988, their direct investments in the United States stood at $102 billion. Japan is the second-largest direct investor with $53 billion, having recently surpassed the Netherlands with $49 billion. The British also accounted for the largest share (39 percent) of the total increase in foreign direct investment between 1987 and 1988; once again, the Japanese ranked second (32 percent).

Partly as a result of this shift to real assets, foreigners have come to control a significant share of the U.S. manufacturing base. Table 2.2 contains estimates of the share of various U.S. industries that are attributable to affiliates of foreign companies.[21] It

Table 2.2
Share of U.S. Industry Attributable to
Affiliates of Foreign Companies, 1987

| | *Percent of all U.S. Business by* | | |
	Employment	*Assets*	*Sales*
All industries	3.6	—	—
All manufacturing	7.3	13.2	11.5
Selected industries:			
Petroleum and coal products	39.5	17.2	16.8
Chemicals and allied products	23.5	30.9	31.2
Stone, clay, and glass products	12.3	31.2	22.2
Primary metal industries	11.8	19.0	19.5
Instruments and related products	10.7	9.7	9.2
Electric and electronic equipment	9.3	10.6	12.2
Food and kindred products	8.8	11.7	8.2
Mining	8.4	—	—
Rubber and plastic products	6.5	13.4	10.3
Motor vehicles and equipment	6.5	—	—

Source: Ned G. Howenstine, "U.S. Affiliates of Foreign Companies: 1987 Benchmark Survey Results," *Survey of Current Business* 69 (July 1989): 116–33.

is, of course, possible to measure industry shares in a variety of ways. Three different measures are the share of employment, assets, and sales. Foreigners still control only a small fraction of all U.S. industry (roughly 3.6 percent, by employment). However, their share of the manufacturing sector is more than twice their overall average. Depending upon how one measures it, foreign affiliates account for more than 30 percent of the manufacturing base in petroleum and coal products, in chemicals and allied products, and in stone, clay, and glass products. In addition, if either assets or sales are considered, the foreign share of the primary metal industries is nearly 20 percent.

It is important to bear in mind that our low rate of saving is not exclusively, or perhaps even primarily, responsible for the rise of direct foreign investment in the United States. Global capital markets became extremely well integrated during the 1980s. At this point, gross capital flows—foreign acquisitions of U.S. assets and U.S. acquisitions of foreign assets—would continue to be enormous even if we brought our capital account into balance by saving a larger fraction of national income. We can avoid foreign ownership of American assets only by pursuing an ill-conceived policy of economic isolationism.

An increasingly visible string of foreign acquisitions has fostered considerable resentment among U.S. citizens and generated support for isolationist policies. In one recent poll, 80 percent of respondents indicated that they favored limiting foreign purchases of American assets, and 40 percent said that they would like to halt this activity altogether.[22] When asked to elaborate, most Americans express a fear that we as a nation are losing control over our economic destiny. This is an emotionally charged statement, and no doubt it strikes a responsive chord in all ot us. But what does it mean in concrete terms? A reading of articles and editorials in popular periodicals reveals five major themes.

First, some people fear that foreigners will make business decisions that run counter to American interests. The most common concerns are that foreign owners will eliminate jobs, fail to maintain and modernize plant and equipment, or divert the company's purchases of parts and supplies to foreign competitors. If American businessmen are imbued with altruism toward their fellow citizens while foreign owners collectively conspire to undermine American prosperity, then this concern is well founded. But in practice, American and foreign owners are equally and primarily motivated by the desire to earn profits. When production is excessive, both scale back employment. When foreign supplies are cheaper, both usually abandon American sources. And when available projects are unprofitable, neither is willing to undertake new investments.

One potentially valid complaint is that foreigners are less adept at managing American labor relations. Even so, horror stories are relatively rare and should become even less common as foreign owners gain experience with American workers. Indeed, if experience to date is a reliable guide, then foreign ownership is generally favorable to American interests. Foreign investors have salvaged a number of floundering American companies by providing access to an abundant supply of cheap financial capital. For example, following its acquisition of the troubled Firestone Tire and Rubber Company, Japan's Bridgestone Corporation announced a $1.5 billion investment program and used its economic muscle to turn Firestone into a profitable venture.

A second and somewhat more subtle concern is that foreigners—particularly the Japanese—may plan strategic acquisitions in high-tech industries. Some analysts fear that U.S. technology will allow Japanese companies to dominate computers, new materials, biotechnology, and other critical emerging industries.[23] In some instances, there are also legitimate national security considerations.

While there is some validity to these concerns, the threat to American industry is almost certainly overstated. So far as I know, there are as yet no documented cases in which foreign parents have stolen new technologies to the detriment of American interests. Nor is this likely to occur on a large scale. The Japanese are developing a global outlook on economic enterprise. As long as new technologies can be applied profitably in the United States, Japanese parent companies do not stand to gain anything from depriving their U.S. affiliates of these technologies. Foreign ownership may accelerate the rate at which new technologies spread to other countries. However, this is a two-edged sword. The U.S. steel industry in particular has recently benefited from the application of Japanese technology and methods of production. In any case, the diffusion of new technology is inevitable. If U.S. companies are to maintain strong, permanent positions in the key high-tech industries, they must learn to compete with foreign companies even when they lack a significant technological advantage. Finally, where national security is at stake, foreign acquisitions can be evaluated on a case-by-case basis.

A third concern is that foreign operations will drive American-owned capacity out of business in order to create and exploit monopoly power in U.S. markets. This concern is entirely groundless. American businesses and consumers are more than ade-

quately protected by antitrust legislation that proscribes monop-
olization and other anticompetitive practices. Enforcement of
antitrust statutes waxes and wanes with political currents.
However, foreign exploitation would be guaranteed to draw a
harsh political response. Foreign investors would soon discover
that this is the quickest route to effective expropriation of capital.

A fourth and somewhat more amorphous concern is that America will lose its status as a "wealthy" nation. Countries that
acquire disproportionately large shares of the world capital stock
may eventually achieve superior standards of living. Alarmists
suggest that a United States owned by foreign nationals will ultimately come to be regarded as a second-class economic power.

It is important to realize that inflows of foreign capital allow
the United States to maintain a higher rate of investment than
it could achieve on its own. This investment contributes to the
creation of high-paying jobs and to the growth of productivity.
If rates of saving remain low while foreign funds dry up, then
the United States will indeed be headed toward second-class status. In the meantime, foreign capital allows America to remain
among the world's economic leaders.

Moreover, as long as foreign capital supports an adequate rate
of investment, individual American workers will continue to en-
joy levels of income comparable to those of their Japanese or
German counterparts. The average American family might well
choose to accumulate less wealth (that is, spend a larger portion
of its income) than a similarly situated Japanese family. However,
this is a matter of choice, and not one of restricted opportunity.
Individual Americans still have the opportunity to accumulate
levels of wealth comparable with those enjoyed by foreign workers of similar socioeconomic status, and some continue to avail
themselves of this opportunity. Thus, the real threat to American economic status is not the infusion of foreign capital but the
possibility that foreign capital will dry up, leaving domestic investment dependent on domestic saving.

Fifth and finally, many Americans experience a visceral reac-
tion to the perception that their country has sunk to selling the
family jewels at "fire sale" prices. There is certainly a great deal
of confusion on this subject. Many commentators have suggest-

ed that the weak dollar makes American assets "good buys" for foreign investors. This is simply nonsensical.[24] The income generated by U.S. assets is also denominated in dollars. When the value of the dollar is low, foreigners pay less for these assets, but they also receive proportionately less in return. Consequently, a weak dollar cannot, in and of itself, make U.S. investments more attractive abroad.[25]

Investment decisions are keyed, not to the prices of assets per se, but rather to the rates of return earned on those assets. The reluctance of Americans to save implies that they demand high rates of return in exchange for financial capital. Foreigners are more content to save, and consequently are willing to settle for lower rates of return. This immediately suggests that foreigners are generally willing to pay more for any given stream of real returns. The international transfer of ownership is therefore simply a matter of supply and demand. There is no national "fire sale"—in general, Americans are not being forced to sell off assets, nor are they doing so with any sense of urgency. By our standards, foreigners are willing to overpay for assets. American investment analysts see this not as a fire sale but a picnic.[26]

None of the concerns about foreign ownership of U.S. assets is particularly well founded. Indeed, the historical precedents generally suggest that high levels of foreign ownership do not produce deleterious consequences. For much of its history, the United States was heavily dependent on inflows of foreign financial capital but managed nevertheless to grow into a dominant economic power. Moreover, the current level of foreign direct investment in the United States (as a percentage of national income) is not high by international standards. For example, a substantial fraction of the Canadian capital stock has for many years been owned by foreigners, yet Canada has remained one of the wealthiest nations in the world.

The American aversion to foreign ownership arises not from sound economic principles but from xenophobia. In simple terms, American citizens have become accustomed to a dominant world position. The deterioration of that position has evoked nationalistic resentment.

While Americans continue to think in terms of "us" and

"them," the Japanese and especially the Europeans are learning to think in global terms. The new economic reality is that, ultimately, a vast number of employees in all countries will come to work for multinational entities. Since these companies will be traded on world capital markets, the notion of a national affiliation will become obsolete. Global economic integration is on the horizon, and the American outlook must adjust to accommodate it.

Until this ideal is achieved, foreign ownership of domestic assets will remain economically relevant. However, by and large, it benefits the host country. While it may be desirable to take some measures in order to protect key technologies, we should not contemplate more general limitations on inflows of foreign capital.

International Competitiveness

Low rates of national saving have impaired the international competitiveness of American industry through two distinct channels. First, rising real interest rates attracted foreign investors, thereby strengthening the demand for U.S. currency. As a result, the dollar appreciated rapidly during the mid-1980s. American goods became expensive relative to foreign goods, making it difficult for American manufacturers to compete in world markets. It should be emphasized again that this shift in the value of currency has not altered the productivity of our industry, or the quality of our productive inputs, and therefore has not impaired our ability to compete at any given rate of exchange. Second, low saving depressed investment. The high cost of financial capital caused many companies to defer maintenance and cancel plans for modernization of plant and equipment. In contrast, higher rates of investment have allowed competitors in other industrialized countries—particularly Japan—to maintain physical capital at peak productivity, while operating at the cutting edge of new technology. As a result, American companies have continued to find themselves at a competitive disadvantage, even though the dollar has fallen sharply during the last few years.

The domestic consequences of deteriorating competitiveness have been severe. When worldwide demand for traded goods shifts

Table 2.3
Employment by Industry

Industry	Employment by Year (in thousands) [a]			
	1970	*1980*	*1985*	*1988*
All industries	78,255	97,708	103,009	110,899
Change		22.4%	7.5%	7.7%
Primary metals	1,248	1,136	798	764
Change		-9.0%	-29.8%	-4.3%
Machinery (except electrical)	1,985	2,491	2,190	2,082
Change		25.5%	-12.1%	-4.9%
Electrical and electronic equipment	1,851	2,083	2,171	2,069
Change		12.5%	4.2%	-4.7%
Motor vehicles and equipment	800	794	875	856
Change		-0.7%	10.2%	-3.3%

[a] Employment is measured as full-time equivalent employees plus self-employed persons.

Sources: U.S. Department of Commerce, *The National Income and Product Accounts of the United States, 1929–1982*, and *Survey of Current Business*, various issues.

to foreign suppliers, U.S. production of these goods falls and employers are compelled to eliminate jobs. Although most terminated workers eventually find alternative employment, many experience significant hardship during the transition. Some are unexpectedly forced to take early retirement and find themselves financially unprepared. In places where towns or cities have been built around a single company or industry, local economic depression results in deterioration of the social fabric. Overall, employment shifts to the nontraded sector, which consists in large part of service industries. Average wages in these industries are lower than in manufacturing, and displaced workers must often settle for low-skill jobs.

Table 2.3 documents the decline of several industries that have

faced stiff competition from abroad. The primary metal industries—particularly steel—have been hit hardest. Since 1970, employment in primary metals has fallen by around 40 percent.
Slightly more than 100,000 jobs disappeared between 1970 and
1980, and employers have eliminated nearly 400,000 additional
jobs since 1980. The machinery industries have also taken a beating. The rate of growth of employment in these industries actually exceeded the economywide average between 1970 and 1980.
However, since 1980, more than 400,000 jobs have disappeared.

Stiff foreign competition has also led to the stagnation of several
other important industries. Although stagnation is less serious
than a sustained contraction, it does threaten job security. In
a rapidly growing industry, adverse market conditions may simply reduce the rate at which new jobs are created. Employers
in stagnant industries are much more likely to lay off workers
during periodic downturns. Even temporary job loss can be a
serious blow to many workers.

Table 2.3 depicts some notable examples of industrial stagnation. Employment in the electrical and electronic equipment
industries grew mildly during the 1970s, but has remained virtually unchanged since 1980. The number of jobs in the auto
industry has grown very little over the last twenty years; indeed,
the year-to-year changes in employment probably reflect fluctuating market conditions rather than sustained growth.

Participants in the hardest-hit industries have been among the
most vocal supporters of protectionist policies. They often cite
artificial barriers to foreign markets—especially Japanese
markets—and unfair competitive practices by foreign companies
as the primary causes of trade imbalances. They argue vehemently
that the U.S. government ought to respond in kind by shielding
domestic markets from foreign competition.

While foreign competition is certainly a serious national concern, protectionism is the wrong solution. Rather than engage
in an extended discussion of protectionist policies that would stray
far from the topic of saving, only two points that are directly
relevant here need be mentioned. First of all, it is essential to
bear in mind that the international capital flow account is the

mirror image of the current account. It is doubtful that America could balance the current account through brute force. But if it did, it would also inadvertently balance the capital account, thereby forcing net domestic investment to equal net national saving. In effect, the supply of foreign capital would dry up. Unless the rate of net national saving rose, net domestic investment would decline by 50 percent or more, sending the economy into a tailspin.

Second, the current account and trade deficits are not primarily attributable to the inaccessibility of certain foreign markets, or to the unfair practices of foreign companies. After all, the United States generally maintained favorable trade balances until the early 1980s; enormous trade deficits are a recent development. While the Japanese and other competitors do shield their markets to some extent, this has always been the case. Likewise, there is absolutely no evidence that foreign business practices have changed dramatically over the last five to ten years. Explanations for the deteriorating competitive position of American companies must therefore lie elsewhere.

To reestablish international competitiveness and redress trade imbalances without disrupting economic prosperity, the United States must achieve a significantly higher rate of national saving. Admittedly, this will entail tangible costs. Americans must get used to lower levels of consumption and higher prices for foreign goods. However, our standard of living will not suffer permanently. In relatively short order, productivity growth should accelerate as high saving provides the financial capital required to refurbish American industry. With a modern and efficient manufacturing base, the United States should eventually be able to sustain a permanently stronger dollar and higher standard of living than it now achieves by selling off its capital stock.

Economic Vulnerability

Low rates of saving have rendered the United States highly dependent on large inflows of foreign capital. The experience of Latin American countries strongly suggests that this is a position of economic vulnerability. Like the United States, many of

these countries failed to achieve high rates of domestic investment despite heavy borrowing on world capital markets. Eventually, their poor economic performances eroded the confidence
of foreign investors. As inflows of foreign capital slowed to a trick-
le, domestic investment fell precipitously, with devastating consequences for output and employment.

It would be foolish to assume that the United States is, by vir-
tue of its economic and political status, completely immune to
the problems encountered by its Latin American neighbors. As
noted earlier, the supply of foreign financial capital to America
could dry up for any one of a number of reasons. Foreign governments may take steps to stem the tide of capital outflows, either
to stimulate investment at home or to strengthen their domestic
currencies. Foreign investors may reach a point of satiation with
American assets. The U.S. government might foolishly move to
limit foreign ownership of American assets, or it might attempt
to redress trade imbalances through protectionism. Even nature
could conspire to reduce inflows of foreign capital. For example, following a catastrophic earthquake in Tokyo, Japanese investors would undoubtedly divert their resources from investments abroad to domestic reconstruction. In any of these cases,
given current rates of saving, the United States would find itself
unable to generate sufficient financial capital domestically, and
the rate of investment would plummet.

A sustained interruption of foreign capital would greatly
depress economic growth; even a temporary interruption would
have an immediate and potentially severe adverse impact on output and employment. This is particularly true in the current
economic environment. Over the last decade, Americans have
accumulated enormous amounts of debt. Many individuals and
corporations would find it difficult if not impossible to carry this
debt in a sluggish economy. This raises the possibility that even
a relatively mild external shock, such as a partial interruption
of foreign financial capital, could snowball into a serious economic contraction.

Several different measures of corporate leverage are available.
One of the most commonly cited statistics is the ratio of debt

to equity. This ratio has not increased markedly during the 1980s. It is therefore tempting to conclude that the corporate sector has not become any more vulnerable to a recession. Unfortunately, this is an illusion. The ratio of debt to equity has remained roughly constant simply because the stock market has performed so well—the value of equity has risen fast enough to keep pace with new corporate borrowing. Moreover, equity values have risen much more rapidly than earnings. As a result, the total carrying costs for corporate debt have become increasingly burdensome.

A statistic known as "interest coverage" provides a much better measure of the corporate debt burden. Interest coverage is equal to pretax income plus interest payments, divided by interest.[27] When this statistic equals ten, total cash flows available for making interest payments are ten times as large as actual payments—thus, the company has a large cushion. On the other hand, when this statistic equals one, total cash flows available for making interest payments are just sufficient to cover these payments. Companies with low interest coverage operate with very small cushions and may be forced to liquidate assets if conditions deteriorate.

Table 2.4 contains data on corporate interest coverage for the 1960s, 1970s, and 1980s. These statistics clearly demonstrate that American corporations have become increasingly burdened by the costs of carrying debt. A sharp downturn could leave many companies unable to cover interest payments. According to some estimates, recessionary conditions similar to those experienced in 1973–74 would bankrupt more that 10 percent of all publicly traded firms.[28] Moreover, even solvent companies might be forced to liquidate assets at unfavorable prices in order to meet obligations to creditors. The result would be a legitimate "fire sale," in which foreign investors would snap up American assets at bargain-basement prices.

Table 2.4 also contains data on household indebtedness. During the 1960s and 1970s, total household liabilities averaged roughly 70 percent of disposable income. This figure jumped to nearly 89 percent in the late 1980s, and reached 92 percent in 1988 (the most recent year for which data are available). It is

Table 2.4
Measures of Private Indebtedness

Sector/Measure	Period				
	1950–59	1960–69	1970–79	1980–84	1985–87/88[a]
Corporate					
Net interest coverage	—	10.2	4.8	3.5	3.1
Gross interest coverage	—	5.5	3.0	2.0	1.7
Households					
Total liabilities as percentage of disposable income	48.1%	69.7%	70.6%	77.1%	88.7%

[a] For net and gross interest coverage, 1985–87; for household liabilities, 1985–88.

Sources: George N. Hatsopoulos, Paul R. Krugman, and James M. Poterba, *Overconsumption: The Challenge to U.S. Economic Policy* (Washington, D.C.: American Business Conference, 1989); Federal Board of Governors, *Balance Sheets for the U.S. Economy, 1948–1988*; Department of Commerce, *The National Income and Product Accounts of the United States, 1929–1982*; and *Survey of Current Business*, various issues.

worth noting that home mortgages account for roughly two-thirds of all household liabilities, while just under one-quarter is attributable to consumer credit. Moreover, most of the increase in personal borrowing is attributable to mortgages. Therefore, it is possible to argue that rising indebtedness is unrelated to economic vulnerability: households own assets (homes) that offset their liabilities (mortgages). However, houses are not highly liquid, and sales become particularly hard to arrange when the economy softens. The nation as a whole would do well to contemplate recent events in the Southwest (particularly Texas), where the ultimate repercussions of recessionary conditions included widespread defaults on mortgage loans and a flood of savings and loan (S&L) failures.

It is apparent that high levels of personal and corporate debt raise the ultimate social costs associated with any adverse external shock to the economy, and that low rates of saving increase our vulnerability to certain kinds of shocks. It is noteworthy that the recent increases in personal and corporate leverage may be related to movements in the rate of saving. In principle, this need not be the case, since financial leverage can be chosen independently of net worth. To put it another way, I can finance current consumption either by borrowing or by selling assets. However, in practice, I may have difficulty selling relatively illiquid assets, such as human capital or owner-occupied housing. Consequently, past a certain point I must borrow in order to finance additional consumption. A decline in saving therefore tends to produce greater personal leverage. For corporations, the causal relationship is probably reversed. When a company swaps debt for equity (for example, in a leveraged buyout), it must pay out a larger fraction of revenues as interest. This reduces residual earnings on equity, thereby depressing corporate retentions. (This effect will be treated at greater length in the next chapter.)

In summary, low rates of saving increase economic vulnerability. Should the economy soften due to some external shock (such as a partial interruption of financial capital), we would probably witness a virtual epidemic of defaults, forced asset sales, and even bankruptcies. Indeed, the very survival of our already crippled S&L industry would be threatened. It is very unlikely that any administration could manage a "soft landing" under these conditions.

The Personal Consequences of Low Saving

Recent statistics on personal saving suggest that an alarming number of Americans have been doing little to prepare for economic adversity or retirement. The financial security of many individuals has come to depend heavily on benefits provided either by employers or by the government. Unfortunately, private and public benefit levels will probably decline substantially during the next decade, and those who have failed to save may well find themselves without adequate protection.

Several economic trends have combined to halt the growth of employee benefits. Increased competition, particularly from abroad, has made employers much more cost conscious. At the same time, workers have demonstrated a willingness to accept benefit reductions rather than face layoffs. The increasingly accommodating posture of American labor has, among other things, produced a remarkable decline in unionization.[29] Many employers have seized the opportunity to slash benefits, particularly in the area of health insurance. Foreign competition has also prompted a shift from manufacturing to services. The service industries are generally even less unionized, and employment is more highly concentrated in small firms. For the most part, smaller firms provide fewer employee benefits.

In response to mounting budgetary pressures, Congress and the administration may also allow the social safety net to become a bit more porous. Fiscal concerns have already resulted in the partial taxation of Social Security benefits, the deferral of cost-of-living adjustments, and the recent turnaround on proposed catastrophic health insurance. As the retirement of the baby-boom generation approaches, sizable reductions in real Social Security benefits, as well as other entitlements, become increasingly likely.[30] Anxiety over federal deficits has also produced a scramble for new sources of revenue, and the tax-exempt status of employee benefits has become a prominent target. If Congress sees fit to eliminate this favorable treatment, then we should expect to see a precipitous decline in the provision of benefits.

If benefits levels do fall substantially, personal saving will become even more essential. When individuals with highly leveraged portfolios do not have adequate insurance (for instance, medical expenses and disability) even relatively mild personal setbacks can result in default or bankruptcy.

Financing consumption during retirement will also become problematic. Even during the high-saving 1960s, some 40 percent of couples and more than 50 percent of unmarried individuals reported that they received no money income from assets after retirement. At age sixty, nearly 30 percent of middle-class individuals lacked sufficient wealth to replace two years' worth of income.[31] Likewise, during the 1970s, most elderly individuals had not accumulated sufficient resources to sustain their accustomed levels of consumption. According to one study, consumption shortly after retirement exceeded the highest sustainable level of consumption by an average of 14 percent. This study also found that most retirees were forced to reduce their expenditures substantially within a few years of retirement.[32]

During the 1960s and 1970s, the United States made enormous progress toward the elusive goal of eliminating poverty among the aged, primarily by expanding the social security system and encouraging the growth of employee benefit programs (especially pension plans). Unfortunately, these gains may be ephemeral. Due to low rates of personal saving and pressures on both public entitlements and employee benefits, economic hardship during retirement will almost certainly become increasingly common. By the turn of the century, the elderly may revert to the status of an economically underprivileged class.

Is It All for the Best?

There are large social and personal costs associated with low rates of national saving. But there are also genuine benefits. When an individual chooses to save less, he accepts a less prosperous future in exchange for a higher current standard of living. Presumably, he has already weighed the relevant costs and benefits and has concluded that the benefits are more important. One of the fundamental guiding principles of U.S. economic policy is respect for free choice, as expressed through free markets. On the basis of this principle, one might be tempted to reject the claim that Americans currently save "too little."

When the free-market mechanism fails to work as it should, government intervention may be justified. Certainly, the U.S. government has departed from laissez-faire principles on many occasions. However, decisions to intervene should not be taken lightly. When arguing for a particular course of public action, it does not suffice to point out that certain private decisions are costly. Since resources are scarce, virtually all decisions entail costs. In general, the presumption must be that individuals understand both costs and benefits better than does the government. To justify prosaving policies, it is therefore necessary to explain why the usual market mechanism has failed to produce a desirable result.

Those who favor higher rates of saving have usually adopted

one of three positions. The first position is that the social benefits from saving exceed the individual benefits. Consequently, decisions based upon comparisons of costs and benefits to individuals yield rates of saving that are inadequate from the social perspective. One important reason for this is that the government taxes capital income (income generated by real or financial assets). Taxpayers save in order to accumulate personal resources. They do not attach much value to the incremental contributions that they make to government revenues, despite the fact that these revenues are socially valuable. Other government policies, such as subsidization of interest payments, achieve the same end. Another explanation for the divergence of individual and social benefits is that saving may create positive "externalities." The term "externality" refers to the impact of one individual's decision on another's well-being. If, for example, my resources fund research that leads to a new discovery, and if I am unable to extract the personal gains of every individual who benefits from this discovery, then the social benefits from this activity will exceed my personal benefits.[33] Likewise, in some instances one individual's investment may indirectly enhance the profitability of another's business enterprise, even though the second individual is not obliged to compensate the first.

A second position often adopted by those who favor higher rates of saving is that individuals do not rationally or systematically weigh costs and benefits. On the contrary, it is sometimes claimed that savings behavior is governed by rules of thumb, and that these rules reflect social and cultural norms. If so, then the government cannot ignore its role as an institution that may foster or perpetuate certain norms. If most individuals fail to consider all of the costs and benefits associated with profligacy, and if the national economy is damaged as a result, then the government may be obliged to actively promote more frugal behavior.

The third and final position is that laissez-faire policies may produce an undesirable distribution of resources across generations. Free markets are supposed to promote efficiency, but efficient resource allocation is not always equitable. If current generations are selfishly impoverishing their successors, perhaps by depleting the capital stock or by bequeathing oppressive levels of external debt, then it is appropriate to call for remedial government action.

All three of these positions have merit. In addition, the historical perspective shows that the principle of laissez-faire has never guided U.S. policy toward saving. Although the causes of low saving are complex, it is clear that the government has contributed through tax policy, budget deficits, and social leadership. The current rate of saving is not the result of an efficient free market, and even if it was, it is difficult to envision circumstances in which it would be considered socially optimal. Consequently, there is ample justification for public policies designed to promote substantially higher rates of national saving.

Chapter 3
Why Do Americans Save So Little?

Since inadequate saving threatens the very foundations of economic prosperity, the current administration must act swiftly and decisively to stimulate the rate of national saving. Unfortunately, this is easier said than done. A wide variety of options, ranging from balanced budget amendments to enhanced IRA provisions, have been proposed. The task before us is to formulate a national saving strategy that embraces the most efficacious and beneficial alternatives.

Theories of Saving

The first step in evaluating the efficacy of alternative policy options is to understand the factors that motivate people to save. Broadly speaking, there are two competing schools of thought concerning the determinants of private saving. One paradigm emphasizes economic and demographic factors. It portrays saving as the mechanism through which individuals rationally allocate their resources between current and future consumption. The other paradigm emphasizes the role of psychology. It characterizes economic and demographic factors as secondary to social, cultural, and experiential influences.

The most widely accepted economic theory of saving is known as the "life-cycle hypothesis."[1] Its central tenet is that individuals formulate long-range financial plans, rationally balancing future needs against current desires. According to this theory,

individuals are particularly sensitive to three concerns that motivate financial planning. First, they expect to retire. If a worker
fails to accumulate significant resources over the course of his
working life, then he cannot hope to maintain his accustomed
standard of living during retirement. Generally speaking, the theory implies that most individuals should do the bulk of their saving for retirement during the mid-life years, when earned income
approaches its peak. Second, their incomes are likely to fluctuate. If an individual wishes to maintain a constant standard of
living, then he must accumulate resources to provide a buffer
for the lean years. Third, expenditures may also fluctuate. From
time to time, most individuals find themselves burdened with
large, temporary financial obligations. Some of these expenses,
such as paying for a child's college education, are predictable.
Other obligations, such as those arising from medical treatment
for severe illnesses, may pop up suddenly and unexpectedly. Individuals must either plan ahead for these expenses by accumulating resources or run the risk of being unable to meet their financial obligations.

The life-cycle hypothesis implies that, in large part, rates of
saving should reflect the interplay of various demographic factors. One of the most important determinants of national saving
should be the age structure of the population. Large concentra-
tions of either young or retired individuals should depress national saving. Conversely, rates of saving should be high in countries with sizable populations of middle-aged individuals. Other
important demographic factors include fertility, life expectancy, and retirement patterns. High rates of fertility are associated with substantial expenditures on dependent children and
should therefore depress national saving. Life expectancy and
retirement patterns together determine the length of the retirement period. According to theory, workers should save more when
they plan to be retired for a greater length of time. Therefore,
longer life expectancies and shorter working lives should both
give rise to higher rates of saving.

The life-cycle hypothesis also implies that national saving should
depend on a number of economic factors, including net worth,

interest rates, capital income taxes, and productivity growth. All else equal, individuals with greater net worth have less reason to save additional resources. Among other things, this implies that rates of saving may decline when investors reap large unanticipated capital gains. Interest rates, together with capital income taxes, determine the rate at which individuals can trade off current consumption for future consumption. In essence, these two factors define the economic benefits of saving. When the benefits are greater (interest rates high, taxes low), individuals should save more.[2] Finally, when the rate of productivity growth is high, economic resources tend to become more concentrated in the hands of younger workers (who can generally adapt better to new technologies, and who will reap the benefits of growth over a longer time horizon), and most workers come to expect larger increases in real wages. Depending upon the specific characteristics of the economy, this could either increase or decrease total saving.

Economic theories of saving do not usually emphasize the roles of institutions. Nevertheless, they do suggest that some institutional arrangements are potentially important. If, for example, the structure of capital markets makes it difficult for consumers to borrow, then net saving should be higher. Institutions like saving and loan companies facilitate borrowing and may thereby depress rates of saving. When private markets for insurance (life, health, disability, and so forth) function efficiently, individuals may have very little need to save as a precaution against fluctuations in income or expenses. Likewise, social insurance programs such as Social Security, Medicare, and unemployment insurance may reduce precautionary motives for saving.

The economic paradigm implies that behavior depends on expectations about the future. Unfortunately, it doesn't explain how those expectations arise. To a large extent, this may be a matter of psychology. In principle, every individual in the United States has access to the same historical information about the economy. If expectations are purely objective, then we should all draw similar conclusions about future economic performance. But in practice, expectations may be colored by personal experience.

Someone who has lived through the Great Depression may well be less optimistic, and hence more conservative, than someone who has only learned about it in school. Firsthand experience changes the way information is framed and may alter the way it is processed. This is not to say that either the optimist or the pessimist is irrational. On the contrary, the point is that expectations arise in part from something beyond an objective notion of rationality. Thus, even if the life-cycle hypothesis is valid, the psychological determinants of expectations may be more important than the economic and demographic factors discussed previously.

Some proponents of the psychological paradigm go a step further and reject the tenet that most individuals rationally formulate complex, long-range financial plans. Self-control and "mental accounting" emerge as the central principles governing saving. In order to avoid temptation, an individual might, for example, restrict future choices by placing funds into a pension plan from which subsequent withdrawals are restricted. Individuals may also mentally separate their resources into a number of distinct accounts, some of which are psychologically easier to invade than others.[3]

The importance of mental accounting is best illustrated by a simple hypothetical situation. Suppose that you are on your way to see a play, and you have paid $40 for tickets. Upon reaching the theater, you discover that you have misplaced the tickets. Would you purchase replacements? Now suppose that you are on your way to the same play, and you intend to pay for the tickets at the theater. Upon arriving, you discover that you have lost $40. Would you still see the play? Objectively, these two situations are identical—in each case, you have lost something worth $40 and must pay an additional $40 for admission. Nevertheless, most individuals say that they would be more likely to see the play if they had lost the money than if they had lost the tickets. Researchers explain this puzzling behavior by noting that individuals assign these losses to different mental accounts.[4] In particular, when an individual purchases tickets, he psychologically allocates resources to entertainment. The loss of tickets depletes the "entertainment account." In contrast, the loss of cash reduces general resources and may therefore have very little impact on entertainment.

If psychological theories of saving are valid, then behavior may be governed primarily by habitual rules regarding the disposition of resources rather than by rational life-cycle planning. An individual may develop self-discipline by cultivating the habit of contributing 5 percent of his earnings to a pension account each month, or he might make periodic deposits into a savings account that he has earmarked for putting his children through college. These habitual rules respond slowly to social norms and to institutions that are designed to foster certain kinds of behavior.

Proponents of the psychological paradigm argue that saving is partly determined by cultural factors. The influences of culture are often expressed through religion and philosophy and may establish either asceticism or extravagance as basic behavioral patterns. To explain rates of saving, one might therefore look to the Protestant work ethic, or to the Confucian ethos of diligence and frugality.

Of course, the importance of culture is tempered by a number of considerations. In addition to the potential role of firsthand, personal experiences, institutional developments may also disrupt traditional patterns of behavior. For example, the development of a consumer credit industry may tempt individuals to invade certain mentally "reserved" accounts in order to spend. On the other hand, institutions such as contributory pension plans create new opportunities for exercising self-discipline. Spending patterns may also be susceptible to public campaigns that extol the virtues of either saving or consumption.

Finally, psychological considerations suggest that the rate of saving may be extremely sensitive to the composition of income and wealth. Changes in composition may shift resources to or from mental accounts that are more susceptible to invasion. For example, an increase in corporate dividends shifts income from undistributed corporate profits (which induce capital gains) to personal disposable income. Many individuals may be more inclined to spend their dividend checks than they are to realize capital gains and spend the proceeds.

Economic and psychological theories have very different implications concerning the efficacy and desirability of particular
public policies. It is therefore essential to determine which
paradigm best accounts for historical and international patterns
of saving.

Explaining Historical Trends

The rate of net national saving for the United States plummeted from roughly 8 percent in the 1960s and 1970s, to 2.7 percent in the late 1980s. Private saving led the decline, falling by
nearly 3.5 percentage points relative to NNP. A useful theoretical paradigm ought to suggest some reasonable explanation for
this drastic change.

Proponents of the economic paradigm have offered several
different explanations. For one thing, the age structure of the
population has changed dramatically over the last two decades.
Some would argue that the most important aspect of this change
has been the aging of the baby-boom generation. During the
1980s, the core of this generation moved into the high-spending,
peak home-buying years (ages 35–44). Conceivably, this could
have depressed aggregate saving. If this does account for recent
trends, then there is cause for optimism. During the 1990s, the
core of the baby-boom generation will move into the 45- to
54-year-old age bracket. Past experience suggests that saving rates
rise rapidly during this phase of the life cycle.[5]

Unfortunately, this explanation does not hold up under closer
scrutiny. First of all, demographic change is an evolutionary
process—and the age composition of the population simply has
not changed rapidly enough to account for the precipitous decline
of saving during the 1980s. Second, the premise of the argument
is faulty. It is true that 35- to 44-year-olds save a smaller fraction of their incomes than do 45- to 65-year-olds. However, the
baby boomers did not grow younger during the 1980s—they aged.
As the core of this generation moved from the 25- to 34-year-old
age bracket to the 35- to 44-year-old bracket, its constituents
should have saved more, not less. Finally, the aging of the baby-
boom generation was not the only relevant aspect of changing

age composition. Among other things, the fraction of the population under age sixteen has declined, while the ranks of the elderly have swelled. One set of economic simulations suggests that the overall impact of changing age composition should have been very slight, and may account for as little as a tenth of a percentage point decline in the rate of net national saving between 1960 and 1985.[6] These simulations also indicate that further changes in the age composition of the population will contribute to slightly lower rates of saving between 1990 and 2000. This outlook provides very little cause for optimism.

A second economic explanation for the decline of saving concerns asset revaluations. According to the life-cycle hypothesis, the purpose of saving is to augment net worth. If wealth rises autonomously, then an individual does not need to save as large a fraction of current income in order to achieve the same degree of augmentation. In other words, so far as the individual is concerned, capital gains are close substitutes for conventional saving. Proponents of the economic paradigm point out that individuals accrued sizable capital gains on corporate equities and residential properties during the 1980s, and they argue that this could in principle explain the decline of private saving as a fraction of disposable income.

Although this argument is theoretically sound, actual capital gains during the 1980s were much too small to account for the decline of private saving. Statistical analysis reveals that rising net worth explains only one-sixth of the recent increase in personal consumption.[7] This is hardly surprising. The fact that capital gains often reflect changes in relative prices, and that some of these changes may actually make the owners of assets worse off, despite apparent increases in wealth, was noted earlier. Moreover, even if one employs a broad-based notion of saving that includes asset revaluations, rates of saving still appear to have fallen appreciably since the 1960s and 1970s.

Asset revaluation and changes in the age structure of the population should have led the observer to expect a small increase in consumption during the 1980s. At the same time, the nation has witnessed declining rates of fertility, trends toward early retirement, increasing life expectancies, substantially higher real rates of return, and the introduction of tax incentives for saving (such as individual retirement accounts [IRAs] and Keogh plans). According to the life-cycle hypothesis, all of these should have produced higher rates of saving. Changes in other relevant variables, such as productivity growth, do not appear to have favored either saving or consumption.[8] The economic paradigm is therefore hard-pressed to account for recent developments.

In contrast, proponents of the psychological paradigm can identify several factors that probably contributed to the decline of saving during the 1980s. Among other things, they point to the impact of personal experience on expectations. Casual observation suggests that generations born after the Great Depression are simply less worried about financial security, and therefore less inclined to save, than those that endured severe economic hardship during the 1930s and 1940s.

Formal analysis of historical trends confirms this impression. According to one recent study, the declining fraction of national wealth held by individuals born before 1939 explains the entire increase in real consumption per household that occurred between 1963 and 1980.[9] This same study suggests that rates of saving in 1980 would have been roughly twice as high if the behavior of younger generations had matched that of the depression cohort. The economic importance of this cohort continued to wane after 1980, presumably causing further erosion of saving rates. However, the generational composition of wealth probably changed too slowly to account for the abruptness of the decline during the 1980s. Other circumstances must have affected the behavior of potential savers.

While the depression is perhaps the most notable landmark in U.S. economic history, it is certainly not the only event that may have shaped the public's basic attitudes toward saving. Just as economic hardship promotes conservatism, prosperity fosters extravagance. It is therefore noteworthy that the unprecedented decline of saving in the United States has coincided with the longest peacetime expansion on record. During the seven years since 1982, real GNP has increased 27 percent, real personal disposable income has advanced 17 percent, and some 19 million new jobs have been created in the nonfarm sector.[10] As a result, many Americans have become accustomed to economic growth and relatively low rates of unemployment, and have forgotten the lessons of less prosperous times.

If indeed the United States has entered a new regime of greater economic stability, then depression-era conservatism is obsolete and lower rates of saving may be justified. Unfortunately, this optimistic outlook is unrealistic. In fact, U.S. economic prosperity hangs by a thread, and inadequate rates of saving could sever that thread. Moreover, momentous events, such as the economic unification of Western Europe and the liberalization of Eastern Europe and the Soviet Union, will profoundly alter the world economy. International coordination of macroeconomic policies—necessitated by rising economic interdependence—will probably be achieved through a process of trial and error. Within the United States, the composition of jobs may change dramatically with shifting patterns of trade. As a result, the 1990s will probably be a period of transition, characterized by substantial instability. Seven years of prosperity have created a false sense of security.

Aside from historical influences, proponents of the psychological paradigm also point to changes in the composition of income as explanations for low rates of saving. Table 3.1 decomposes private disposable income into four categories: personal interest income, transfers received net of taxes paid, other personal income, and undistributed corporate profits. Several patterns are evident. First and foremost, personal interest income has risen dramatically as a percentage of private disposable income, especially between the 1970s and 1980s. During the same period, transfers net of taxes remained relatively constant, while other income declined steadily. Finally, the data exhibit a twenty-year decline in undistributed corporate profits, followed by a slight upturn in the late 1980s.

Economic theories of saving generally imply that these changes in the composition of income should have no impact on spending patterns. In contrast, the psychological paradigm suggests that

Table 3.1
Composition of Private Disposable Income

Ratio to Private Disposable Income of:	Period				
	1950–59	1960–69	1970–79	1980–84	1985–89
Personal interest income	5.2%	7.6%	10.3%	15.5%	16.3%
Transfers to individuals (net of personal taxes)	-7.8%	-8.1%	-5.6%	-4.8%	-5.4%
Transfers to individuals	6.3%	8.8%	14.3%	17.2%	16.6%
Personal taxes[a]	14.2%	16.9%	19.9%	22.0%	22.0%
Other personal income	98.8%	95.7%	91.8%	87.1%	86.5%
Undistributed corporate profits	3.9%	4.8%	3.4%	2.2%	2.6%

[a] Including contributions to social insurance

Sources: Department of Commerce, *The National Income and Product Accounts of the United States, 1929–1982*, and *Survey of Current Business*, various issues.

some types of income may be more spendable than others. Specifically, individuals may have difficulty resisting the temptation to spend unless they have to take explicit steps in order to access income. As a result, they may save a very small fraction of items like interest income but a very large fraction of undistributed corporate profits (that is, they may be reluctant to realize the associated capital gains in order to finance consumption). It is conceivable that the substitution of interest income for undistributed corporate profits and other private income has reduced the scope for self-discipline, thereby elevating consumption.[11]

One other aspect of Table 3.1 merits comment. The apparent stability of transfers net of taxes masks an increase in both taxes and transfers. This might help to account for the decline of saving, even within the economic paradigm. On balance, the poor and the elderly tend to be net beneficiaries from the tax/transfer system. As a result, an increase in both taxes and transfers redistributes disposable income to individuals who are less inclined to save. Even so, this effect is probably of little quantitative importance. Between the 1970s and early 1980s, taxes and transfers rose by two to three percentage points (expressed as fractions of private disposable income). Assuming that taxpayers save 10 percent of their incomes while transfer recipients save nothing, a redistribution of this magnitude would depress the rate of saving by perhaps 0.2 percent—a tiny fraction of the actual decline. Moreover, the saving rate fell even further between the early and late 1980s, despite the fact that neither taxes nor transfers rose.

The psychological paradigm also suggests that changes in the composition of wealth may have stimulated consumption during the 1980s. In particular, investors swapped huge amounts of corporate equity for debt. Net issues of new equity for the corporate sector hovered near zero until 1983. At that point, equity retirements and additions to debt both skyrocketed. In 1987, corporations retired $77 billion worth of equity, while debt grew by $154 billion. Projections for 1988 reveal even more rapid growth of corporate leverage.[12] These trends reflect two separate developments: the wave of leveraged buyout activity and the growing tendency for companies to repurchase stock.

When a stockholder tenders his shares (either voluntarily or involuntarily) in a buyout or a repurchase arrangement, he converts wealth to cash, at least temporarily. Economic theories of saving imply that this transaction should not affect behavior. If the investor originally had no plans to liquidate wealth in order to finance consumption, then he should simply reinvest the proceeds of the sale. But from a psychological perspective, the conversion shifts resources between mental accounts. In particular, it transforms wealth into cash, and places this cash in the hands of the investor. At that point, the investor may well be tempted to consume at least a portion of the proceeds. Indeed, the available evidence indicates that this temptation is quite powerful. Ordinarily, when wealth increases by one dollar, current consumption rises by about three cents. In contrast, the typical investor consumes roughly fifty to sixty cents out of each dollar that he realizes in a forced conversion of corporate equity.[13]

Changes in the composition of income and wealth have been quantitatively important. By one estimate, the rise in personal disposable income, led by the increase in interest income, accounts for roughly one-third of the increase in the ratio of consumption to NNP that occurred between the 1970s and late 1980s. The same study indicates that forced debt-for-equity conversions explain another one-sixth of the increase.[14] Consequently, when taken together, compositional factors may account for more than half of the recent decline in the rate of saving.

While these were proximate causes for the decline of saving, they too resulted from more basic changes in the economic environment. During the late 1970s and 1980s, personal interest income rose for at least three reasons. First, interest rates climbed rapidly. Rates of return on three-month Treasury bills reached a peak of just over 14 percent in 1981, after averaging only 5.9 percent between 1970 and 1978.[15] The importance of this effect had largely dissipated by the late 1980s, when rates once again dipped below 6 percent.[16] Second, accumulating debts burdened the federal government with increasing interest payments. Net interest payments from the government sector to the private sector nearly doubled between the 1970s and late 1980s (see Appendix Table A.4). However, this represented an increase relative to NNP of slightly less than 1 percent, against a rise in personal interest income of roughly 5 percent. Third, mounting debts resulted in much higher interest payments from corporations to households. For the corporate sector as a whole, the ratio of net interest payments to pretax income soared from 11.4 percent in the 1960s, to 24.0 in the 1970s, to 42.3 percent in the early 1980s, to 48.4 percent—nearly half—in the late 1980s.[17]

The pervasive substitution of debt for equity has thus affected consumption both directly, by altering the composition of wealth, and indirectly, by increasing the importance of interest income. Consequently, some of the causes of declining rates of saving must be rooted in recent changes in corporate capital structure.

Throughout recent history, the U.S. tax system has heavily favored debt over equity. The basic features of the tax system have undergone little change. With respect to debt, interest payments are deductible at the corporate level, but are taxed as personal income upon receipt. In contrast, equity income is taxed twice.

First, it is subject to the corporate income tax, regardless of whether it is retained or distributed as dividends. Second, residual earnings are taxed at the personal level. Dividends are treated as ordinary personal income. Retained earnings induce capital gains, and the government taxes these at realization. This "double taxation" creates strong incentives to increase leverage.

Although these incentives have always existed, they have grown more powerful during the 1980s. Large reductions in marginal personal tax rates, combined with the elimination of provisions that allowed for the partial exclusion of capital gains, have tipped the scales still further in favor of debt.

Some simple calculations serve to illustrate this point. Suppose that corporate securities are held by an individual who falls into the top tax bracket. In 1980, this individual would have paid 70 cents on each incremental dollar of income. As a bondholder, he would have received 30 cents on each dollar of gross return generated by an investment. As a stockholder, his return would have been subjected to a 46 percent tax at the corporate level. The residual—54 cents on the dollar—might have been either retained or distributed. Retentions generate capital gains. In 1980, 60 percent of these gains were excluded from taxation at the personal level. Assuming that the individual would have realized all gains immediately, he would have paid 28 cents in taxes on each dollar of retained earnings. For dividends, the government would have assessed 70 cents on the dollar. Assuming equal division of earnings between dividends and capital gains, the equity holder would have received approximately 27 cents on each dollar of gross return generated by an investment.[18] Since this is 3 cents lower than the corresponding figure for debt, the tax system favored high leverage.

In 1990, an individual in the top tax bracket paid only 28 cents in taxes on each dollar of incremental income. As a bondholder, such an individual receives 72 cents on each dollar of gross return generated by an investment. As a stockholder, his return is now subject to a tax of 34 percent at the corporate level. Since the capital gains exemption has been eliminated, the residual (66 cents) is taxed as ordinary personal income (at 28 percent, pro-

vided capital gains are realized immediately). Consequently, the
equity holder receives 48 cents on each dollar of gross return
generated by an investment. This is 24 cents lower than the corresponding figure for debt. For this investor, the relative advantage of using debt has increased about eightfold since 1980.

Capital markets have responded strongly to these tax incentives. During the 1980s, we have witnessed the rise of the junk
bond market, the explosion of leveraged buyouts, and the development of various financial instruments and institutions that
are designed to reduce the costs of bankruptcy. The resulting
increase in corporate leverage has profoundly altered the composition of personal wealth and private income, thereby significantly depressing rates of saving in the United States.

In summary, economic theories are hard-pressed to account
for the decline of saving during the 1980s. In contrast, the psychological paradigm offers two plausible explanations. First, the
declining fraction of wealth held by individuals born before 1939
has reduced the importance of depression-era conservatism. At
the same time, the longest peacetime expansion on record has
promoted a false sense of security and stability, reducing the perceived need for saving. Second, changes in the composition of
income and wealth have shifted resources between mental accounts, thereby increasing the temptation to consume. These
changes are in large part attributable to increases in corporate
leverage, which in turn can be traced to several recent rounds
of tax reform.

Although these explanations fit the facts, there still exists the
possibility that saving declined in the 1980s for reasons that have
not been considered. Economists understand savings behavior
imperfectly. Consequently, it is conceivable that the rate of saving could rebound as suddenly and as mysteriously as it declined.
Likewise, the efficacy of any given policy designed to stimulate
private saving is uncertain. Yet it would be a mistake to adopt
a passive stance and hope that recent trends will simply reverse
themselves without external encouragement. Thus, government
should take an active role, and attempt to stimulate private saving through a program that is guided by our best—although admittedly imperfect—understanding of behavior.

Explaining International Differences

While the United States saves significantly less than the developed nations of Western Europe, comparisons with Japan are particularly distressing. Just as the Japanese achieved prosperity after World War II by mimicking features of the U.S. economy, Americans should now examine the workings of the Japanese economy in order to learn from its successes before attempting to formulate a national saving strategy. Why are the Japanese so much more frugal than Americans?

Economic theories of saving offer a variety of potential answers to this question. One set of explanations emphasizes Japanese demographics. Relative to other developed countries, Japan has small populations of both young (that is, those who have not yet reached working age) and elderly individuals. Several studies suggest that differences in the age structure of the population may account for a large portion of the gap between rates of saving in the United States and Japan.[19] Several other demographic factors presumably contribute to this gap. Life expectancies in Japan are among the longest in the world. The average age difference between husbands and wives is unusually large, and this creates a greater need to save as a precaution against widowhood. Finally, Japanese families are more inclined to adopt shared living arrangements, wherein parents and mature children form single households. This yields economies of scale in consumption, permitting households to save larger fractions of their income.

Upon closer examination, the demographic factors mentioned above do not emerge as key determinants of Japanese saving rates. The age composition of the population matters only if rates of saving differ by age. According to theory, these rates should be very low for young workers, high for the middle-aged, and low, if not negative, for the elderly; consequently, the composition of the Japanese population would seem to favor high saving. But in fact, Japanese behavior does not conform to the theory. Table 3.2 presents rates of saving broken down by age for Japan and the United States. American households exhibit the predicted life-cycle pattern, but Japanese households save a virtually constant fraction of income irrespective of age. Rates of saving in

Table 3.2
Age-Specific Rates of Saving for U.S. and Japanese Households

Age of Family Head	Saving Rate (%)	
	U.S., 1972–73	Japan, 1974
Less than 24	-15	25
25–34	5	21
35–44	10	21
45–54	17	21
55–64	20	21
65 and up	13	21

Source: Fumio Hayashi, "Why Is Japan's Saving Rate So Apparently High?" in Stanley Fischer, ed., *NBER Macroeconomics Annual 1986* (Cambridge, Mass.: MIT Press, 1986).

Japan averaged 21 percent in every age category except for households headed by individuals under twenty-four. Moreover, this youngest group saved more, not less. The remarkable stability of saving rates across age cohorts strongly suggests that behavior in Japan is governed by habitual rules of thumb (such as "save one-fifth of income"), rather than by rational economic planning. Consequently, it is not at all surprising that the life-cycle hypothesis does a poor job of accounting for historical movements in the Japanese rate of saving.[20]

The other demographic factors mentioned also explain a very small fraction of the difference between Japan and the United States. While the Japanese have long life expectancies, they also tend to continue working until an advanced age.[21] Continued attachment to the work force reduces the amount of time that an individual will spend fully retired, offsetting the effect of greater life expectancy. Differences between the ages of spouses and the prevalence of shared living arrangements have both declined during periods when the Japanese saving rate rose sharply. This correlation may not be entirely coincidental: when individuals belong to closely knit extended families, they may be able to rely on relatives during periods of hardship, and may therefore have less incentive to save.[22]

The economic paradigm also suggests that saving should depend upon net wealth. For a given level of income, greater wealth reduces the need to save. World War II devastated the Japanese capital stock. In contrast, the U.S. capital stock was largely spared, and Americans enjoyed a high ratio of wealth to income after the war. It is conceivable that Japan has simply been playing catch-up in terms of wealth—the Japanese may have maintained high levels of saving in order to achieve for themselves and their children standards of living comparable to those of U.S. citizens.

At first glance, the data do not appear to support this hypothesis. Japan's ratio of wealth to income is currently more than twice that of the United States, and has exceeded the U.S. ratio since at least the mid-1950s.[23] According to theory, Japan should have saved less relative to national income, not more.

A more careful examination of the data reveals that this conclusion is unwarranted. An unusually large fraction of Japanese net worth—two-thirds in 1987, compared with only one-quarter for the United States—consists of land. Since land is not a reproducible asset, its stock remains roughly fixed. Unless the productivity of land changes, increases in its price cannot contribute to national wealth in any real sense. Therefore, when comparing ratios of income to wealth across countries, it is arguably appropriate to exclude the value of land as well as service flows associated with land. Figure 3.1 displays historical data on the ratio of wealth to income, adjusted to exclude real estate concerns. For the United States, this ratio has remained roughly constant throughout the postwar period and until recently has substantially exceeded the corresponding ratio for Japan. Even so, the Japanese have steadily closed the gap, and as of 1987, the two data series have essentially converged. Figure 3.1 certainly invites the interpretation that Japan has been catching up with the United States.

Despite this evidence, postwar reconstruction probably accounts for a very small fraction of the difference between the saving rates of the United States and Japan. Economic theory suggests that saving in Japan should have peaked immediately after the war, when the ratio of wealth to income hit a historic low. In fact, the rate of saving in Japan rose steadily for twenty-five years,

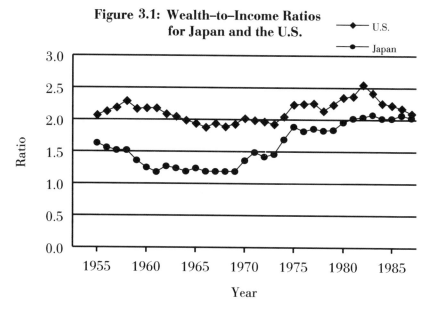

Figure 3.1: Wealth–to–Income Ratios
for Japan and the U.S.

Note: Wealth excludes the value of land, and income excludes imputed
rents from land.

Source: Fumio Hayashi, private communication

reaching its apex in the early 1970s. It may be possible to explain part of this lag by arguing that, at least initially, the Japanese
needed to consume a large fraction of income merely to achieve
subsistence—only later did higher levels of income permit discretionary saving.[24] Yet it is difficult to explain why the effects
of reconstruction should be so protracted. Certainly, forty-five
years after the war one cannot continue to attribute differences
to an initial handicap. Many European countries were equally
devastated by World War II, yet the Japanese experience appears
to be unique. Even though wealth-to-income ratios were converg-
ing, the gap between U.S. and Japanese saving rates widened during the 1980s instead of narrowing as the catch-up theory would
predict.

    Some economists have also attributed high rates of saving in
Japan to rapid economic growth.[25] If consumers seek a constant
target ratio of wealth to income, then faster rates of economic

growth necessitate higher rates of saving. But high productivity growth leads to rising wages, and this reduces the need to save. With more rapid growth, consumers would probably seek a lower target ratio of wealth to income. The net effect of growth on saving is therefore ambiguous.

It has also been argued that growth concentrates income in the hands of younger workers who, under some conditions (such as low life-cycle wage growth), are more inclined to save. But these conditions are not satisfied in Japan. The wages of Japanese workers rise quite steeply with age (up until retirement from primary employment). The life-cycle hypothesis implies that these workers should save very little when young and accumulate resources rapidly immediately before retirement. An increase in economic growth would then concentrate resources in the hands of individuals who save very little, thereby stimulating consumption instead of saving.[26] Moreover, we have already seen that, in practice, rates of saving in Japan are unrelated to age.

In light of these remarks, it is hardly surprising that, historically, there has been no clear correlation between Japanese saving and growth. Indeed, saving rose sharply when growth declined around 1974, and the continued decline of growth rates since the mid-1970s has been accompanied by only a moderate dip in the rate of saving. In the long run, high rates of saving have unquestionably contributed to Japanese growth. But there is very little reason to believe that high rates of growth have produced high saving.

The high and rising cost of housing has also been identified as a potentially important determinant of rates of saving in Japan. Since the Japanese were slow to develop a home mortgage market, young workers were compelled to accumulate substantial resources prior to purchasing homes. In principle, this could have contributed to higher rates of saving. But the available evidence indicates that housing costs account for a negligible fraction of the difference in savings behavior between the United States and Japan.[27] Table 3.3 displays rates of saving for several different categories of Japanese households. The data clearly demonstrate that Japanese homeowners do not save more than renters with

Table 3.3
Saving Rates for Various Classes of Japanese Households

Class of Household	Saving Rate (%)			
	1979		1984	
	Urban	Rural	Urban	Rural
Homeowners	18	19	18	20
Renters without purchase plans	19	19	18	20
Renters with purchase plans	25	24	19	21

Source: Fumio Hayashi, "Why Is Japan's Saving Rate So Apparently High?" in Stanley Fischer, ed., NBER Macroeconomics Annual 1986 (Cambridge, Mass.: MIT Press, 1986).

no plans to purchase homes. Although renters with purchase plans saved a significantly higher fraction of income in 1979, this difference had entirely dissipated by 1984, perhaps reflecting the development of mortgage markets. Moreover, if housing costs explain high rates of saving, then one would expect these rates to be lower in rural areas, where housing is cheaper. In fact, this has not been the case. As shown in Table 3.3, rates of saving for urban and rural households did not differ significantly in either 1979 or 1984, regardless of home purchase plans.

Some economists ascribe Japan's high rate of saving to favorable tax treatment of capital income. Until recently, the Japanese government provided numerous tax breaks for various forms of saving. Interest income and distributions of profits from bonds, debentures, some varieties of investment trusts, and deposits in certain types of special accounts were all exempt from income taxation, up to generous limits. Together, these provisions permitted individuals to invest well over $100,000 each year without paying taxes on the associated interest, and even this statutory limit was relatively easy to circumvent. In addition, other forms of capital income, including capital gains on land, housing, and equities were largely tax-free.[28] Most of these tax breaks were abolished in the sweeping (and hugely unpopular) tax reform that took effect on April 1, 1988. Currently, Japanese investors pay a flat 20 percent withholding tax on all interest income.

The economic paradigm implies that capital income taxation affects saving by altering the after-tax rate of return available to investors. The quantitative importance of this effect depends upon a behavioral parameter known by economists as the "interest elasticity of saving." This parameter indicates the percentage change in saving that results from a 1 percent increase in the after-tax rate of return to investors. Measurement of the interest elasticity has proved highly controversial. The weight of the evidence points to a very low interest elasticity of saving; in other words, after-tax rates of return have little bearing on saving. For Japan in particular, there appears to be very little correlation between spending patterns and available rates of return.[29] It is therefore very unlikely that tax incentives account for much of the difference between rates of saving in the United States and Japan, at least directly. There may be some important indirect effects that warrant examination later.

According to the economic paradigm, there should also be a relationship between rates of private saving and the structure of social insurance programs. When the government provides either larger retirement benefits or a more comprehensive safety net, it reduces incentives for a private individual to save on his own behalf. During the 1960s and early 1970s, Japan's social security system was extremely underdeveloped. However, it was thoroughly upgraded in 1973, and for the last seventeen years it has been more closely comparable with the systems of most other industrialized countries. During this same period, public confidence in the U.S. Social Security system has deteriorated markedly. While the adequacy of social insurance programs may once have explained a portion of the savings gap between the United States and Japan, it is no longer an important consideration.

None of the factors discussed so far, including demographics, postwar reconstruction, rapid economic growth, housing costs, tax incentives, and social insurance programs, accounts adequate-

ly for either the magnitude or persistence of the difference between rates of saving in the United States and Japan. Proponents
of the economic paradigm make further points about incentives
and deterrents, but the accumulated research renders such explanations unpersuasive.[30] This evidence compels us to consider
the possibility that the root causes of Japanese frugality lie in
psychology rather than in pure economics.

It has become a commonplace assertion that Japanese frugality arises from deeply rooted cultural values. These values are
often ascribed to the influences of Confucianism, Buddhism,
Shintoism, and the like. Since these influences were at work
throughout Asia, some commentators have argued that culture
and tradition account for the preponderance of high rates of saving in this part of the world. There is some very sketchy evidence
that supports this view. Rates of saving for Japanese-Americans
are around five percentage points higher than those of other eth-
nic groups. Moreover, several researchers have found that, within Japan, saving is correlated with attitudes and behaviors that
reflect the strength of traditional values.[31]

Unfortunately, in the current context, "culture" has simply
become a catchphrase for influences that social scientists have
failed to understand. Attributing high rates of saving to Japanese
culture amounts to invoking a principle of Asian inscrutability,
and prevents us from learning some valuable lessons from the
Japanese experience.

The role of traditional, deeply rooted cultural values has been
vastly overstated. Recall that rates of saving in Japan have varied
enormously over the last fifty years. During the interwar period, as well as in the years immediately following World War II,
the Japanese saved less than Americans. Rates of saving in Japan
rose steeply during the 1960s. Yet this was a decade of Westerni-
zation, during which the influences of traditional Japanese culture waned. Similarly, Korea, Taiwan, and Singapore saved very
little as recently as 1960, and have only lately earned reputations as countries with high rates of saving. It certainly appears,
if culture is the chief determinant of frugality, that cultural influences can change dramatically within a very short period of

time. It should then be possible to identify the causes of these changes, and to ask whether public policy can induce a similar transformation in the United States.

After World War II, the Japanese government resolved to shape cultural norms directly and launched a national campaign to promote saving. To orchestrate this campaign, it established several new agencies, including the Central Council for Savings Promotion, the Savings Promotion Department of the Bank of Japan, and the Savings Promotion Center of the Ministry of Finance. Promotional activities have included monthly seminars that extol the virtues of saving and provide workers with financial guidance, sponsorship of children's banks, and the appointment of private citizens as savings promotion leaders. These agencies have also prepared and disseminated magazines, booklets, leaflets, posters, advertisements, films, and the like, all of which are designed to build and reinforce the values of conservatism and frugality.

By themselves, these promotional activities probably would not have produced high rates of saving in Japan. Fortunately for the government, certain institutional arrangements rendered the Japanese population receptive to the national campaign. One extremely important factor was the widespread use of the "bonus system."[32] A large proportion of Japanese workers have traditionally received semiannual bonuses as part of their compensation. During the 1950s, these bonuses accounted for a much larger fraction of total employee compensation (roughly 16 percent) than in any other industrialized country. Investigators have consistently found that Japanese workers save a large fraction of bonus income: most households closely adhere to the rule of thumb that half of bonus income should be spent and half saved.

According to the economic paradigm, the timing of employee compensation should not affect either consumption or saving.[33] But from a psychological perspective, the bonus system is critically important. First of all, it trains employees to save. Few if any individuals are inclined to spend such an enormous portion of their total annual compensation in a very short period of time. Therefore, at a minimum, employees must plan explicitly to spread their bonuses out over the year. In essence, the bonus system forces Japanese workers to practice a particular behavioral pattern; saving becomes an accustomed activity. Second, the bonus system encourages the development of other institutional arrangements that foster saving. Japanese banks and other financial institutions wage intense advertising campaigns at bonus time, aggressively marketing various financial instruments in order to attract deposits. Many employers also offer payroll saving plans, which in some cases require employees to deposit a portion of their bonuses for a specified period of time. Third, this artificial division of compensation helps workers to partition income into distinct mental accounts. By developing rules of thumb regarding the disposition of bonus income, employees find it easier to exercise self-discipline.

Researchers who have studied historical correlations conclude that the bonus system has raised the rate of saving in Japan by as much as three percentage points. These estimates are almost certainly conservative. Bear in mind that the bonus system has operated within the context of Japan's saving promotion activities. The government encouraged a specific pattern of behavior, and bonuses provided workers with ideal opportunities to practice it. It seems likely that once workers formed the habit of frugality, they carried it over to other types of income. Unfortunately, this indirect effect is very difficult to measure.

Several other circumstances of public and private policy also coaxed Japanese households into the government's scheme. Due to the inadequacy of social insurance and the unavailability of consumer credit, individuals readily recognized the need to save and were open to financial guidance. The marketing campaigns of the financial sector also exploited the favorable tax treatment of capital income.

During that last two decades, most of the institutions mentioned above have changed dramatically. In response to international pressure, the Japanese government has de-emphasized the promotion of saving. Japan greatly expanded its social insurance system in 1973 and has abolished most tax incentives for saving during the 1980s. The fraction of employee compensation paid as bonuses has declined to about 5 percent. Moreover, consumer credit has become increasingly available. Yet Japan's rate of saving has remained high. Those who are accustomed to thinking in terms of the economic paradigm find this puzzling. Once the incentives and institutions that supported high rates of saving are dismantled, shouldn't these rates decline swiftly? The psychological paradigm has no difficulty accounting for persistent patterns of behavior. It suggests that the direct and immediate impact of incentives and other arrangements may be much less important than their longer-run effects on the formation of habits and behavioral norms. Institutional change should reduce rates of saving in Japan, but this will occur slowly as new habits evolve.

Traditional economic factors do not explain why the Japanese are so much more frugal than Americans. Nor are the differences between Japan and the United States attributable to the immutable and inscrutable influences of "culture." Rather, the Japanese government actively and systematically promoted saving. Because of a variety of institutional arrangements, the Japanese public was particularly receptive to the government's message. Together, these policies created an environment that was favorable to the exercise of self-discipline, and in which the repetition of certain behavioral patterns led to the acquisition of robust habits. Japan has, by design, created a nation of savers.

In contrast, the U.S. government has traditionally portrayed consumption as the beneficial driving force behind macroeconomic expansion. Specific policies, such as the subsidization of home mortgages (for example, through the savings and loan system) and the tax deductibility of consumer interest generated a highly aggressive credit industry. Consumers have found it increasingly easy to cross the lines between distinct mental accounts by borrowing at favorable terms. Institutional developments within the United States have therefore made it difficult for individuals to exercise self-discipline. As if by design, we have created a nation of spenders.

Chapter 4
Policy Options

The task of restoring adequate rates of saving in the United States poses a major challenge to those who formulate national economic policy. Widespread concern over declining investment, deteriorating international competitiveness, foreign ownership of American businesses, and other economic woes has spawned sporadic attempts to stimulate saving through piecemeal policies. Taken as a whole, U.S. policy regarding saving remains uncoordinated, inconsistent, and generally ineffective. As long as Americans lack a coherent national saving strategy, the prospects for significant, sustained improvement are slim.

A chapter devoted to policy prescriptions and proposals to increase saving should begin by emphasizing the importance of policy coordination. A rapid increase in the rate of saving could have some undesirable side effects. Traditional Keynesian arguments suggest that high rates of saving may depress economic activity. In addition, there is some reason to believe that our economy might misallocate incremental domestic financial capital. Fortunately, it is possible to avoid these pitfalls through proper management of monetary policy and the adoption of appropriate investment incentives.

A national saving strategy should promote both public and private saving. The surest way to increase saving is to bring federal deficits under control. Unfortunately, from a political standpoint, this is an extremely difficult undertaking. While the ratio of federal deficits to GNP will probably decline over the next five years, the United States should not expect to achieve balanced budgets until the late 1990s at the earliest. Moreover, even if we could eliminate budget deficits instantaneously, the rate of national saving would still fall far short of its historical average. A credible national strategy must therefore rely heavily on policies designed to stimulate private saving, even though the efficacy of these policies is uncertain.

Following the example of postwar Japan, the U.S. government must actively and systematically promote private saving. The situation requires nothing less than a national campaign designed to reshape social norms, backed by substantive, high-profile economic incentives. In addition, the government must encourage institutional changes that are conducive to the exercise of financial self-discipline. In short, an effective national saving strategy should coax the American public into developing the habit of saving.

Coordinating National Economic Policy

Although most economists believe that the United States saves too little, some insist that excessive saving poses a much more serious threat to economic prosperity. This point of view is the legacy of John Maynard Keynes. Writing during the Great Depression, Keynes argued that high rates of saving depress aggregate demand, thereby contributing to economic stagnation. Following the depression, fashionable Keynesian ideas included the "paradox of thrift," which asserts that low rates of saving actually promote aggregate investment by stimulating demand.

Relatively few modern Keynesians believe that a high rate of saving is necessarily inconsistent with high levels of employment, output, and investment. After all, Japan, Korea, and several other Asian countries have managed to save extremely large portions of their GNP without provoking a Keynesian debacle. Even the United States generally sustained adequate levels of aggregate demand during the 1950s and 1960s, when rates of saving were several times greater than those observed during the 1980s.

Historical and international precedents notwithstanding, a few Keynesians insist that a sharp increase in the rate of saving could potentially provoke a recession. If individuals begin to save more, then the demand for consumer goods will decline, and the companies that produce these goods will scale back production and employment. Ideally, the forces of competition should then reallocate underutilized resources to the production of investment goods, such as new plant and equipment. Unfortunately, it may be very difficult to orchestrate this transition. Indeed, once employers have observed a decline in the demand for consumer products, they may become even less inclined to pursue new investment projects. Eventually, changing prices and wages should direct resources to their most productive uses. However, the economy may operate well below capacity for a protracted period of time while the necessary adjustments take place.

Despite this possibility, the promotion of saving should still rank as the nation's top economic priority. Keynesian concerns simply alert us to the importance of coordinating national economic policy.[1] In particular, the government can offset the undesirable side effects of high saving by using monetary policy to manage the level of aggregate demand. When rates of saving begin to rise, the Federal Reserve system should respond by expanding the money supply. This should reduce interest rates and raise investment, expediting the reallocation of resources to the production of physical capital. It is worth stressing that by failing to adopt an accommodating policy, the Federal Reserve could defeat the entire purpose of policies designed to raise the rate of saving. Yet, as long as policymakers have the foresight to pursue the appropriate mix of monetary and fiscal policies, it should be possible to increase the rate of saving significantly without impairing macroeconomic performance.

Even if the United States manages to avoid aggravating the current recession, higher rates of saving would not necessarily benefit the economy. Since taxes and problems of imperfect information distort capital markets, there is no guarantee that incremental funds would be allocated to the projects that generate the greatest social returns. This concern raises an important question: in practice, how would our economy use an additional dollar of financial capital? The available evidence suggests that slightly more than one-third of each incremental dollar would eventually go

toward reducing net inflows of foreign capital, while the remainder would augment net investment.[2] Consequently, if the
United States succeeds in raising the rate of net national saving
from 2.7 percent to 8 percent, it would probably invest as large
a fraction of GNP as it did during the 1950s and 1960s, and both
the international capital and current account imbalances would
all but disappear.

Unfortunately, even a substantial increase in aggregate investment can mask a severe misallocation of resources between competing projects. It is therefore essential to identify the types of
investments that would benefit from an increase in the supply
of financial capital. The data at hand indicate that residential
housing would account for between one-half and two-thirds of
incremental investment. However, according to some recent estimates, the social rate of return on additional investment in housing is only about one-half of the corresponding return on non-
housing investments.[3] In part, this reflects housing's historically
favorable tax treatment compared to other investments. Few
economists would argue that the American housing stock is in
the aggregate deficient relative to that of any other developed
country.[4] Society as a whole stands to gain very little from policies that would divert an even larger slice of our productive capacity into the construction of residential housing.

The United States urgently needs to stimulate capital formation within the business sector. Yet for each dollar of additional
saving, net investment in plant and equipment may rise by as
little as twenty cents. This observation has led some economists
to argue that the rate of saving is an inappropriate policy target,
and that Congress and the administration would do better to focus on investment incentives. This would be a serious mistake.
Unless the rate of saving rises, policies that stimulate domestic
investment will exacerbate international capital and current account imbalances. It is unwise to rely too heavily on inflows of
foreign financial capital. Ultimately, domestic saving will constrain domestic investment.

Fortunately, the United States need not resign itself to spending two dollars on residential housing for every additional dollar of business investment. In particular, the nation can increase

the domestic supply of financial capital through policies that target the rate of saving while simultaneously managing the allocation of funds through the adoption of appropriate investment incentives. By coordinating national economic policy, it should be possible to direct a larger share of savings toward much-needed investment in plant and equipment.

Public Saving

A quick review of NIPA statistics raises the possibility that the United States could achieve a satisfactory rate of saving simply by balancing the federal budget. During the late 1980s, net national saving averaged 2.7 percent of net national product—the private sector saved 5.6 percent of NNP, but the government sector borrowed more than half of this (2.9 percent of NNP). Federal deficits averaged 4.3 percent of NNP, while the state and local sector consistently operated with a surplus (1.4 percent of NNP). If the federal government had balanced its budget, then the government sector as a whole would have run a surplus equal to 1.4 percent of NNP. Assuming no change in the level of private saving, national saving would have totaled 7.0 percent of NNP (1.4 percent plus 5.6 percent). This figure is only slightly below the rates that prevailed during the 1950s, 1960s, and 1970s. Many economists have therefore emphasized that Congress should adhere to its self-imposed Gramm-Rudman deficit reduction targets, and some have even argued in favor of accelerating the timetable for balancing the budget.

Unfortunately, the statistical argument here is flawed, since private saving depends, at least to some extent, on public saving. Suppose, for example, that Congress chooses to balance the budget by imposing higher taxes. Most taxpayers would find themselves with less disposable income. If taxpayers tend to consume seventy cents out of each additional dollar of disposable income, then for each dollar of tax revenues, private saving would decline by thirty cents. Thus, public saving would displace private saving at the rate of thirty cents on the dollar.

Some policy analysts have argued that public saving actually crowds out private saving dollar for dollar. If this is true, then the elimination of federal deficits will have absolutely no impact on the rate of national saving. It is therefore important to examine this "crowding-out" argument (also known as "Ricardian equivalence") in some detail, in order to assess its validity.[5]

Proponents of Ricardian equivalence begin with the premise that the public must ultimately bear the burden of paying for federal programs, regardless of whether Congress raises taxes or authorizes additional borrowing. Deficits can postpone the day of reckoning but cannot alter the ultimate price tag associated with any program.[6] Consequently, government borrowing does not make taxpayers any wealthier, despite the fact that it may increase their after-tax incomes. As long as taxpayers understand and believe this argument, it would be foolish for them to consume more today simply because the government has borrowed on their behalf. Instead, they should save their tax rebates, and use principal and interest to pay off higher taxes when the debt matures.

This reasoning suggests that the government cannot alter private consumption by substituting taxes for deficits. Public consumption likewise will not change. Since aggregate demand is unaffected, NNP should remain fixed as well. But national saving equals the difference between NNP and total consumption. Since national saving holds steady, proponents of the Ricardian doctrine logically conclude that public saving crowds out private saving dollar for dollar.

The argument for Ricardian equivalence is simple, elegant, and almost certainly mistaken. The Ricardian hypothesis is predicated on at least three highly implausible assumptions.[7] First, individual taxpayers must be extraordinarily rational and farsighted. No allowance is made for the psychological impact of postponing or accelerating tax payments. Second, credit markets must work extremely well to offset the effects of tax changes on spending patterns. When the current income of any particular taxpayer is unusually low, he may wish to borrow in order to finance consumption. If he is unable to obtain credit at favorable terms, then his disposable income will constrain his expenditures. Evidence from studies indicates that as much as 20 percent of the taxpaying population may fall into this category. These individuals will almost certainly spend less in response to a tax rise. Third, the government must repay deficits in relatively short order. Even though the public ultimately bears the full cost for any federal program, deficits can shift this burden to later generations, in which case current taxpayers might justifiably feel wealthier. Of course, if a particular individual cares about his children enough, he may realize that the postponement of taxes does not benefit his family. If the vast majority of individuals come to this realization, then Ricardian equivalence will continue to hold.[8] However, theory and evidence both suggest that economic ties within families are not strong enough to rescue the Ricardian doctrine.[9]

The accumulated research strongly supports the view that private consumption responds to changes in public saving. Although economists do not have the luxury of testing alternative theories under laboratory conditions, policymakers occasionally oblige by inadvertently devising a nearly ideal experiment. Reagan's program of tax relief during the early 1980s is an excellent case in point. These measures did not affect government spending; rather, the administration simply substituted borrowing for taxes on an extremely large scale. Moreover, statutory tax reductions enacted in 1981 were phased in over a three-year period. Under the Ricardian view, private consumption should have been unaffected. Even allowing for minor imperfections in the assumptions about rationality, farsightedness, and access to credit markets, any surge in consumption should have occurred immediately after the measures were approved. In fact, consumption rose only 1.7 percent in 1981. It jumped 2.5 percent in 1982 when tax relief began to take effect, and surged 5.1 percent in 1983 after the remaining provisions had been implemented.[10] This sequence of events invites a very natural interpretation: consumer spending responded to concurrent changes in disposable income.

Even if the Ricardian hypothesis is false, it does not follow that additional public saving raises national saving dollar for dollar, either. The actual effect probably lies in the neighborhood of thirty to fifty cents on the dollar, and few if any economists would argue that it exceeds seventy cents.[11] Although the elimination of federal deficits would not have raised the rate of national saving to 7 percent during the late 1980s (as suggested at the outset of this section), it would nevertheless have had a significant impact.

Unfortunately, the pursuit of a balanced federal budget could well produce some undesirable side effects. There are, of course, the Keynesian concerns mentioned earlier, but these can be addressed through the appropriate use of monetary policy. The greatest risk is that the higher taxes that are integral to any deficit reduction package likely to be considered in Washington would alleviate fiscal pressures, prompting Congress to raise spending still further. This upward ratcheting of government spending has been a recurring theme in budgetary politics. Among other things, it describes much of the legislative history of the Social Security system. In the past, Congress has either increased benefits or expanded coverage whenever the Social Security trust fund accumulated significant resources. Clearly, revenue enhancement serves little purpose unless Congress is capable of resisting political temptation and exercising fiscal discipline.

Another, more important consideration is that Congress might attempt to reduce deficits by raising additional revenue through capital income taxes. Many politicians see the favorable treatment of life insurance, employee benefits (including pensions), and retirement accounts as tax loopholes. By eliminating these highly vulnerable provisions, and by shifting a still larger fraction of the tax burden to corporations, Congress could make progress toward balancing the budget. But this would defeat the primary purpose of deficit reduction. There is no point to raising the level of public saving if incentives for private saving and capital formation are sacrificed in the process. The United States requires a coordinated national saving initiative, not one that is self-defeating.

In any event, the political feasibility of balancing the budget by raising additional revenues is open to question. The success of President Bush's "read my lips" campaign underscores the public's resistance to increased taxation. Congress and the administration have now indicated a willingness to enact higher taxes, and it is likely that further progress will be made on this front. However, one must place current proposals in perspective. Measures that would add $10 billion or $20 billion per year to federal revenues are widely regarded as major political steps. Yet $10 billion represents only 7.0 percent of the federal deficit, and only 0.2 percent of GNP. If the ultimate goal is to raise the rate of national saving by five percentage points (relative to GNP), then this is a mere drop in the bucket. Some commentators have called for the adoption of a new, broad-based tax designed to raise perhaps $100 billion to $200 billion in new revenues. The most common proposal is for a value-added tax (VAT), which would generate substantial revenue without discouraging saving or capital formation. However, the prospects for adoption of a VAT are remote.

All things considered, the federal government can and should reduce deficits by raising more revenue through carefully chosen taxes that do not burden capital income (for example, taxes on gasoline consumption or pollution emissions). However, this will have only a modest impact on the rate of national saving. Tax increases must be accompanied by reductions in federal spending, as well as by measures designed to stimulate private saving.

Unfortunately, the prospects for significantly reducing the deficit by cutting federal programs are limited. Proposals to reduce spending inevitably precipitate battles with special interest groups. As the federal government has tightened its belt, these groups have marshaled their forces in order to protect their most cherished programs. Further progress is unlikely unless policymakers demonstrate a willingness to scale back politically sensitive programs, such as entitlements or the military budget.

Most politicians regard entitlements as sacrosanct. Congress did manage to slip some thinly veiled benefit reductions into the 1983 amendments to the Social Security Act, but this has been the exception rather than the rule.[12] Escalating budgetary pressures will probably compel further cuts. However, it is doubtful that these cuts will be large enough to affect either the federal deficit or the rate of national saving significantly. The 1983 Social Security amendments also provided for the accumulation of an enormous trust fund, intended to finance the retirement of the baby-boom generation. Given historical patterns, Congress will need to exercise an unprecedented level of self-discipline merely to hold the line on benefits. As long as the trust fund contains significant resources, large-scale reductions in benefits are probably not politically feasible.

The military budget is far more vulnerable than entitlements. This is a recent development; the world changed fundamentally and irrevocably during the second half of 1989. As the Warsaw Pact dissolves, Americans are reexamining the need for a monolithic defense force. If moderates continue to gain influence in Eastern Europe and the Soviet Union, pressure for reductions in military spending will mount. Prudence dictates, however, placing the potential "peace dividend" in perspective. The national defense budget for 1989 totaled roughly $300 billion, while the federal deficit weighed in at $160 billion. Therefore, Congress would have had to scale back military spending by more than 50 percent in order to achieve a balanced budget. It is unlikely that political developments around the world will all work in our favor or that conflicts will stabilize quickly enough to justify cuts of this magnitude within the next few years. Indeed, the war with Iraq seems to have dashed hopes for reaping a "peace dividend" in the near future.

If Congress attempts to balance the federal budget by cutting other programs, there is a major risk that its actions will be self-defeating. Earlier, the importance of public investment as one channel through which our society provides for its future was noted. Reduced spending on infrastructure, highways, education, and the like would allow an increase in the officially measured rate of national saving by slashing federal deficits. However, it would also reduce the accumulation of public capital, thereby impairing the nation's ability to provide for future needs.

Moreover, a decade of monolithic deficits has not imbued our lawmakers with the spirit of fiscal responsibility. Rather, Congress has responded to budgetary pressures by tinkering with the books, and has even resorted to moving certain items off-budget in order to assure nominal compliance with Gramm-Rudman targets. Consequently, even if Congress substantially reduces outlays on current programs, increased spending on other politically sensitive activities may simply take up the slack.[13]

If Congress and the administration pursue responsible fiscal management—if they make carefully chosen cuts in existing domestic programs while holding the line on new spending, and if world events permit them to pursue a program of planned reductions in military spending—then federal deficits should decline significantly over the next few years. It is, however, difficult to envision politically feasible cuts that would be large enough to balance the current budget. Fortunately, there is an additional factor working in our favor. If real spending grows more slowly than real GNP, and if the ratio of revenues to GNP remains constant, then economic growth will eventually balance the budget. Suppose, for example, that the government enacts no changes in statutes governing tax revenues or entitlement spending, and that other appropriations simply keep pace with inflation. Then, according to the bipartisan Congressional Budget Office, the federal deficit should fall from $220 billion in 1990 to $128 billion in 1995. This may seem like mild progress. But during the same period, GNP should grow from roughly $5.3 trillion to just over $7 trillion. Thus, as a fraction of GNP, federal deficits should decline from 4.1 percent to 1.8 percent—a far cry from the 5.3 percent figure posted in 1985. Moreover, if the government adheres to the discretionary spending limits enacted in the Omnibus Budget Reconciliation Act of 1990, then the federal deficit should fall to $57 billion by 1995—a mere 0.8 percent of GNP.[14] If in addition state and local governments continue to run surpluses in excess of 1 percent of GNP, the government sector as a whole should find itself slightly in the black by 1995.

In the best of all possible worlds, lawmakers would be able to overcome all political obstacles and balance the federal budget immediately. Unfortunately, the impact on national saving might well be disappointing because of citizens' propensity to consume from their tax savings. Suppose that, instead of running deficits averaging 4.3 percent of NNP, the federal government had balanced its budget during the late 1980s, and that states and localities had nevertheless continued to run surpluses. Assuming that each dollar of public saving contributes thirty cents to national saving, the rate of national saving would have been only 1.3 percentage points higher (4.0 percent instead of 2.7 percent). Even if public saving contributed to the national aggregate at the rate of fifty cents on the dollar, federal budget surpluses would have had to average 6.3 percent of NNP in order to achieve an 8 percent rate of national saving.[15] Put in perspective, the federal government could not have realized this objective even if it had eliminated all spending on goods and services. Moreover, at that rate federal authorities would have had to buy back the entire federal debt in relatively short order. Chronic surpluses would then have necessitated large-scale public ownership of either private or foreign securities. Managing such a massive intervention into financial markets would have raised a number of ticklish political problems (for example, whose securities should the government purchase?).

Consideration of the prospects for deficit reduction leads to a single, inescapable conclusion: if we are to succeed in raising the rate of national saving to its historical average, the private sector must lead the way. This does not mean that Congress ought to abandon its efforts to exercise fiscal restraint; it is essential that lawmakers demonstrate their commitment to a national saving initiative by continuing to pursue the elusive objective of a balanced budget. But deficit cuts are insufficient in and of themselves to raise capital accumulation to desirable levels.

Private Saving

If the rate of private saving continues to languish in the neighborhood of 5 to 6 percent of NNP, America's economic strength will deteriorate rapidly. The federal government must therefore take drastic and immediate steps to stimulate saving on the part of individuals and corporations. These measures should be firmly grounded in, and justified by, a theory of saving that accounts for observed behavior, including the recent and precipitous decline of private saving.

Proponents of the economic paradigm of individual and corporate behavior believe that the scope for government intervention is limited. Clearly, the government can do little to alter many factors that this paradigm singles out as key determinants of saving. For example, neither demographics nor the rate of productivity growth fall under the direct and immediate control of Congress or the president. Moreover, the composition of private saving is, under this view, of little substantive relevance. In particular, even if corporations were encouraged to retain more of their earnings, stockholders would realize that corporations were saving on their behalf, and would in response reduce personal saving by an offsetting amount, leaving total private saving unaffected.

The economic paradigm isolates one policy strategy as potentially workable: augment incentives to save by taking steps to raise the after-tax rate of return. This requires either higher interest rates or lower capital income taxes. The first alternative is extremely unattractive, since it would discourage investment. As a result, many economists insist that the federal government must stimulate private saving by reducing the rate of taxation on capital income.

Several specific proposals have been advanced. The most extreme option would be to eliminate capital income taxation altogether and to replace the existing system with a "consumption tax." One relatively simple way to accomplish this is to allow taxpayers to deduct all saving prior to calculating income tax liabilities. A discussion of the advantages and disadvantages of a consumption tax is beyond the scope of this paper;[16] moreover, the prospects for adoption are negligible.

A number of less drastic alternatives are also available. The Bush administration, as well as many members of Congress, favors a reduction of tax rates on realized capital gains and an expansion of special tax-exempt savings accounts. Martin Feldstein, former chairman of the Council of Economic Advisers, has argued forcefully that, in addition, Congress should tax real capital income rather than nominal income.[17] He points out that the inflationary component of investment income actually represents a return of principal—by taxing this component, the federal government heavily penalizes saving. Likewise, corporations are permitted to deduct nominal interest payments, rather than real payments, for the purpose of calculating tax liabilities. In this way, the government subsidizes corporate borrowing.

Unfortunately, a general reduction of capital income taxes might do little to stimulate a flow of additional saving. Until the mid-1970s, most economists believed that saving was essentially unresponsive to the available after-tax returns on investments (that is, they suspected that the interest elasticity of saving was close to zero). Several scholars have since challenged the accepted wisdom on both theoretical and empirical grounds.[18] This challenge has provoked an active debate and has stimulated additional research. Although a preponderance of this research has confirmed the traditional view,[19] none of the existing evidence is completely convincing. Even so, it seems likely that saving is not very sensitive to rates of return. In part, this conclusion reflects introspection. Suppose, for example, that you are attempting to decide whether or not to save an additional $1000 in the current year. Suppose also that you can invest this sum in an account that yields an 8 percent rate of return, but that you would have to pay taxes on this income at the rate of 28 percent. If Congress cut your capital income tax rate in half (to 14 percent), would this have an important effect on your decision? To answer this question, consider the impact of tax relief on your incentive to save. Since your tax rate falls by fourteen percentage points, your after-tax income will rise by 14 percent of 8 percent, or 1.1 percent of your principal. For a $1000 investment, this is equivalent to just under one dollar of additional income per month. It is hard to believe that this "kicker" would induce very many people to make the additional investment.

The possibility that the after-tax rate of return does not significantly affect the level of saving is too great to dismiss. In addition, a general reduction of capital income tax rates might generate a number of undesirable side effects. Opponents of this strategy emphasize two potential consequences.

First, capital income taxes fall disproportionately on wealthy individuals. As a result, preferential treatment of capital income is widely regarded as a tax dodge for the rich. It would be difficult for Congress to cut taxes on interest, rents, dividends, and capital gains without contributing to the perception that the system is unfair. Because of this, the prospects for a significant, broad-based reduction of capital income taxes are extremely remote.

Second, capital income tax relief might reduce revenues, impairing the ongoing effort to combat federal deficits. Further deterioration of the federal budgetary position would depress public saving, potentially offsetting any increase in private saving. Ultimately, the policy could well turn out to be self-defeating.

Those who favor reduced rates of capital income taxation have responded by arguing that federal receipts would decline little, if at all. Some maintain that even the complete elimination of capital income taxes would at worst leave total revenues unaffected.[20] Others have suggested that Congress could eliminate particular taxes without sacrificing revenue.[21] Generally, these arguments are based on the premise that individuals respond to capital income taxes by behaving in ways that reduce their total tax liabilities.

The case for reduced capital gains taxation has been couched in precisely these terms. Currently, the United States taxes gains only at realization (that is, when an investor sells an asset). With a lower tax rate, the Treasury would collect less revenue per dollar of realized gain. However, several studies have suggested that investors are more likely to realize accrued gains when tax rates are lower. An increase in the frequency of realization would contribute to revenue. According to some estimates, this second effect may actually outweigh the first effect, at least in the short term, in which case one could raise revenue by reducing tax rates on capital gains.[22]

Despite much political rhetoric, the advocates of a reduction in capital gains taxes do not have a convincing case. Most economists agree that changes in the rate of capital gains taxation affect the timing of realizations. For example, if an investor expects the rate to decline (perhaps because tax reductions have been enacted but not yet implemented), he will tend to hang on to assets that he would otherwise sell. Even so, many economists believe that a *permanent* reduction in the rate of capital gains

taxation would have very little effect on the frequency of realization. And it is this permanent effect that is, after all, most
relevant to the debate over federal revenue. Unfortunately, existing studies measure a blend of these permanent and transito-
ry effects.[23] Exaggerated claims of revenue neutrality therefore
reflect either bold speculation or wishful thinking rather than
objective interpretation of the evidence.

Those who support reduced taxation of capital gains also ignore other indirect effects on federal revenue. Preferential treatment of capital gains would induce many corporations to reduce
dividends and raise retentions.[24] Since dividends are taxed
more heavily than capital gains, federal receipts would fall.

Not enough empirical information has been gathered to rule
out the possibility that Congress could reduce the tax burden
on capital income without sacrificing revenue. Unfortunately,
there is also a good chance that revenues would decline precipitously. In this respect, capital income tax relief is a risky venture.

If economic incentives have little impact on private saving, and
if the adoption of these incentives entails significant risks, then
the economic paradigm offers little in the way of a constructive
solution to current difficulties. But since this paradigm, as explained in the last chapter, cannot account adequately for historical trends or for international differences in rates of saving, it
is natural to look elsewhere for policy guidance. The competing
psychological paradigm offers a different perspective on methods
of influencing people to save.

In order to appreciate the importance of psychology in the context of private saving, consider the following: Prior to the 1980s,
most whole-life insurance policies allowed individuals to borrow
against accumulated cash value at rates that were specified up
front. When interest rates climbed steeply in the late 1970s, these
provisions gave many policyholders opportunities to borrow at
extremely low rates. Indeed, it was possible to reinvest the borrowed funds at market rates, use the proceeds to pay off the loan
within a couple of years, and walk away with a substantial profit,
all without exposing oneself to any risk. Yet fewer than 10 percent of the policyholders who had this opportunity actually took

advantage of it.[25] There can be little doubt that the reluctance to borrow against life insurance policies reflects behavioral norms or rules of thumb rather than economic optimization. In effect, individuals impose self-discipline by exploiting their reluctance to invade the cash value of life insurance policies.

Just as psychology can work against rational optimization (as in the case of insurance policy loans), it can also reinforce economic incentives. Individual retirement accounts (IRAs) provide an example of this principle.

Following their introduction, the popularity of IRAs grew rapidly. Contributions jumped from $5 billion in 1981 to $38 billion in 1986. Congress then adopted legislation that limited the tax advantages of these accounts for many families. Subsequently, contributions declined sharply. Only 7 percent of all families contributed to an IRA in 1987, down from 15 percent during the preceding year. Two concerns appear to have motivated the decision to tighten restrictions on IRAs. First, many observers believed that IRAs primarily benefited the wealthy. Second, a number of economic experts argued that IRAs added little to aggregate saving. Rather, they maintained that the volume of IRA contributions reflected a shift of existing assets into tax-favored accounts. Anecdotal evidence even suggested that some individuals borrowed money in order to exploit IRAs as a tax dodge.

The first concern appears to have been exaggerated. In practice, two-thirds of all IRA accounts were held by individuals with annual incomes below $50,000. As for the second concern, economic theory supports the view that IRAs primarily provide incentives for asset shifting instead of for greater saving. Rules governing eligibility for tax-exempt status specify a maximum allowable contribution for each taxpayer. Any individual who contributes this maximum amount does not receive favorable tax treatment for income generated by incremental saving. Such an individual has a strong incentive to exploit the IRA tax shelter by diverting his money from other investments but no incentive to save a larger fraction of his income. Nevertheless, a series of careful empirical studies have gone against theory in contending that the bulk of IRA contributions actually represented net additions to national saving.[26] These reports suggested that few individuals shifted existing assets into IRA accounts, or increased their total indebtedness, in order to finance contributions. The most recent of these studies concluded that reduced consumption provided the resources for two-thirds of all IRA contributions, while reduced tax liabilities provided another third. Since it is difficult to believe that no asset shifting occurred at all, many analysts are skeptical about the validity of this finding. Unfortunately, it is too early to know whether or not these results will stand up under further scrutiny.

Taken at face value, the evidence on IRAs presents an intriguing puzzle: if the after-tax rate of return does not have a significant impact on saving, then why were IRAs so successful? Standard economic analysis provides few if any clues. To understand the popularity of IRAs, the psychological paradigm must be called into play.

Congress and the administration introduced IRAs with a great deal of public fanfare. Television, newspapers, and magazines devoted an extraordinary amount of time and attention to this topic. Financial institutions soon joined the media blitz, hoping to capture a share of the rapidly expanding market. Promotional strategies were designed to help potential investors appreciate the tax benefits of IRAs through simple, concrete illustrations. In short, taxpayers were hit with a barrage of messages that played upon a variety of emotions running from guilt to the satisfaction of beating the IRS to naked self-interest, and many were simply swept along with the tide of public enthusiasm.

A detailed examination of the public's response to IRAs reveals several patterns that confirm the importance of psychological influences. For one thing, contributions to IRAs were concentrated at the end of the tax year. This makes little financial sense—if one intends to contribute to an IRA, it is best to do so as early as possible, in order to maximize tax-free accumulation. Yet it is easy to understand the attractiveness of IRAs at tax time, since they can be used to reduce a taxpayer's immediate liabilities. From a psychological standpoint, the inclination to contribute ought to be particularly strong for individuals who discover that they owe money to the IRS (that is, those with insufficient withholding and estimated tax payments). In fact, taxpayers with year-end liabilities were much more likely to make contributions to an IRA than were those who received a refund.[27]

Investment patterns also provide some indirect evidence on the importance of marketing. Most advertisements and promotional literature emphasized the $2000 limit on contributions. In fact, many families faced limits of $2250, or $4000. Of the 14 million families that contributed to an IRA in 1985, 5.5 million could have sheltered more than $2000 but chose to save exactly $2000 nevertheless.[28] This cannot be coincidence. Rather, it appears that the media blitz had begun to establish a social norm.

Some economists believe that high-profile financial instruments such as the IRA produce a "recognition effect," whereby participants acquire a more general appreciation for the importance of saving.[29] An alternative theory is that IRAs encourage taxpayers to practice saving, so that financial self-discipline becomes an accustomed mode of behavior. In either case, total contributions to tax-favored accounts might actually understate the true impact of the IRA program on national saving. One recent study has examined this possibility by comparing rates of private saving for the United States and Canada. As it happens, these rates diverged demonstrably when Canada instituted a system of special, tax-favored accounts. Statistical analysis of these data reveals that for each dollar saved in a special account (including IRAs for the United States), national saving rose by one and a half dollars.[30]

IRAs provide a clear example of the principle that psychological factors can inflate the importance of economic incentives. In particular, it is possible to market saving in the same manner as consumer goods. Japan learned this lesson shortly after World War II, and it now boasts one of the greatest rates of saving in the developed world. It is high time that the United States followed suit.

The experience of the 1980s makes it abundantly clear that IRAs are not, by themselves, sufficient to restore an adequate

adequate rate of private saving. Unfortunately, U.S. economic policy has often worked at cross-purposes with respect to saving: some policies promote saving while others discourage it.

A coordinated national initiative designed to reshape social and psychological attitudes toward saving is needed. This initiative should consist of the following.

Expansion and Modification of Special, Tax-favored Accounts

The public should have access to a variety of instruments that permit tax-sheltered saving. The design of these instruments should adhere to several important principles:

1. It should fundamentally alter existing rules governing the eligibility of contributions to tax-favored accounts. By specifying maximum allowable contributions, current programs invite asset shifting and blunt the effectiveness of economic incentives. Earlier, I argued that these incentives are probably less important than various psychological factors that influence the rate of saving. Yet economic factors should not be written off as irrelevant. The Japanese have achieved high rates of saving by exploiting synergies between psychology and economics. Ideally, these influences should be mutually reinforcing.

To maximize economic incentives, the United States should establish a system of tax-favored accounts with the following features: Incremental contributions to these accounts should be eligible for favorable treatment only if the taxpayer's total saving exceeds some fraction of his total income. In this way, the government could provide tangible incentives for additional saving while at the same time avoiding the large loss of revenue that might well accompany a general reduction of capital income taxes. In the interest of equity, conditions for eligibility could be made more demanding for wealthier individuals. For example, low-income taxpayers might receive favorable treatment on all contributions, whereas taxpayers in the highest bracket might be required to save more than 50 percent of income before qualifying for tax breaks on further increments. Limits on contributions should either be extremely high (for example, 90 percent of income) or nonexistent. In short, rules governing eligibility should specify a floor, not a ceiling.

2. Tax-favored accounts should be dedicated to specific, readily identified purposes, such as retirement, college, or the purchase of a home or auto. This system would establish a correspondence between mental accounting and actual financial decision making, thereby discouraging investors from thinking about tax-favored savings as a substitute for other forms of personal wealth. With this format, it is more likely that contributions to special accounts would represent net additions to private saving. Narrowly focused accounts would also encourage individuals to rely on personal saving in several areas where borrowing is currently the preferred mode of finance. Finally, if the accounts are designed to serve objectives that are clearly of interest to middle-income individuals, and if Congress sets reasonable limits on contributions, then the public may be less inclined to perceive the program as a tax dodge for the rich (witness the popularity of IRAs).

3. Special accounts should be tied to objectives that are relevant for taxpayers of all ages. Young individuals are not sufficiently motivated by the desire to provide for retirement. Most are preoccupied with more pressing issues, such as financing the purchase of a home or planning for college expenses. Special accounts should target these concerns. It is also essential to reach individuals as early in life as possible, in order to build habits of frugal behavior. The Japanese have successfully demonstrated this principle by sponsoring children's banks. To attract the attention of high school and college students, Congress should consider creating special accounts earmarked for educational expenses and automobile purchases.[31]

4. In addition to receiving tax-free accumulation, individuals should be allowed to deduct contributions to special accounts from taxable income up front. The IRS would then tax the principal (and cumulative interest) at withdrawal. IRAs have exactly

this structure. An alternative scheme would be to allow no deductions up front, and to impose a tax on cumulative interest only upon withdrawal. This option is, in effect, currently available for some purposes through the use of whole-life insurance policies. From an economic point of view, these two schemes are practically identical—as long as the taxpayer's marginal tax rate doesn't change, the government takes the same percentage of assets, whether now or later. However, from a psychological point of view, the distinction is critical. IRAs were popular in large part because they allowed individuals to reduce tax liabilities immediately. Whole-life insurance does not have the same appeal.

5. Special accounts should be introduced with a great deal of fanfare. The federal government must, at least initially, do its part to engage the public's attention and imagination. Once the new products are sufficiently well established, the marketing efforts of competing financial institutions should suffice to maintain public enthusiasm.

The Bush administration has recently indicated that it supports the creation of "Family Savings Accounts" (FSAs), which would allow individuals to earn tax-free income by squirreling money away for a specified number of years. Individual taxpayers would be allowed to make nondeductible contributions to an FSA of up to $2500 per year. Earnings in these accounts would accumulate tax-free. Furthermore, taxpayers would be permitted to withdraw earnings tax-free, provided that the contributions generating these earnings are held in the account for at least seven years. Withdrawals of earnings on contributions held in the account for less than seven years would be included in gross income. For contributions held less than three years, there would also be a 10 percent early withdrawal tax. High-income taxpayers would not be eligible for the program.

The Bush FSA proposal is deficient in several critical respects. First, as with IRAs, eligible contributions would be subject to a ceiling rather than a floor. This would attenuate economic incentives for higher saving and invite asset shifting rather than genuine incremental saving.

Second, the proposal does not provide wealthier individuals with any incentive to save. These individuals currently account for the bulk of personal saving. In addition, they tend to be more sophisticated financially and therefore more likely to respond to economic incentives. Certainly, government cannot offer FSAs to this group without creating justifiable concerns about the distribution of the tax burden. However, there is a solution. If, as suggested earlier, eligible contributions are subject to a floor rather than a ceiling, and if this floor rises in accordance with income, then it is possible to enhance incentives for high-income taxpayers without offering great windfalls.

Third, FSAs fail to exploit the psychology of mental accounting. The Bush administration favors this proposal because, in contrast to IRAs, it provides a highly flexible, general-purpose vehicle for saving. But to minimize asset shifting and maximize incremental contributions to net saving, the government must encourage individuals to distinguish psychologically between special accounts and other forms of saving. By failing to earmark accounts for specific purposes, the Bush proposal removes the most important distinguishing characteristics of tax-favored vehicles. There is thus a substantial risk that contributions to these generic accounts would simply substitute for other forms of saving. Without properly structured psychological incentives, the availability of a higher rate of return probably would not, by itself, significantly affect behavior.

Fourth, the Bush proposal does not permit taxpayers to deduct contributions to FSAs when calculating taxable income. Instead, it offers tax-free withdrawal of principal. As I have indicated, these two different methods of structuring incentives, though nearly equivalent from a financial point of view, have very different psychological impacts. Recent experience suggests that taxpayers strongly prefer to receive tax breaks up front. It is therefore likely that FSAs will be less effective than IRAs.

Overall, the Bush administration's FSA proposal is not structured to maximize economic incentives, or to capitalize on psychology. Although it could conceivably have a measurable impact on private saving, it would also contribute to the federal deficit by reducing tax revenues. So even if the program stimulates private saving, there is no guarantee that it would bolster national saving. In contrast, a program designed around the five principles enunciated in this section would have maximal economic and psychological impact. Moreover, the use of eligibility floors would minimize adverse effects on revenues and public saving.

Elimination of Incentives for Personal Borrowing

In the past, the United States has promoted personal borrowing by allowing taxpayers to take deductions for consumer interest and mortgage payments and by encouraging the growth of the savings and loan industry. One simple way to raise national saving is to make borrowing less attractive.

Congress has already phased out the tax deductibility of consumer interest payments. This will probably have only a small direct effect on consumer borrowing. There may, however, be some important indirect effects. Economic institutions rise and fall in response to changing targets of opportunity. In particular, the consumer credit industry sprang up to exploit the tax deductibility of interest. Economic incentives combined with appealing marketing strategies to create a booming demand for credit. In the absence of tax breaks, marketing will become more problematic, and the credit industry will probably decline.

It is also time to reconsider the advisability of allowing homeowners to deduct mortgage interest payments. This is a politically sensitive subject, since tax breaks help many families to achieve the "American dream" of owning a house. However, the issue is not *whether* to subsidize the acquisition of houses, but rather, *how* to do it. The special, tax-favored savings accounts dedicated to home purchases mentioned earlier should be viewed as a substitute for the current system of mortgage deductions, not as a complement. In the process of subsidizing homeownership, government can either train taxpayers to borrow or teach them to save. Historically, the United States has only encouraged borrowing.

The current crisis in the savings and loan industry also offers us an opportunity to rethink federal policy regarding financial intermediaries. For years, S&Ls were required to hold big portions of their portfolios in the form of home mortgages. This policy effectively subsidized homeownership by diverting financial capital into the mortgage market. More recently, many of the restrictions on S&Ls have been relaxed. A growing number of economic experts question the wisdom of continuing to draw artificial distinctions between S&Ls and commercial banks. At a minimum, financial statutes ought to be rewritten to terminate the remaining implicit subsidies for home loans.

Pension Policy

Pension funds hold just over 10 percent of the value of all U.S. assets. While this is certainly an enormous figure, it vastly understates the extent to which Americans save through pensions. Between 1980 and 1984, net acquisitions of assets by private, state, and local pension funds averaged more than 90 percent of NIPA personal saving.[32] During the same period, the real value of pension assets (in 1982 dollars) climbed by $297 billion, while national wealth rose only $287 billion. Thus, for this four-year period, pensions accounted for more than 100 percent of the increment to national wealth. Between 1980 and 1987 (the most recent year for which data are available), more than half of the increase in national wealth ($720 billion out of $1.4 trillion) was attributable to pension funds.[33]

Pension contributions receive extremely favorable treatment under federal tax law. Although most individuals do not respond directly to these incentives, pensions have institutionalized saving for many workers in the sense that the accumulation of resources no longer represents a sequence of conscious choices. The phenomenal growth of the pension system is largely attributable to tax incentives; if Congress were to weaken the tax advantages of pensions, then the growth of this system would slow, and might even reverse. In view of the economic importance of pensions, this would be a national tragedy. In short, the favorable treatment of employee pension plans must be protected at all costs.

National policy also affects the structure of retirement plans. There are currently two distinct types of pensions. In a "defined benefit" plan, employers do not make explicit contributions on behalf of individual workers, nor do workers contribute anything themselves. Rather, benefits are calculated as a function of earnings during the last few years of employment. In a "defined contribution" plan, each worker accumulates assets in a separate account. Often, employers and workers both contribute to these accounts. In some cases, the employer simply adds a multiple of the worker's contribution.

A considerable majority of workers are solely or primarily covered by defined benefit plans. Even so, the defined contribution approach has steadily gained popularity. Much of this growth has taken place in the form of optional secondary plans, usually for workers who have primary defined benefit coverage.[34] Further growth of defined contribution plans—both primary and secondary—should be encouraged for two reasons.

1. Participation in a defined benefit plan is entirely passive. Since workers do not make explicit contributions, saving cannot become an accustomed, familiar, or habitual mode of behavior. Defined contribution plans—particularly those with generous matching provisions—require workers to assume a more active role, both in authorizing contributions and (for some plans) in determining portfolio composition. Through participation in a defined contribution plan, workers learn to save.

2. The response of asset accumulation in defined benefit plans to changes in interest rates is quite peculiar. In particular, when rates of return rise, total contributions fall. This phenomenon helps to explain why aggregate U.S. saving is so insensitive to interest rates.[35] As a result of this insensitivity, the U.S. economy is significantly more vulnerable to interruptions of foreign financial capital. Should the supply of foreign capital decline, a low interest elasticity of saving implies that interest rates will rise steeply and investment will drop precipitously. With a larger elasticity, increased domestic saving would take up some of the slack, thereby muting the impact on economic activity.

Corporate Tax Policy

The Tax Reform Act of 1986 included a number of provisions that affected the level of corporate saving. First, it significantly increased corporate income tax liabilities, reducing the pool of funds that corporations might have retained.[36] Second, by eliminating the favorable treatment of realized capital gains, the act encouraged corporations to retain smaller proportions of earnings and raise dividends. Third, it altered the relative tax treatment of debt and equity. The direction of this last effect is somewhat unclear. Taken together, these provisions probably depressed corporate saving by $36 billion in 1989.[37]

Some economists believe that changes in corporate saving have no effect on national saving. They point out that corporations merely retain earnings on behalf of their owners, and that the owners are perfectly capable of saving for themselves. Others insist that the composition of income is psychologically meaningful. They argue that corporate retentions and dividends belong to distinct mental accounts, and that stockholders are more inclined to spend dividends than sell off shares. By and large, the available evidence confirms the importance of psychological motivations. In particular, when corporate saving falls by one dollar, private saving drops by about twenty-five cents.[38] Conversely, a doubling of the rate of corporate saving that prevailed during the late 1980s would raise national saving by roughly half a percentage point relative to NNP.

Policies designed to encourage corporate retentions should therefore play an important supporting role in our national saving initiative. The most natural instrument for manipulating retentions is the corporate tax system. Realistically, any reforms that reduce corporate tax revenues have little chance for passage. In addition, while tinkering with the tax system, policymakers must be sure to preserve incentives for corporate investment.

One option is to reduce the attractiveness of dividends relative to retentions, presumably by reinstating the favorable treatment of capital gains. While this may not stimulate additional personal saving, it will prompt corporations to cut dividends. Unfortunately, as discussed earlier, there is a strong possibility that lower tax rates for capital gains would significantly depress federal revenues.

The second option is to eliminate the tax advantages of debt. Corporations would respond by reducing leverage, thereby raising interest coverage. Incremental earnings would likely boost both retentions and dividends. As the supply of corporate bonds contracts, interest might well decline as a fraction of personal income, reversing the long-standing trend noted in Table 3.1.

The simplest way to penalize debt is to drop the tax deductibility of corporate interest payments. But this would dramatically raise the cost of financial capital, in turn discouraging investment. Alternatively, legislators could implement one of many plans for integrating the corporate and personal tax systems. Many tax integration proposals would place debt and equity on an equal footing without raising the cost of capital. Still, most of them would reduce the overall tax burden, depressing corporate tax revenues. In the current political climate, the outlook for tax integration is bleak.

Fortunately, it is possible to eliminate the advantages of debt without greatly affecting either corporate tax revenues or the cost of capital. Specifically, this would entail the partial or complete elimination of corporate interest deductibility, an acceleration of depreciation allowances, and the reinstatement of an investment tax credit (ITC). The logic of this strategy is straightforward: if government raises the tax burden on debt while comparably lowering the burden on equity, total revenues and average investment incentives will remain roughly constant. Accelerated depreciation and the ITC reduce the cost of capital regardless of whether the corporation uses debt or equity, while limitations on interest deductibility affect only debt. An appropriate combination of these provisions will therefore yield the desired result.

One final point deserves emphasis. Instead of accelerating depreciation allowances and reinstating the ITC, Congress could also reduce the cost of equity capital by cutting the statutory corporate tax rate. But lowering this rate would reduce the tax burden on existing capital as well as new capital. Tax breaks for existing capital do not improve investment incentives. Both accelerated depreciation and the ITC are much more efficient ways to encourage investment, since they only provide favorable treatment for new capital. For this reason, the Tax Reform Act of 1986 moved the corporate tax system in precisely the wrong direction.

A National Campaign

Throughout this discussion, I have emphasized that a national saving initiative must exploit the psychology of saving. To a large extent, this is a matter of marketing. The United States must follow the example of Japan and institute a high-profile, public campaign designed to promote more frugal behavior. There are many domestic precedents for this endeavor. Previous campaigns have focused on a variety of topics, including seatbelts, drunk driving, energy conservation, high-cholesterol diets, drug use, and smoking. Successful campaigns have combined public information with economic incentives (the best example of this is the drive for energy conservation). The promotion of private saving is ideally suited for this two-pronged approach. Congress and the administration must publicly embrace the promotion of saving as a top economic priority, and systematically set about the task of reshaping social norms. However, as a first step, the federal government must make good progress toward bringing its own budget into balance. A profligate government cannot successfully preach thrift to the rest of the nation.

Notes

Chapter 1

1. These statistics are taken from the U.S. National Income and Product Accounts (NIPA), published periodically by the Department of Commerce in the *Survey of Current Business*. A historical summary of NIPA statistics appears in *The National Income and Product Accounts of the United States, 1929–1982*, also published by the Commerce Department.

2. Net national product is a commonly used measure of total national output. It is closely related to the more familiar concept of gross national product (GNP). The difference between NNP and GNP is equal to total depreciation on existing plant and equipment. Consequently, it is appropriate to measure net saving relative to NNP and gross saving relative to GNP.

3. The 3.7 percent figure is based on the assumption that one dollar of public saving contributes thirty cents to national saving. The available evidence generally supports this assumption (see chapter 4). Even if public saving contributed dollar-for-dollar to national saving, the total elimination of government deficits would have increased the rate of national saving to only 5.6 percent. The reader should also bear in mind that the public sector ran significant deficits during the 1970s. Thus, eliminating deficits goes well beyond a return to the policies of the preceding decade.

4. Gross domestic product is the value of final goods and services produced within a country. It differs from GNP in that part of GNP is earned abroad. Although it would be preferable to scale net national saving by some measure of net output, the OECD has adopted the

convention of expressing saving relative to GDP. This convention does not affect any qualitative patterns.

5. These countries include Belgium, Denmark, France, Germany, Greece, Ireland, Italy, Luxembourg, the Netherlands, Portugal, Spain, the United Kingdom, Austria, Finland, Iceland, Norway, Sweden, Switzerland, and Turkey.

6. Gross saving rates for developing countries are based upon data collected by the International Monetary Fund. See Susan Collins, "Saving Behavior in Ten Developing Countries," in B. D. Bernheim and J. Shoven, eds., *National Saving and Economic Performance* (Chicago: University of Chicago Press, forthcoming).

7. See Jeffrey Williamson, "Why Do Koreans Save 'So Little'?" *Journal of Development Economics* 6, no. 3 (September 1979): 343–62.

8. See Robert E. Lipsey and Irving B. Kravis, "Is the U.S. a Spendthrift Nation?" National Bureau of Economic Research Working Paper no. 2274, Cambridge, Mass., June 1987.

9. See Collins, "Saving Behavior in Ten Developing Countries."

10. See Patric Hendershott and Joe Peek, "Private Saving in the United States: 1950–1985," National Bureau of Economic Research Working Paper no. 2294, Cambridge, Mass., June 1987.

11. This discussion of differences between the accounting practices of the United States and Japan is based upon work by Professor Fumio Hayashi. See Fumio Hayashi, "Why Is Japan's Saving Rate So Apparently High?" in Stanley Fischer, ed., *NBER Macroeconomics Annual 1986* (Cambridge, Mass.: MIT Press, 1986), and Hayashi, "Is Japan's Saving Rate High?" *Quarterly Review, Federal Reserve Bank of Minneapolis*, Spring 1989.

12. See Deutsche Bundesbank, "The Saving Ratio of Households in the Federal Republic of Germany: An International Comparison," *Monthly Report of the Deutsche Bundesbank*, Frankfurt, January 1984.

13. See Derek W. Blades and Peter Sturm, "The Concept and Measurement of Savings: The United States and Other Industrialized Countries," in *Saving and Government Policy*, Federal Reserve Bank of Boston, October 1982; Hendershott and Peek, "Private Saving in the United States"; and Lipsey and Kravis, "Is the U.S. a Spendthrift Nation?"

14. The quantitative importance of research and development is somewhat smaller than it might appear. Because of data limitations, the final line of Table 1.1 is based on a sample of ten countries, rather than eleven. For those countries, the official measure of gross capital

formation amounted to 23.3 percent of GDP rather than 23.5 percent. Thus, the three adjustments collectively reduce the gap between the United States and other countries by 1.4 percentage points rather than 1.6 points.

15. See the Hudson Institute, *Workforce 2000* (Indianapolis: Hudson Institute, 1989).

16. If, however, the capital gain for the second corporation reflects retained earnings of $1 per share, then the Commerce Department would count this as corporate saving.

17. To illustrate, suppose that the actual rate of saving is 5 percent. Then a 1 percent error in measuring income translates into a 20 percent error for saving.

18. Recall that stock-based measures of saving are calculated as the difference between estimates of total wealth for two distinct points in time. In recent years, aggregate net worth has averaged slightly more than three times GNP. Supposing once again that the actual rate of net saving is 5 percent, a 1 percent error in measuring either initial or final wealth would translate into a 60 percent error for estimated saving.

19. See E. L. Feige, "The Meaning of the 'Underground Economy' and the Full Compliance Deficit," in W. Gaertner and A. Wenig, eds., *Studies in Contemporary Economics: The Economics of the Shadow Economy* (Berlin: Springer-Verlag, 1983).

20. Board of Governors, Federal Reserve System, *Balance Sheets for the U.S. Economy, 1948–1987*, Washington, D.C., October 1988.

21. Depending upon exactly what it is that one is trying to measure, there are a number of different ways to use this data. See John B. Shoven, "Saving in the U.S. Economy," in Michael L. and Susan M. Wachter, eds., *Removing Obstacles to Economic Growth* (Philadelphia: University of Pennsylvania Press, 1984); Alan J. Auerbach, "Saving in the U.S.: Some Conceptual Issues," in Patric Hendershott, ed., *The Level and Composition of Household Saving* (Cambridge, Mass.: Ballinger, 1984); Michael J. Boskin, "Issues in the Measurement and Interpretation of Saving and Wealth," National Bureau of Economic Research Working Paper no. 2633, Cambridge, Mass., June 1988; and David Bradford, "Market Value vs. Financial Accounting Measures of National Saving," National Bureau of Economic Research Working Paper no. 2906, Cambridge, Mass., March 1989.

22. See Hayashi, "Is Japan's Saving Rate High?"

23. At any given point in time, companies may find themselves with

too much physical capital, or too little physical capital. When capital is excessive, replacement cost exceeds market value. When capital is below the level required to maximize profits, market value exceeds replacement cost.

24. I discuss data on physical assets owned by the government, as well as par-to-market adjustments, further on. A slightly different use of the national balance sheet data allows for carrying all corporate assets at market value rather than replacement value. With this alternative treatment of the data, one finds that the yearly change in national wealth averaged 8.8 percent of GNP between 1961 and 1970, 8.9 percent between 1971 and 1980, and only 5.5 percent between 1981 and 1987. See Bradford, "Market Value vs. Financial Accounting Measures of National Saving."

25. In the first example, an increase in the interest rate reduces the price of future goods relative to current goods. In the second example, the price of computers falls relative to other goods. In the third example, the price of land rises relative to other goods. Capital gains and losses do not change the total amount of goods and services produced in the economy in any of these examples.

26. Ironically, state and local budgeting procedures do generally distinguish between capital and current outlays, even though the Commerce Department and Federal Reserve do not.

27. See Michael J. Boskin, Marc S. Robinson, and Alan M. Huber, "Government Saving, Capital Formation and Wealth in the United States, 1947–1985," National Bureau of Economic Research Working Paper no. 2352, Cambridge, Mass., August 1987.

28. See ibid.

29. It is worth mentioning that these bailout costs represent liabilities that were accumulated over a long period of time. Ideally, liabilities should be added to deficits as they accrue. In this case, the government simply waited until 1989 to recognize FSLIC liabilities, thereby creating the false impression that its total liabilities have surged.

30. See Boskin, Robinson, and Huber, "Government Saving, Capital Formation and Wealth."

31. See Hendershott and Peek, "Private Saving in the United States."

32. See Boskin, Robinson, and Huber, "Government Saving, Capital Formation and Wealth."

33. Even with both the inflation rate adjustment and the debatable interest rate adjustment, the private sector still accounts for 50 percent of the decline in national saving.

Chapter 2

1. I use the term "financial capital" to denote the funds that are available for financing the purchase of new plant and equipment (sometimes referred to as "physical capital").

2. See, for example, Martin S. Feldstein and Charles Y. Horioka, "Domestic Saving and International Capital Flows," *Economic Journal* 90, no. 358 (June 1980): 314–29.

3. Department of Commerce, *Survey of Current Business*, Washington, D.C., March 1983.

4. See, for example, Arnold C. Harberger, "Perspectives on Capital and Technology in Less Developed Countries," in M. J. Artis and A. R. Nobay, eds., *Contemporary Economic Analysis* (London: Croom Helm, 1978).

5. This point was first clarified by Jeffrey Frankel, "International Capital Mobility and Crowding-out in the U.S. Economy: Imperfect Integration of Financial Markets or of Goods Markets?" in R. Hafer, ed., *How Open Is the U.S. Economy?* (Lexington, Mass.: Lexington Books, 1986). Perfect mobility of financial capital implies only that investors should earn the same expected return (measured in domestic currency) on equally risky investments (where the measure of risk includes exchange rate fluctuations). Alternatively, if an investor uses currency futures to hedge exchange rate fluctuations, he should earn the same return on domestic and foreign bonds, as long as the bonds share the same default risks. The difference between these returns is known as the "covered interest rate differential." The available evidence does indeed indicate that these differentials have disappeared during the 1980s, at least for industrialized countries. Consequently, international capital markets appear to have become completely integrated. See Jeffrey A. Frankel, "Quantifying International Capital Mobility in the 1980's," in B. D. Bernheim and J. Shoven, eds., *National Saving and Economic Performance* (Chicago: NBER–University of Chicago Press, forthcoming).

6. As discussed later in this chapter, low saving contributes to current account deficits by raising the real value of the domestic currency. If investors regard trade imbalances as temporary, then they may well believe that depreciation of the domestic currency will be required to boost exports and depress imports. It is worth mentioning that a widespread expectation of real currency depreciation can arise only if there are barriers to trade (technically, this requires the failure of a condition known as "purchasing power parity"). Thus, the incomplete integration of goods markets has important implications for international capital mobility.

7. Explicit expropriation of foreign-owned U.S. assets is extremely unlikely. However, it is possible to accomplish the same objective implicitly through a number of acceptable mechanisms, such as higher rates of capital income taxation and more favorable laws regarding unionization and labor negotiations. As foreign ownership of the U.S. capital stock increases, these options become increasingly attractive to domestic politicians.

8. Foreign control of domestic assets is politically unpopular. Large capital inflows are also associated with a strong domestic currency, which damages the traded-goods sector. (These points are discussed at greater length later in this chapter.)

9. Since capital inflows are associated with a strong domestic currency, it follows that capital outflows weaken the currency. This reduces the purchasing power of domestic consumers. In addition, investment at home creates jobs, raises the level of wages, and generates larger contributions to tax revenues. For these reasons, governments may restrict or discourage capital outflows.

10. For an extended discussion, see Lawrence H. Summers, "Tax Policy and International Competitiveness," in Jacob A. Frenkel, ed., International Aspects of Fiscal Policies (Chicago: University of Chicago Press, 1988).

11. See Martin Feldstein and Phillipe Bacchetta, "National Saving and International Investment," National Bureau of Economic Research Working Paper no. 3164, Cambridge, Mass., November 1989.

12. Although this principle may at first seem mysterious, it is in fact quite transparent. Imagine that a Japanese investor purchases an American-held asset, paying the owner in yen. The previous owner then uses these yen to buy consumer goods from a Japanese manufacturer. At the end of these two transactions, all yen have been restored to Japanese nationals. In essence, the United States has simply swapped an asset for consumer goods. The transfer of the asset to Japanese owners constitutes an inflow of foreign capital to the United States. The transfer of the goods to American consumers adds to imports. If nothing else happened, net foreign investment would fall and the trade deficit would rise by identical amounts. In practice, there are significant differences between the current account balance and net foreign investment, as calculated by the Department of Commerce. This is attributed to a "statistical discrepancy."

13. Due to the structure of the corporate and personal tax systems, the cost of financial capital may also depend upon the rate of inflation, and therefore indirectly upon the nominal interest rate.

14. See Mervyn A. King and Don Fullerton, *The Taxation of Income from Capital* (Chicago: NBER–University of Chicago Press, 1984), as well as two papers by B. D. Bernheim and J. Shoven: "Taxation and the Cost of Capital: An International Comparison," in Charles E. Walker and Mark A. Bloomfield, eds., *The Consumption Tax: A Better Alternative?* (Cambridge, Mass.: Ballinger, 1987), and "Comparisons of the Cost of Capital in the U.S. and Japan: The Roles of Risk and Taxes," Center for Economic and Policy Research (CEPR) Discussion Paper no. 179, Palo Alto, Calif., September 1989.

15. The difference between net investment and gross investment is the capital consumption allowance. As discussed in the Appendix, this difference increased steadily between the 1950s and 1980s due to the changing composition of investment.

16. Net foreign investment measures net *outflows* of capital. Therefore, a fall in net foreign investment represents an increase in net inflows.

17. Suppose that net foreign investment in the United States falls to zero. (This does not imply that all foreign investment dries up. Gross flows might still be large, but inflows and outflows would offset each other.) Then net domestic investment would equal net national saving. During the last five years, net national saving has averaged slightly less than 50 percent of net domestic investment.

18. The 10 percent figure represents a long-run or "steady-state" effect, and is obtained by making calculations similar to those appearing in Martin S. Feldstein, "Social Security, Induced Retirement, and Aggregate Capital Accumulation," *Journal of Political Economy* 82, no. 5 (September/October 1974): 905–26. Other work suggests that most of the long-run effect will be felt within twenty to thirty years; see B. D. Bernheim, "A Note on Dynamic Tax Incidence," *Quarterly Journal of Economics* 96, no. 4 (November 1981): 705–23.

19. See Michael J. Boskin, "Theoretical and Empirical Issues in the Measurement, Evaluation, and Interpretation of Post-War U.S. Saving," CEPR Publication no. 52, Palo Alto, Calif., 1986. Boskin's calculations are based upon utilitarian optimal growth models.

20. See Russell B. Scholl, "The International Investment Position of the United States in 1988," *Survey of Current Business* 69, June 1989. Some economists have argued that the official figures overstate the net asset position of foreigners, but they generally concede that the United States is now a net debtor nation. See Robert Eisner and Paul J. Pieper, "The World's Greatest Debtor Nation?" *The Review of Economics and Finance*, forthcoming.

21. According to the Commerce Department, "a U.S. affiliate is a

U.S. business enterprise in which a single foreign person owns or controls, directly or indirectly, 10 percent or more of the voting securities if an incorporated business enterprise or an equivalent interest if an unincorporated business enterprise." See Ned G. Howenstine, "U.S. Affiliates of Foreign Companies: 1987 Benchmark Survey Results," *Survey of Current Business* 69 (June 1989): 116.

22. See Jaclyn Fierman, "The Selling of America," *Fortune*, May 23, 1988, p. 54.

23. See "Is the U.S. Selling Its High-Tech Soul to Japan?" *Business Week*, June 26, 1989, pp. 117–18.

24. Indeed, higher rates of saving would simultaneously depress the value of the dollar and reduce net inflows of foreign capital.

25. In principle, a weak dollar can make U.S. assets more attractive to foreigners if they believe that the dollar will appreciate (this would make future returns relatively more valuable to foreign owners). In practice, most economists believe that the dollar will have to depreciate further in order to redress the current account imbalance.

26. See John J. Curran, "What Foreigners Will Buy Next," *Fortune*, February 13, 1989, pp. 94–98.

27. Net interest coverage subtracts interest received from gross interest payments. Since borrowers may default during a downturn, and since a company would nevertheless have to cover interest payments in order to remain solvent, gross interest coverage probably provides a superior measure of economic vulnerability.

28. See Ben S. Bernanke and John Y. Campbell, "Is There a Corporate Debt Crisis?" *Brookings Papers on Economic Activity*, Washington, D.C., 1988: 1, pp. 83–125.

29. According to the Bureau of Labor Statistics, union membership dropped from 22.5 percent of all U.S. workers in 1980 to 16.8 percent in 1988. In the private sector, union membership has fallen to about 13 percent, the lowest rate in over forty years.

30. The long-run fiscal outlook for the Social Security system remains bleak, despite legislative measures taken in 1983. See Michael J. Boskin, *Too Many Promises: The Uncertain Future of Social Security* (Homewood, Ill.: Dow Jones–Irwin, 1986).

31. See Peter A. Diamond, "A Framework for Social Security Analysis," *Journal of Public Economics* 8, no. 3 (December 1977): 275–98.

32. See Daniel S. Hamermesh, "Consumption During Retirement: The Missing Link in the Life Cycle," *Review of Economics and Statistics* 66, no. 1 (February 1984): 1–7. This finding is, however, somewhat

controversial. Other economists have reached more optimistic conclusions. See Laurence J. Kotlikoff, Avia Spivak, and Lawrence H. Summers, "The Adequacy of Saving," *American Economic Review* 72, no. 5 (December 1982): 1056–69.

33. Through patents and licensing, someone who owns the rights to an invention may be able to extract some of the gains received by many individuals who benefit from the invention. However, in most situations it is not possible to extract all of these benefits.

Chapter 3

1. Professor Franco Modigliani of the Massachusetts Institute of Technology was awarded the Nobel Prize in Economics for several achievements, including his pioneering work on the life-cycle hypothesis. See Franco Modigliani and Richard Brumberg, "Utility Analysis and the Consumption Function: An Interpretation of Cross-Section Data," in Kenneth K. Kurihara, ed., *Post-Keynesian Economics* (New Brunswick, N.J.: Rutgers University Press, 1954).

2. In fact, the life-cycle hypothesis does not unambiguously predict that saving should rise (fall) with interest rates (tax rates). Higher interest rates affect saving through two separate channels. In the text, I have described the "substitution effect": individuals will tend to save more because each dollar of saving yields a larger benefit in terms of future consumption. On the other hand, when interest rates rise, individuals can attain satisfactory levels of consumption in the future even if they reduce their current saving. As a result, some individuals may choose to consume more and save less. This is known as the "income effect." In theory, the income effect could exceed the substitution effect, so that higher interest rates could depress saving. This is an issue that must be resolved through analysis of data. I discuss the existing evidence on this subject in Chapter 4.

3. See Hersh M. Shefrin and Richard H. Thaler, "The Behavioral Life Cycle Hypothesis," *Economic Inquiry* 26 (October 1988): 609–43.

4. See Daniel Kahneman and Amos Tversky, "The Psychology of Preferences," *Scientific American*, January 1982, pp. 166–72.

5. For an analysis that reasons along these lines, see the Hudson Institute, *Workforce 2000* (Indianapolis: Hudson Institute, 1989).

6. See Alan J. Auerbach, Laurence J. Kotlikoff, Robert P. Hagemann, and Giuseppe Nicoletti, "The Economic Dynamics of an Ageing Population: The Case of Four OECD Countries," *OECD Economic Studies* 12 (Spring 1989): 97–130.

7. See George N. Hatsopoulos, Paul R. Krugman, and James M. Poterba, *Overconsumption: The Challenge to U.S. Policy* (Washington, D.C.: American Business Conference, 1989).

8. According to the Council of Economic Advisers, *Economic Report of the President* (Washington, D.C.: U.S. Government Printing Office, January 1989), productivity growth fell from an average of 3.4 percent in the mid-1960s (1963–69) to 1.3 percent in the mid-1970s (1973–77) to roughly zero in the late 1970s and early 1980s. One might therefore be tempted to conclude that lower productivity growth has produced lower rates of saving. However, saving continued to decline during the 1980s despite the fact that the rate of productivity growth rebounded to an average of 2.1 percent between 1983 and 1987.

9. See Michael J. Boskin and Lawrence J. Lau, "An Analysis of Postwar U.S. Consumption and Saving, Parts I and II," NBER Working Papers no. 2605 and 2606, Cambridge, Mass., June 1988.

10. See the Council of Economic Advisers, *Economic Report of the President*.

11. A substantial fraction of personal interest income is actually received by financial intermediaries and imputed to individuals in the National Income Accounts. The psychological paradigm suggests that the propensity to consume from this imputed income should be quite low, since it is naturally allocated to a separate mental account, and hence is more difficult to invade. However, the evidence suggests that, overall, rising personal interest income has contributed significantly to the decline of saving.

12. See Hatsopoulos, Krugman, and Poterba, *Overconsumption*.

13. See James Poterba, "Dividends, Capital Gains, and the Corporate Veil: Evidence from OECD Nations," in B. D. Bernheim and J. Shoven, eds., *National Saving and Economic Performance* (Chicago: NBER–University of Chicago Press, forthcoming), and Hatsopoulos, Krugman, and Poterba, *Overconsumption*.

14. See Hatsopoulos, Krugman, and Poterba, *Overconsumption*.

15. Council of Economic Advisers, *Economic Report of the President*.

16. Although real interest rates (the difference between nominal rates and the rate of inflation) remained high throughout the 1980s, this would not account for the pattern displayed in Table 3.1. Moreover, psychological theories suggest that consumption should be more closely related to nominal rates than to real rates, since nominal rates determine cash flow.

17. These statistics are calculated from data on net interest coverage

for the corporate sector, taken from Hatsopoulos, Krugman, and Poterba, *Overconsumption.*
    18. The calculations are as follows:

$$0.46i + 0.54i \times ([0.4 \times 0.7 \times 0.5] + [0.7 \times 0.5]) = \text{approx. } 0.73i$$

where i represents the investor's gross return. Assuming half of the
residual (after corporate tax) earnings is retained (40 percent of this
is taxed at 70 percent) and half is distributed (taxed entirely at 70 percent), the equation reveals that 73 percent of the investor's gross earnings on equity are taxed away.
    19. See Charles Y. Horioka, "Why Is Japan's Private Saving Rate
So High?" in R. Sato and T. Negishi, eds., *Recent Developments in
Japanese Economics* (Tokyo: Harcourt Brace Jovanovich Japan/Aca-
demic Press, 1988), as well as Franco Modigliani and Arlie Sterling,
"Determinants of Private Saving with Special Reference to the Role
of Social Security: Cross-Country Tests," in F. Modigliani and R. Hem-
ming, eds., *The Determinants of National Saving and Wealth* (Lon-
don: Macmillan Press, 1983).
    20. See Fumio Hayashi, "Why Is Japan's Saving Rate So Apparently
High?" in Stanley Fischer, ed., *NBER Macroeconomics Annual 1986*
(Cambridge, Mass.: MIT Press, 1986).
    21. Although the Japanese typically retire early from primary em-
ployment, they also tend to embark on second careers after retirement.
As a result, in 1975 the labor force participation rate for males aged
sixty-five and over was 50 percent in Japan—twice the OECD average.
See Charles Y. Horioka, "Why Is Japan's Household Saving Rate So
High? A Literature Survey," CEPR publication no. 145, Palo Alto, Calif.,
December 1988.
    22. See Laurence J. Kotlikoff and Avia Spivak, "The Family as an
Incomplete Annuities Market," *Journal of Political Economy* 89, no.
2 (April 1981): 372–91.
    23. See Fumio Hayashi, "Is Japan's Saving Rate High?" *Quarterly
Review, Federal Reserve Bank of Minneapolis*, Spring 1989.
    24. See Lawrence J. Christiano, "Understanding Japan's Saving Rate:
The Reconstruction Hypothesis," *Quarterly Review, Federal Reserve
Bank of Minneapolis* (Spring 1989): 10–25.
    25. For example, Modigliani and Sterling, "Determinants of Private
Saving," attribute a large fraction of the difference between the Unit-
ed States and Japan to rates of growth.

26. This prediction is consistent with economic simulations performed by Fumio Hayashi. See Hayashi, "Why Is Japan's Saving Rate So Apparently High?"

27. See Charles Y. Horioka, "Saving for Housing Purchase in Japan," *Journal of the Japanese and International Economics* 2 (1988): 351–84.

28. For additional details on the Japanese system of capital income taxation, see J. Shoven and T. Tachibanaki, "The Taxation of Income from Capital in Japan," in J. Shoven, ed., *Government Policy towards Industry in the United States and Japan* (Cambridge: Cambridge University Press, 1988).

29. See Hayashi, "Why Is Japan's Saving Rate So Apparently High?"

30. See Horioka, "Why Is Japan's Household Saving Rate So High?" for a more extensive discussion of possible explanations of Japan's high rate of saving.

31. The existing evidence on this point is summarized by Horioka, in "Why Is Japan's Household Saving Rate So High?"

32. See Horioka, "Why Is Japan's Household Saving Rate So High?" for a more detailed review of the existing evidence concerning the effects of the Japanese bonus system.

33. In principle, the economic paradigm could account for high propensities to save out of bonus income if bonuses were sufficiently random. But in practice, there is virtually no uncertainty concerning whether or not employees will receive bonuses. Dates of payment are known in advance, and amounts are predictable.

Chapter 4

1. Many economists have addressed the problem of selecting an appropriate "policy mix." References include Arthur M. Okun, "Rules and Roles for Fiscal and Monetary Policy," in James J. Diamond, ed., *Issues in Fiscal and Monetary Policy: The Eclectic Economist Views the Controversy* (Chicago: De Paul University, 1971), and Warren L. Smith, "Monetary and Fiscal Policies for Economic Growth," in Walter W. Heller, ed., *Perspectives on Economic Growth* (New York: Random House, 1968).

2. See Lawrence Summers, "Issues in National Savings Policy," National Bureau of Economic Research Working Paper no. 1710, Cambridge, Mass., September 1985.

3. See Edwin S. Mills, "Social Returns to Housing and Other Fixed Capital," *Journal of the American Real Estate and Urban Economics Association* 17, no. 2 (Summer 1989): 197–211.

4. Many believe that the stock of low-income housing is inadequate. However, there is very little reason to suspect that the availability of new financial capital would, by itself, alleviate this situation. The problems of homelessness and availability of low-income housing should be addressed through a reallocation of resources currently devoted to residential construction, and not through a net increase in the resources devoted to this activity.

5. The idea that public saving may not affect national saving can be traced to the writings of David Ricardo. The resurgence of interest in Ricardian equivalence is primarily attributable to the work of Robert Barro, "Are Government Bonds Net Wealth?" *Journal of Political Economy* 82, no. 6 (November/December 1974): 1095–1117.

6. Of course, when the government borrows it must also pay interest, and in that sense deficits do raise the ultimate cost of government projects. However, borrowing does not alter the present discounted value of the payments that must be made to finance a particular project (present discounted value refers to the sum of nominal cash flows that a project will generate over its lifetime, discounted at the nominal rate of interest).

7. There are many objections to Ricardian equivalence other than the three listed here. For a more extensive discussion, see Willem H. Buiter and James Tobin, "Debt Neutrality: A Brief Review of Doctrine and Evidence," in George M. von Furstenberg, ed., *Social Security versus Private Saving* (Cambridge, Mass.: Ballinger, 1981); and B. Douglas Bernheim, "Ricardian Equivalence: An Evaluation of Theory and Evidence," in Stanley Fischer, ed., *NBER Macroeconomics Annual 1987* (Cambridge, Mass.: MIT Press, 1987).

8. This observation is credited to Barro, "Are Government Bonds Net Wealth?"

9. See B. Douglas Bernheim and Kyle Bagwell, "Is Everything Neutral?" *Journal of Political Economy* 96, no. 2 (April 1988): 308–38; and Bernheim, "Ricardian Equivalence."

10. See James M. Poterba and Lawrence H. Summers, "Finite Lifetimes and the Effects of Budget Deficits on National Savings," *Journal of Monetary Economics* 20, no. 2 (September 1987): 369–91.

11. See Bernheim, "Ricardian Equivalence."

12. Among other things, the 1983 amendments introduced taxation of Social Security benefits and delayed cost-of-living adjustments. Both of these measures amount to de facto benefit reductions.

13. The most obvious candidate is health care. Escalating medical

costs and demographic changes will add significantly to the costs of existing programs. Recent estimates indicate that the health insurance portion of Social Security faces a long-run deficit that will average 5.2 percent of payroll over the next seventy-five years, and could run as high as 12.5 percent of payroll. See Michael J. Boskin, *Too Many Promises: The Uncertain Future of Social Security* (Homewood, Ill.: Dow Jones–Irwin, 1986). At the same time, larger populations of elderly individuals will create growing pressure for an expansion of benefits. An increasing number of younger individuals in the lower- and middle-income brackets may also join the ranks of those who support some form of national health insurance.

14. See Congressional Budget Office, *The Economic Budget Outlook: Fiscal Years 1992–1996* (Washington, D.C.: Government Printing Office, January 1991). It should be noted that the CBO projects a $46 billion surplus in 1995 from the operation of deposit insurance funds due to proceeds from selling the assets of failed institutions. This budgetary "bonus" will be short-lived.

15. An 8 percent rate of national saving would have been 5.3 percentage points above actual experience. If public saving contributed to national saving at the rate of fifty cents on the dollar, then, all else equal, government saving would have had to have been 10.6 percent of NNP higher than it actually was to achieve the 8 percent target. Since federal saving was actually −4.3 percent of NNP, this implies that surpluses of 6.3 percent would have been necessary.

16. The interested reader is referred to the U.S. Treasury, *Blueprints for Basic Tax Reform* (Washington, D.C.: Government Printing Office, 1977).

17. See Martin Feldstein, "Tax Policies for the 1990's: Personal Saving, Business Investment, and Corporate Debt," NBER Working Paper no. 2837, Cambridge, Mass., February 1989.

18. In an analysis of aggregate data for the United States, Michael Boskin estimated a substantial elasticity of saving. See Michael J. Boskin, "Taxation, Saving, and the Rate of Interest," *Journal of Political Economy* 86, no. 2, part 2 (April 1978): S3–27. Subsequently, Lawrence Summers argued that this estimate probably understates the true elasticity by a wide margin. In particular, he pointed out that higher rates of return reduce the present value of future earnings. The resulting decline of current wealth, broadly defined, may cause many individuals to scale back current consumption. See Lawrence H. Summers, "Capital Taxation and Accumulation in a Life Cycle Growth Model," *American Economic Review* 71, no. 4 (September 1981): 533–44.

37. See Poterba, "Tax Policy and Corporate Saving."

38. See ibid. Some conflicting evidence is provided by Alan J. Auerbach and Kevin Hasset, "Corporate Saving and Shareholder Consumption," NBER Working Paper no. 2994, Cambridge, Mass., June 1989.

Appendix
A Detailed Review of Official Data on U.S. Saving

The purpose of this Appendix is to provide more detailed statistics relating to some of the issues raised in Chapter 1. It consists of two parts. The first part reviews the historical record on U.S. saving, based upon data from the National Income and Product Accounts.* The second part provides more elaborate international comparisons, drawing on statistics published by the OECD.

The Historical Record

Figure A.1 tracks net and gross national saving for the United States as fractions of GNP.† While these rates are somewhat volatile, several patterns are evident. The rate of gross national saving remained fairly constant from 1950 through the late 1970s but has declined steadily since 1978. The rate of net national saving also exhibits a long period of relative stability, followed by steady deterioration. There are, however, two important differences. First, the rate of net saving began to decline roughly five or six years sooner. Second, net saving has declined more dramatically than gross saving.

---

* All data for 1989 are based upon first-quarter performance.

† Usually, it makes more sense to scale net saving by net national product (NNP), and indeed I follow this practice throughout most of this book. For the moment, however, I prefer to scale gross and net saving by the same variable (GNP), so that I can discuss the difference between them (which equals the capital consumption allowance).

The difference between these two series is the capital consumption allowance, which represents the Commerce Department's best estimate of depreciation. This allowance rose significantly from the late 1960s through 1980, thereby causing net saving to fall further and sooner than gross saving. Since the accuracy of the data on depreciation is open to question, one might well wonder whether increasing capital consumption allowances reflect spurious statistical factors rather than actual economic events. In fact, this phenomenon is not a statistical aberration. During the 1960s and 1970s, business investment shifted toward shorter-lived assets, and continuing capital accumulation produced higher capital-to-output ratios. Both trends significantly raised depreciation as a fraction of GNP.

Table A.1 contains average rates of saving for the 1950s, 1960s, 1970s, early 1980s, and late 1980s. These data allow us to track long-run trends with greater quantitative precision.

Net national saving increased slightly between the 1950s and 1960s, reflecting both a rise in gross saving and a decline in capital consumption allowances. These allowances mushroomed during the following decade. The impact of this development on net saving was somewhat offset by a further increase in gross saving.

Much more dramatic changes occurred between the 1970s and early 1980s. Gross saving plummeted by an additional 1.5 percentage points, while capital consumption allowances continued to leap upward, adding another 1.9 points. The combined impact of these trends cut the rate of net national saving by nearly 50 percent.

By the late 1980s, net saving had fallen to a paltry 2.5 percent of GNP—roughly one-third of the rate observed during the three previous decades. It is notable that the trend toward higher capital consumption allowances actually reversed between the early and late 1980s—net saving has declined during the past five years entirely because the rate of gross saving has continued to deteriorate rapidly.

Overall, the rate of net national saving (expressed as a fraction of GNP) has declined by 4.6 percentage points since the 1970s. Roughly 80 percent of this change is attributable to falling rates of gross saving. Rising capital consumption allowances account for roughly 20 percent of the decline. Thus, regardless of whether one nets out depreciation, national saving in the United States is extremely low by historical standards.

Figure A.2 tracks various components of net national saving as fractions of net national product (NNP). Between 1950 and the early 1970s, one can discern a gradual tendency for the government to save less (that is, to run smaller surpluses and larger deficits).* This trend accelerated dramatically in the early 1980s due to the Reagan administration's budgetary policies. Private saving rose slightly from the 1950s through the early 1970s; however, it then began to decline rapidly. This trend resulted from falling rates of personal and corporate saving.

The data in Table A.2 allow us to decompose historical trends with greater quantitative precision. Since the 1950s, 1960s, and 1970s were periods of relative stability, I will focus on more recent events. Between the 1970s and early 1980s, the ratio of net national saving to NNP fell by a whopping 3.7 percentage points. The private sector accounted for slightly more than half of this decline (1.9 points), with the personal and corporate sectors making roughly equal contributions. Enormous federal deficits produced a striking decline in public saving. Even so, this accounted for slightly less than half of the total effect (1.8 points).

Between the early 1980s and late 1980s, net national saving fell by an additional 1.5 percentage points. This occurred despite the fact that public saving actually stabilized as a fraction of NNP. As is evident from Table A.2, the continued decline was entirely attributable to a sharp drop in the ratio of personal saving to NNP.

Overall, the ratio of net national saving to NNP plummeted from 7.9 percent to 2.7 percent—a staggering 5.2 percentage points—between the 1970s and late 1980s. Roughly 3.3 percentage points, or nearly two-thirds of the total change, was attributable to declining ratios of private saving to NNP. Of that amount, 2.7 percentage points—more than half of the total change—

---

* Statistical analysis of the data reveal that the trend accounted for slightly less than a one percentage point decline in government saving (expressed relative to NNP) during the twenty-five-year period from 1950 to 1974.

represented plunging rates of personal saving (expressed as fractions of NNP). Skyrocketing public deficits accounted for little more than one-third of the total change in rates of net national saving.

The statistics discussed so far do not necessarily absolve the government of primary responsibility for our current troubles. It is easiest to illustrate this point by describing a purely hypothetical set of events. If the government consumed more goods and services (relative to NNP), and if it financed this consumption through a mix of new taxes and deficits, then public saving would certainly decline as a fraction of NNP. But private disposable income would also fall relative to NNP. As a result, the ratio of private saving to NNP would decline, even if the propensity to save out of private income remained constant. A decomposition of national saving might then reveal that private saving had fallen more than public saving. Even so, the major responsibility for declining rates of national saving would clearly lie with the government. To put it simply, when the public sector consumes more, the nation saves less.

In reality, events in the United States bear little or no resemblance to this hypothetical scenario. Declining national saving primarily reflects escalating *private* consumption, not public consumption. Table A.3 contains data on the consumption of final goods and services by the private, federal, and state and local government sectors. The ratio of private consumption to NNP was relatively stable from the 1950s to the 1970s. However, between the 1970s and late 1980s, it leaped from 69.3 percent to 74.0 percent—an increase of 4.7 percentage points. In contrast, consumption by the federal government rose a mere 0.8 percentage points (from 9.5 percent to 10.3 percent), while consumption by state and local governments remained virtually constant. Moreover, most of the increase in public consumption during the 1980s consisted of defense spending, a large part of which is arguably investment.

During the same period, the public sector began to run large deficits. Since public consumption of goods and services increased only moderately, net receipts from the private sector must have fallen. Table A.4 confirms this speculation. Between the 1970s and late 1980s, government revenues rose by roughly 1.8 percentage points. This was, however, entirely offset by a 1.9 percentage point increase in transfers to individuals. On top of that, net interest payments to individuals and businesses increased by nearly a percentage point. As a result, the total cash flow available to finance public consumption dropped a full point, from 21.7 percent to 20.7 percent of NNP. Slightly more than half of the 1.8 percentage point increase in government deficits is therefore attributable to declining net receipts from the private sector; the remainder reflects increased public expenditures on final goods and services.

Table A.5 documents several striking patterns. As the government's net receipts from the private sector fell during the 1970s and 1980s, private disposable income actually increased.* If there had been no change in the propensity to save out of this income, the ratio of private saving to NNP would have risen. In fact, the propensity to save plummeted from 11.1 percent during the 1970s to 6.9 percent in the 1980s, more than offsetting the increase in disposable income. Personal disposable income increased even more sharply than private disposable income as a whole, from 77.3 percent of NNP in the 1970s to 79.8 percent in the late 1980s. Unfortunately, the propensity to save out of personal disposable income plunged from 8.0 percent to 4.3 percent, resulting in the sharp decline of personal saving relative to NNP noted earlier.

International Comparisons

Figure A.3 depicts rates of net national saving as percentages of GDP for the United States, Japan, and European members of the OECD. Clearly, the United States has saved very little relative to other developed countries throughout the postwar period. A closer inspection of this figure reveals several interesting patterns. Between the 1960s and early 1970s, the rate of saving fell slightly for the United States, but rose for Europe, and rose sharply for Japan. As a result, the difference between rates for

---

* Private disposable income is equal to personal disposable income plus undistributed corporate profits.

the United States and other countries peaked during the 1968–73 period. Since the early 1970s, saving rates have fallen steadily throughout most of the developed world, including Japan. The differential between the United States and other countries narrowed during the mid- to late 1970s, but widened once again in the 1980s.

Figure A.4 displays data on rates of gross saving. As mentioned in Chapter 1, the decline of gross saving rates for the United States did not begin in earnest until the 1980s. However, the patterns in Figures A.3 and A.4 are similar in most other respects. Since 1960, the United States has consistently saved far less (as a percentage of GDP) than Europe and Japan. The differential between the United States and these other countries peaked during the late 1960s and early 1970s, narrowed somewhat during the mid- to late 1970s, and widened again during the 1980s.

Differences between the United States and other countries are primarily attributable to private-sector activity rather than the government sector. Figure A.5 displays household saving as a percentage of disposable income for the United States, OECD Europe, and Japan. Households saved significantly less in the United States throughout the period considered. The differentials between the United States and other developed countries peaked during the mid- to late 1970s, roughly five years after the peak for national saving rate differentials, and the household saving gap has closed only slightly during the 1980s.

Figure A.6 provides a comparison of government saving (net lending) as a percentage of GDP for the same set of developed countries. During the 1960s and early 1970s, U.S. government deficits were slightly larger, but this explains only a small fraction of the differences noted in Figures A.3 and A.4. During the mid- to late 1970s, the government sector actually borrowed less in the United States than in OECD Europe and Japan. Finally, despite skyrocketing budget deficits during the 1980s, the U.S. government still borrowed less than its counterparts in OECD Europe, and only a percentage point more than the Japanese government.

Table A.1
National Saving for the United States, Gross and Net

	Period				
	1950–59	*1960–69*	*1970–79*	*1980–84*	*1985–89*
Gross National Saving (% of GNP)	16.1	16.3	16.7	15.2	13.0
Net National Saving (% of GNP)	7.4	7.9	7.1	3.8	2.5
Capital Consumption Allowances (% of GNP)	8.7	8.4	9.6	11.5	10.6

Source: U.S. Department of Commerce, *The National Income and Product Accounts of the United States, 1929–1982*, and *Survey of Current Business*, various issues.

Table A.2
Sectoral Components of Net National Saving for the United States

Component of Saving, as a Percentage of NNP	Period				
	1950–59	*1960–69*	*1970–79*	*1980–84*	*1985–89*
Net National Saving	8.1	8.6	7.9	4.2	2.7
Net Private Saving	8.2	8.9	8.9	7.0	5.6
Net Personal Saving	5.2	5.1	6.2	5.3	3.5
Net Corporate Saving	3.0	3.8	2.7	1.8	2.2
Government Saving	-0.1	-0.3	-1.1	-2.8	-2.9
Federal Saving	0.1	-0.3	-1.9	-4.2	-4.3
State and Local Government Saving	-0.2	0.0	0.9	1.4	1.4

Source: Department of Commerce, *The National Income and Product Accounts of the United States, 1929–1982*, and *Survey of Current Business*, various issues.

Table A.3
Consumption as a Percentage of NNP

Sector	Period				
	1950–59	1960–69	1970–79	1980–84	1985–89
Private Consumption	69.7	68.5	69.3	72.5	74.0
Government Consumption*	21.8	23.0	22.8	23.1	23.6
Federal	13.6	12.1	9.5	10.1	10.3
State and Local	8.2	10.9	13.3	13.0	13.4

* Includes all payments to foreigners

Source: Department of Commerce, The National Income and Product Accounts of the United States, 1929–1982, and Survey of Current Business, various issues.

Table A.4
Government Accounts

	Period				
	1950–59	1960–69	1970–79	1980–84	1985–89
Net receipts from private sector / NNP	21.7%	22.7%	21.7%	20.3%	20.7%
Revenues*	27.7%	30.5%	33.7%	35.2%	35.5%
Transfer payments**	4.7%	6.5%	11.0%	13.5%	12.9%
Net interest***	1.4%	1.2%	1.0%	1.4%	1.9%
Government consumption / NNP	21.8%	23.0%	22.8%	23.1%	23.6%
Government deficit / NNP	0.1%	0.3%	1.1%	2.8%	2.9%

*   Includes current surplus of government enterprises
**   Excludes transfers to foreigners (this appears as government consumption)
*** Includes dividend payments to the government; excludes interest payments to foreigners (this appears as government consumption)

Source: Department of Commerce, The National Income and Product Accounts of the United States, 1929–1982, and Survey of Current Business, various issues.

Table A.5
Private Income and Saving

Ratio of			Period				
(1)	*to*	*(2)*	*1950–59*	*1960–69*	*1970–79*	*1980–84*	*1985–89*
Private Disposable Income*		NNP	79.2%	79.1%	80.1%	81.6%	81.9%
Private Saving		Private Disposable Income	10.4%	11.2%	11.1%	8.6%	6.9%
Personal Disposable Income		NNP	76.1%	75.3%	77.3%	79.8%	79.8%
Personal Saving		Personal Disposable Income	6.8%	6.7%	8.0%	6.6%	4.3%

* Private disposable income equals personal disposable income plus undistributed corporate profits

Source: Department of Commerce, *The National Income and Product Accounts of the United States, 1929–1982,* and *Survey of Current Business,* various issues.

Figure A.1: National Saving for the U.S.

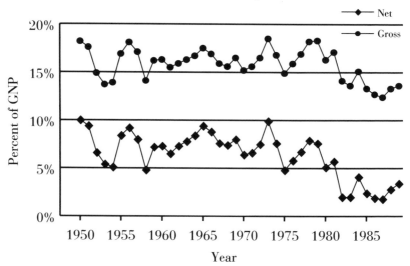

Source: U.S. Department of Commerce, *The National Income and Product Accounts of the United States, 1929-1982*, and *Survey of Current Business*, various issues.

Figure A.2: Components of Net Savings for the U.S.

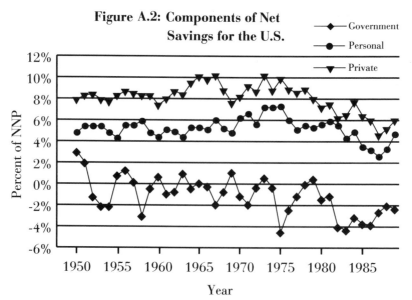

Source: U.S. Department of Commerce, *The National Income and Product Accounts of the United States, 1929-1982*, and *Survey of Current Business*, various issues.

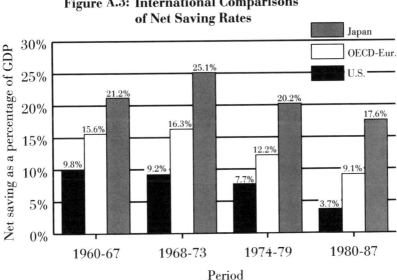

Figure A.3: International Comparisons of Net Saving Rates

Source: Organization for Economic Cooperation and Development, *Economic Outlook, Historical Statistics*, 1988

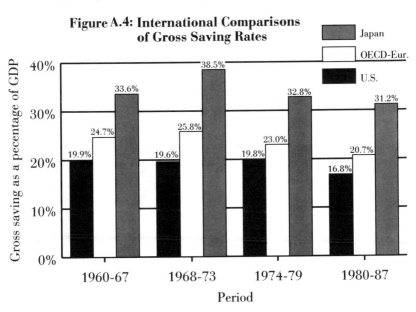

Figure A.4: International Comparisons of Gross Saving Rates

Source: Organization for Economic Cooperation and Development, *Economic Outlook, Historical Statistics*, 1988

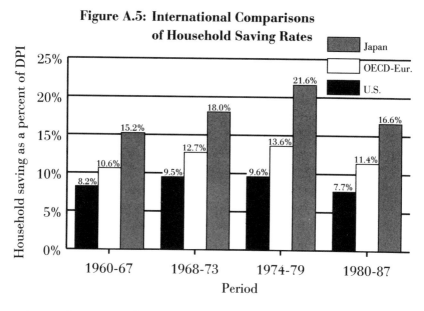

Figure A.5: International Comparisons of Household Saving Rates

Source: Organization for Economic Cooperation and Development, *Economic Outlook, Historical Statistics*, 1988

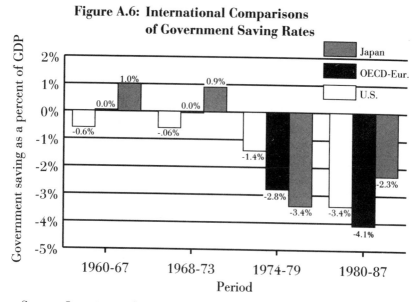

Figure A.6: International Comparisons of Government Saving Rates

Source: Organization for Economic Cooperation and Development, *Economic Outlook, Historical Statistics*, 1988

Index

153

The Japanese
Money Market

The Japanese Money Market

Robert F. Emery

LexingtonBooks
D.C. Heath and Company
Lexington, Massachusetts
Toronto

Library of Congress Cataloging in Publication Data

Emery, Robert F. (Robert Firestone), 1927–
  The Japanese money market.

  Bibliography: p.
  Includes index.
  1. Money market—Japan.   I. Title.
HG1275.E43   1983   332'.0412'0952   83–48452
ISBN 0–669–07208–7

Copyright © 1984 by D.C. Heath and Company

Published simultaneously in Canada

Printed in the United States of America

International Standard Book Number: 0–669–07208–7

Library of Congress Catalog Card Number: 83–48452

Dedicated with affection to my wife,
Phyllis Swanson Emery

Contents

Figures and Tables

Preface

Several factors prompted the writing of this book, one of the most important being the need to fill a large gap. While several books have been written on the money markets of the major Western countries, no book has been written in English—so far as I am aware—solely about the Japanese money market. This work is an attempt to fill that gap.

In addition, important developments have been occurring in the Japanese money market since 1971, especially the establishment of two new markets (bill discount and negotiable certificates of deposit) and the very rapid growth of the Tokyo dollar call market since 1978. Thus, one can no longer view the Japanese money market as consisting mainly of the yen call-money market plus a small amount of *gensaki* trading. Instead, the domestic money market must now be viewed as comprising four main components—each approximately the same size.

Another important development has been the substantial liberalization of the market since 1978, with the authorities no longer exercising close control over interest rates in the call-money and bill-discount markets. These developments could well be laying the groundwork for the establishment of a bona fide offshore market during the 1980s. If Japan does establish an offshore banking center similar to the United States' international banking facility, and the yen is included as one of the trading currencies, the domestic money market is likely to become even more important than it is now.

One of the aims of this book is to provide as much relevant information as possible on all components of the Japanese money market. Each of the major components of the market is analyzed in separate chapters, and in the last chapter there is an analysis of the entire market. Although an attempt has been made to be as accurate as possible about the information provided in the book, it is possible that some reports used as source material may not have been correct. Since much of the information is based on several sources that have proved internally consistent, presumably any inaccuracies are relatively few and minor.

It is hoped that this book will reveal important statistical gaps in the information available on the Japanese money market. This in turn may encourage the publication by the authorities of regular—and readily available—data to fill these gaps. An example is the lack of readily available data on the turnover, and the amount of funds outstanding, in the Tokyo dollar call market.

I am grateful to many persons, both in Japan and the United States, who provided me with information for this book and I regret that I cannot express my appreciation to each one. However, I would especially like to thank Mr. Noriyuki Toyama, executive director, Bank of Japan, and the Bank of Japan staff in Tokyo and New York City. Others who have provided me with valuable assistance are Mr. Kageaki Akashi, advisor to Tanshi Kyokai, Mr. Tomoo Yanagita of Tokyo Tanshi, and Mr. Shigeru Mori of Nomura Securities Company, Ltd.

I accept the responsibility for any errors or serious omissions that the book may contain. This book represents my views and does not necessarily represent the official views of the Board of Governors of the Federal Reserve System or other members of its staff.

1 Introduction

The main purpose of this book is to examine in some detail, and to provide extensive information on, the Japanese money market—particularly its major components. At present, the amount of information published in English on the money market is limited and is generally scattered in various sources, most of which are not easily available. To the best of my knowledge, no book has been published in English that deals solely with the Japanese money market. This book is an attempt to fill that gap.

In order to provide an appropriate framework for the money market, the book contains a short description of Japan's financial institutions and indicates how the money market relates to these institutions. I have not attempted to detail the nature and operation of Japan's capital market (that is, the stock and bond markets) since my main focus is strictly on the money market. I have emphasized herein the organization of the money market, its main participants, the types of instruments used, and the important developments in the market during the postwar period. In brief, the book attempts to provide as complete information as possible on all of the important aspects of the money market—one of Japan's major financial institutions—with analysis of its past, present, and future role in the Japanese economy.

The book is organized so as to present two background chapters and then five chapters on the various components of the market. The three concluding chapters deal with official control of the market, money-market interest rates, and an extensive assessment of the market.

Chapter 2 contains a brief survey of the Japanese financial system, a short overview of the various components of the money market, and a detailed explanation of the Tanshi companies (that is, the money-market brokers). Chapter 3 discusses important money-market developments since 1945, with special emphasis on the 1970s, when several new components of the market were established. Data are also presented on the rate of growth of the market as a whole, as well as the rates of growth in each of the four main components of the market.

Chapters 4 through 6 deal with three of the main money-market components, namely the bill-discount market, the yen call-money market and the *gensaki* (bond-repurchase) market. Some of the major topics covered in each of the chapters are the organization of the market, its participants, typical terms, the nature of the money-market instruments, and an analysis of this particular component of the money market. Chapter 7 deals solely with the Tokyo dollar call market, which is, in essence, an interbank market in short-term foreign-currency funds. The chapter explains the origin and nature of the market, who the major participants are, the mechanics of a market transaction, and recent trends regarding the size and volume of activity in the market.

The relatively new negotiable certificate of deposit (NCD) market is discussed in chapter 8, which also describes the short-term government-securities market, the interbank-deposit system, and the moribund market in bank-guaranteed export and import bills. Except for the NCD market, none of these markets constitutes a bona fide money market.

For many years the Japanese money market has been strongly influenced and—in certain instances—controlled by Japan's two main financial authorities. These are the Bank of Japan (that is, the central bank) and the Ministry of Finance. So important is official influence and control of the Japanese money market that all of chapter 9 is devoted to the subject.

Chapter 10 discusses the structure and trends in money-market interest rates, with the main focus regarding the structure of the rates being on the period during the 1970s and the early 1980s. Interest-rate features in the individual components of the money market are also discussed, along with an analysis of rate levels and volatility.

The last chapter contains a comprehensive assessment of the money market. The rate of growth of the market is put in perspective through a comparison with other economic and financial aggregates, and the pace of diversification of the various money-market instruments is examined. The chapter includes discussion of whether the money market has met the needs of most borrowers and lenders, as well as the various gaps in the market. Likely future developments in the market are also explored, along with an action program for further development of the market.

2 An Overview of the Market

To put Japan's money market in proper perspective and explain its relationship to other financial institutions, it is important to understand the existing framework of Japan's financial institutions. The Bank of Japan—the country's central bank—uses a classification system that can be employed to better understand this framework.[1]

The Bank of Japan divides the country's financial institutions into eight categories. These are: (1) The Bank of Japan; (2) all banks; (3) financial institutions for small business; (4) financial institutions for agriculture, forestry, and fishery; (5) securities-finance institutions; (6) insurance companies; (7) government financial institutions; and (8) government financial units. Some of these—such as categories (2) and (4), as well as securities companies that are included in category (5)—play an important role in the money market. Others, particularly categories (7) and (8), play only a small, if any, role in the money market.

The Bank of Japan plays a major role in two components of the money market, namely, the call-money market and the bill-discount market. Also, as the central bank of the country, it closely monitors developments in the remaining components of the money market.

Category (2)—all banks—includes four types of banks. These are city banks, regional banks, trust banks, and long-term-credit banks. As the name implies, the city banks are the large major banks located in Japan's major cities. Since the early 1970s, there have been thirteen such banks. The city banks have a large number of branches, which at the end of 1981 totaled over 2,600. The regional banks—known until the mid-1970s as local banks—are located in the smaller cities and towns. Each regional bank is based in a prefecture, but is able to extend its operations into neighboring prefectures. At the end of 1981 there were sixty-three regional banks with over 5,400 branches. The trust banks are small in number—only seven—but their total assets are substantial and, as their name implies, they perform trust functions. The three long-term credit banks, established under the Long-Term Credit Bank Law, extend medium- to long-term credits which they finance mainly by issuing debentures.

Categories (3) and (4)—financial institutions for small business and the primary industries—include various types of credit cooperatives, savings

3

banks, and specialized banks. They play an important role in supplying funds to the money market—especially the call-money and bill-discount markets.

Category (5)—securities-finance institutions—includes three securities-finance companies and about 230 securities companies. The main business of the securities-finance companies is to provide money or securities to the many securities companies, while the latter serve as brokers and dealers in the buying, selling, and flotation of securities.

Category (6)—the insurance companies—includes about twenty-one life-insurance companies and twenty-two non-life-insurance companies. Like categories (3) and (4), they are also suppliers of funds to the money market.

The financial institutions in categories (7) and (8) are not involved to any significant extent in the money market. Category (7)—government financial institutions—includes twelve specialized financial institutions, such as the Japan Development Bank and the Export-Import Bank of Japan. Category (8)—government financial units—includes the Postal Savings System, the Postal Life Insurance and Annuity System, and the Trust Fund Bureau. These institutions mainly invest government funds from postal savings, welfare annuity payments, and other sources, in government securities.

While the previously mentioned financial institutions are listed in the Bank of Japan's regular monthly publication, additional historical information is also provided in the bank's yearly publication entitled *Economic Statistics Annual.* [2]

Unfortunately, the Bank of Japan list of financial institutions excludes some institutions that play an important role in the money market. These are the foreign-branch banks, [3] the Tanshi companies (that is, short-term money brokers) and the *Tanshi Kyokai* (the money brokers' association). These will be discussed later in the chapter.

The Four Main Components of the Money Market

There are four components of the Japanese domestic money market which are both substantial in size and bona fide money markets. These are the bill-discount, call-money, *gensaki,* and NCD (negotiable certificate of deposit) markets.

There are other potential or theoretical components of the money market. However, they are either not bona fide money markets [4] (for example, the interbank-deposit market, the short-term-government-securities market and the market in bank-guaranteed export and import bills), or they are bona fide, but deal in foreign rather than domestic currencies. This is the case with the Tokyo dollar call market, which has been growing rapidly in relative importance. These other possible components of the money market will be discussed in the next section.

For all practical purposes, Japan's money market consists of the following four components: (1) the bill-discount market, (2) the call-money market, (3) the *gensaki* market (that is, bond trading with repurchase agreement), and (4) the market in NCDs. Most observers would agree that these four components comprise Japan's money market. Accordingly, any subsequent reference to Japan's money market refers to this four-component market.

Although Japan's money market has become freer, or less subject to restrictions, in recent years, it is not as open a money market as those in the United States and the United Kingdom. For example, only financial institutions can participate in Japan's bill-discount and call-money markets. Nevertheless, the Japanese money market does play an important role in providing both an outlet and a source of short-term funds in Japan, despite being more closely controlled by the government authorities.

Although it is somewhat risky to do so, the nature of Japan's money market can be grasped more readily by comparison with certain parts of the U.S. money market.

For example:

1. Japan's bill-discount market is roughly comparable to the United States' bankers' acceptance market.
2. Japan's call-money market is roughly comparable to the United States' Federal Funds market.
3. Japan's *gensaki* market is roughly comparable to the United States' repurchase-agreement market.
4. Japan's NCD market is comparable to the Unites States' NCD market.

One reason that Japan's bill-discount market is not fully comparable to the U.S. bankers' acceptance market is that, while both markets utilize bills of exchange as the underlying instrument, the Japanese banks do not formally guarantee payment should the payer default. Although, in general, the banks would pay the obligation if there were a default. In addition, the bulk of the financing in the bill-discount market is accomplished through an accommodation bill (that is, one large covering bill for many smaller bills) rather than through an ordinary bill.

Japan's call-money market is roughly similar to the U.S. Federal Funds market in that banks in both countries with excess funds lend them to other banks (often the banks in large cities) that are short of funds. However, in the United States the transaction is carried out through entries on the books of the Federal Reserve Banks in response to telephone or computer-terminal instructions, while in Japan the underlying instrument is a promissory note secured by appropriate collateral.

Japan's *gensaki* market is similar to the U.S. market in that both markets involve the short-term sale of securities (by the borrower), coupled with an agreement by the borrower to repurchase the securities at a fixed future date at a negotiated price. Although both markets have existed for many years, the *gensaki* market only became quantitatively important in Japan in the early 1970s, while the repurchase-agreement market in the United States became quantitatively important even more recently, that is, late in 1975 (not counting the active use made of the market during the credit squeeze of the late 1960s).

The NCD markets are very similar for both countries, except that there are more controls in Japan on the market. These controls include limits: on the total amount that can be issued, on the minimum size of each certificate, and on the time period (a minimum of three months to a maximum of six months) for NCD maturities. Whereas the U.S. market in NCDs first began to function about two decades ago in the early 1960s, the Japanese market was established as recently as May 1979.

The relative importance of the different components of the money market has changed substantially over the years, but for 1982 the amounts outstanding were as shown in table 2-1. Additional details on the size of the market and its rate of growth in the postwar period are provided in chapter 3.

Compared with the U.S. money market, the Japanese money market is both smaller in scale and more limited in the variety of money-market instruments available. At the end of 1980 the total amount of funds outstanding in the U.S. money market was $620 billion, which—converted at the prevailing exchange rate—was about eight times larger than the Japanese money market.[5] Even when measured by the size of the respective

Table 2-1
Balances Outstanding in the Money Market, 1982

	Billions of Yen	*Billions of Dollars*	*Percent Share*
Bill Discount	3,867	16.3	22.7
Gensaki	4,304	18.2	25.2
Call Money	4,528	19.1	26.6
NCD	4,342	18.3	25.5
Total	17,041	71.9	100.0

Adapted from table 3-2.

Note: Data in yen converted to U.S. dollars at a rate of 236.75 yen to the dollar.

economies, the Japanese market is much smaller. In 1980 the amount of funds outstanding in the U.S. money market was equivalent to 24 percent of U.S. nominal gross national product (GNP), whereas in Japan the respective proportion was 6 percent. However, when compared with the amount of credit extended in Japan by all banks (as defined earlier), the Japanese money market is significant. At the end of 1980 the amount of funds outstanding in the Japanese money market was equivalent to 9 percent of the total credits outstanding of all banks.

The Bill-Discount Market

Japan's bill-discount market is an open market in domestic bills of exchange of companies listed on the Tokyo stock exchange that have been discounted by banks. Most types of bills of exchange (commercial, trade, industrial, et cetera) are eligible for trading in the market except for purely financial paper. The main instrument utilized in the market is an *accommodation bill* rather than an *original bill* (both types are explained in chapter 4). The usual maturities in the market range from two to four months.

The participants in the market are limited to financial institutions resident in Japan, including the Bank of Japan. Excluded are individuals and nonfinancial institutions—whether resident or nonresident. The main borrowers are the thirteen large city banks, with some borrowing by the foreign-branch banks. The lenders consist of a large number of financial institutions, with the more prominent being the credit associations, financial institutions for agriculture, and the trust banks. The bill-discount market is described in detail in chapter 4.

Call-Money Market

This is a market in very short-term funds (currently up to two months' maturity) that has been in operation since the turn of the century, making it the oldest component of the money market. Borrowing in the market is carried out through an exchange of promissory notes secured by readily marketable collateral such as government bonds, other prime securities, and commercial bills. In principle this collateral should be the same type of collateral as that accepted by the Bank of Japan in its lending operations.

About 85 percent of the borrowing in the market is done by the city banks, with most of the rest being done by foreign and regional banks. On the supply side, there are about a half-dozen major lenders. These include trust banks, regional banks, financial institutions for agriculture and forestry, long-term-credit banks, insurance companies, and mutual savings banks.

The call-money market was, in effect, split in half in May 1971, with the longer-term part of the market (two- to four-month maturities) transformed into the bill-discount market. The remaining half, with maturities up to two months, largely remained unchanged and is the present-day call-money market. A more-complete description and analysis of the call-money market is provided in chapter 5.

The Gensaki Market

This market is a bond-repurchase market that consists of bond trading coupled with a repurchase agreement. Thus, a borrower sells an authorized bond with an agreement that he will repurchase the bond within a fixed period at a specified price. The *gensaki* transactions generally have a maturity of one to three months, with the yield to the lender determined primarily by the difference between the selling and the repurchase price. The two main types of bonds traded in the market are discount and coupon-bearing bonds; convertible bonds are not eligible for trading.

Unlike the bill-discount and call-money markets, nonfinancial business enterprises are allowed to participate in the *gensaki* market, but participation by individuals is not permitted. Since May 1979 nonresidents have been allowed to participate in the market with no restraints by means of *minimum maturities* for the bonds purchased.

Securities companies play a very important role in the market, both as intermediaries and as major borrowers. Other borrowers include the city banks, business enterprises, and insurance companies. The main lenders in the market have been the nonfinancial industrial corporations and other nonfinancial enterprises, including foreign companies. The *gensaki* market is treated more fully in chapter 6.

The NCD Market

This is a market in yen-denominated NCDs, which was established in May 1979. A secondary market in NCDs began to develop in the first half of 1981. In this secondary market, NCD transactions with repurchase agreements tend to be more popular than outright transactions.

The instrument employed in the market is a certificate of deposit that, in principle, is negotiable, that is, capable of being sold by its owner before maturity. Japanese NCDs cannot be redeemed before maturity, but they can be used as collateral for loans. Maturities are restricted to a three- to six-month period and the minimum for a single certificate is ¥500 million (or \$2.5 million at an exchange rate of 200 yen to the U.S. dollar).

The financial institutions authorized to participate in the NCD market are the city, regional, trust, foreign, and long-term-credit banks, as well as credit associations and mutual-loan and savings banks. The main borrowers have been the city, foreign, trust, and long-term-credit banks. Overall limits have been set by the Ministry of Finance on the issue of NCDs, and for each financial institution—other than foreign banks—this is equivalent to 75 percent of the institution's net worth, effective January 1984. The main lenders are the trading companies and Japanese manufacturers—especially the large automobile and electronic firms. Additional details are provided in chapter 8.

Other Components of the Money Market

As indicated earlier, there are other possible components of the money market in Japan, but they either involve foreign currencies or they are not bona fide money markets. These are the Tokyo dollar call market, the interbank-deposit market, the short-term-government-securities market and the market in bank-guaranteed export and import bills.

The Tokyo Dollar Call Market

This is a market that was established to facilitate the borrowing and lending of short-term foreign-currency funds in Japan. It is, in essence, a closely regulated extension of the Eurocurrency market to Japan. As a result of official restraints, the market is not open to nonbank financial institutions or to nonresidents, and—unlike the Eurocurrency market—interest earnings are not exempt from Japanese withholding taxes.

Established on 17 April 1972, the main purpose of the market has been to give small local banks easier access to the Eurocurrency market so that they can clear their foreign-exchange position daily, as required by official regulations. Prior to April 1972 there was no domestic market for interbank loans in foreign currency.

The dollar call market is basically a telephone market where brokerage firms arrange interbank foreign-currency loans or borrowings. Although there is no collateral underlying the transaction, there is an exchange of written statements of the transaction.

In addition to the Tanshi companies that serve as brokers in the market, there are six different types of banks that participate in the market. These are the city, regional, trust, foreign, long-term-credit, and mutual-loan and savings banks. The major borrowers in the market have been the trust, regional, and mutual-loan and savings banks. The main lenders have been the city and foreign-branch banks.

Despite its name, the market is not confined to transactions in U.S. dollars. Roughly 10 percent of the transactions are denominated in other major currencies such as the West German deutsche mark, the Swiss franc, and the British pound. Although the maximum maturity for transactions in the market is six months, roughly 90 percent of the maturities are for seven days or less. The minimum amount for each transaction is $100,000, and the interest rates in the Tokyo dollar call market tend to parallel those in the Eurocurrency market, though at a slightly higher (by 1/16 to 1/8 percentage point) level.

The Market for Interbank Deposits

Some observers of the Japanese financial system have included the system of interbank deposits as part of the money market.[6] Although briefly prominent in 1972, this system is not actually a part of Japan's bona fide money market, and is included here only for the sake of completeness.

The interbank-deposit market consists of term deposits that banks place directly with each other, mostly with six-month maturities. This operation is on a direct bank-to-bank basis, without intermediaries, and lacks the usual elements of an open money market. The main suppliers of funds are the small- and medium-sized financial institutions, and the main borrowers are the large city banks. Profits appear to be the main motivating force behind the system, rather than any requirement that the smaller banks maintain compensating balances with their correspondent banks.

In the early 1970s, the Bank of Japan was concerned that this system of interbank deposits might become a conduit of funds to the city banks that the Bank of Japan might not be able to control. However, this concern has disappeared as the interbank-deposit system has been relatively unimportant compared with the total amount of funds available to all financial institutions.

The Short-Term-Government-Securities Market

As is the case with the interbank-deposit system, the short-term-government-securities market is not considered a part of the bona fide money market in Japan. This is because it lacks the usual characteristics of an open money market. In addition, yields in the market are controlled by the government and set at levels below other short-term rates. There is virtually no secondary market in short-term government securities, and the bulk of the short-term securities are held by the Bank of Japan and the government's Trust Fund Bureau.

Three types of short-term bills are issued by the government: (1) treasury bills, (2) food bills, and (3) foreign-exchange-fund bills. Treasury bills are issued when the government experiences temporary fund shortages. Food bills are related to the government's agricultural-price-support program and are issued when the government needs funds to purchase the crops. Foreign-exchange-fund bills are issued to finance temporary shortages in the government's Foreign Exchange Fund caused by adverse balance-of-payments developments.

The usual maturity on all three types of bills is sixty days, and individual bill denominations range between ¥1 million and ¥500 million (or $4,000 and $2.0 million at an exchange rate of 250 yen to the U.S. dollar). The yield on all three types of bills is tightly controlled by the government and is deliberately held below the yields on the major money-market instruments.

Because of the inadequate yield, the holdings of the bills by private financial institutions are relatively low. Roughly 90 percent of the bills are held by government entities, such as the Bank of Japan and the Ministry of Finance's Trust Fund Bureau. When private investors do purchase bills, the Japanese securities companies serve as intermediaries.

Short-term government securities generally comprise only a minor part of the total national government debt. However, the volume of short-term debt does fluctuate sharply at times. Since most investors hold the bills until maturity, there is virtually no secondary market in short-term government securities in Japan. Until the yields on bills are allowed to rise to more-realistic levels, the development of a secondary market in bills appears unlikely.

Bank-Guaranteed Export and Import Bills

Japan's money market does not include a bankers' acceptance market, as such. However, since 1973 the Bank of Japan has been attempting to develop a market in yen-denominated export and import bills guaranteed by banks. In 1973 the Bank of Japan authorized the commercial banks to guarantee such bills and the bank also was granted the authority to carry out open-market operations in such bills.

There are several reasons why the Bank of Japan has been interested in developing a market in bank-guaranteed export and import bills. These include the desire to reduce the foreign-exchange-rate risks for Japanese traders, to contribute to a wider use of the yen in international financing, and to increase the volume of funds available for trade financing.

However, despite various actions by the Bank of Japan—such as authorizing the use of cover bills (*hyoshi tegata*) in this market—the volume of transactions in the market has been small (see chapter 8). Some of the factors that have restrained the growth of the market include the limited negotiability of the bills in this market and the high cost of funds to potential borrowers.

No major developments have occurred in recent years in this market. At this time, the prospects for developing the market do not appear very promising.

The Tanshi Companies and the Call-Money Association (Tanshi Kyokai)

Any discussion of the Japanese money market would be incomplete if it excluded the Tanshi companies. These are the companies that serve as intermediaries in the market between lenders and borrowers. They have performed their intermediary role—mostly as brokers rather than dealers[7]—since the money market first began to operate around the turn of the century. Since their commission fee as brokers has remained relatively unchanged over the years, their earnings have fluctuated with the volume of transactions in the market.

This chapter is aimed at providing a general overview of the money market; however, the Tanshi companies—being only intermediaries and not principals—are not discussed in very much detail in any subsequent chapter. Therefore this section is designed to provide a full discussion of the Tanshi companies, as well as their association, namely, the Call-Money Association (*Tanshi Kyokai*).

Each Tanshi company can best be described as a group of money-market brokers. By bringing together the lenders and borrowers of funds, especially in the call-money and bill discount markets, they play an almost indispensable role in the money market. By connecting financial institutions with each other, they greatly facilitate the flow of funds.

During the period prior to the Second World War, the Tanshi companies served as brokers in the call-money market. After Japan's foreign-exchange market was reestablished in 1952, the Tanshi companies began to serve as foreign-exchange brokers.[8] However, they also continued to operate as domestic-money-market brokers. When the bill-discount market was established in 1971, they also took on the task of serving as the brokers for that market. Their activities were further increased in 1972 when they became active as brokers in the Tokyo dollar call market. More recently they have also begun to serve as both brokers and dealers in the new NCD market.

Although a Tanshi company's prime function is to act as an intermediary in the money market, it also operates in close cooperation with the Bank of Japan. Thus a secondary function is to serve as an ". . . agent for the monetary policy exercised by the financial authorities, such as the Bank of Japan's open-market operation."[9] The Tanshi companies, in turn, are under the direct supervision of the Ministry of Finance.

In most of the postwar period, there have been only six Tanshi companies operating in Japan.[10] In November 1962 these companies decided to establish a formal association known as *Tanshi Kyokai.* The full name in English is Association of Call Loan and Discount Companies, but *Tanshi Kyokai* will be referred to here as simply the Call-Money Association.

The association basically guards the interests of the Tanshi companies in their dealings with the Bank of Japan, the Ministry of Finance and other financial groups. In performing this function, it serves as a formal point of contact with the government on official matters. In more general terms, the Call-Money Association was reportedly established in 1962 ". . . with a view to further improvement of the short-money business, together with contributing to the development of the money market."[11] It decides on the dealing practices and procedures of the Tanshi companies. Membership is limited to those money-market companies that have been deemed eligible for transactions—and, hence, maintaining an account—with the Bank of Japan. In 1982 the eligible companies consisted of the six listed in an earlier footnote.

There is no single location in Tokyo for the Tanshi companies; rather, they are scattered about the financial district and their business offices constitute the actual market place for transactions in the money market. The Tanshi companies have borrowing privileges at the Bank of Japan, which they are able to use, at times, to finance their inventory of money-market instruments.

Table 2-2 provides a listing of the six Tanshi companies and indicates which are active in the various components of the money market. All of the companies are active in the bill-discount, call-money, and NCD markets. None are active in the *gensaki* market. With regard to the Tokyo dollar call market, all are active except for Tokyo Tanshi. In 1978 Tokyo Tanshi established a subsidiary—Tokyo Forex—which is active in both the foreign-exchange brokerage business and the Tokyo dollar call market.

Conclusion

The four bona fide components of Japan's money market are the bill-discount, call-money, *gensaki,* and NCD markets. Except for the call-money market, all other components have only been important, or estab-

Table 2–2

Tanshi Companies Active in Certain Components of the Money Market

Tanshi Companies	Bill-Discount Market	Gensaki Market	Call-Money Market	NCD	Dollar Call Market
Yamane	Active	Inactive	Active	Active	Active
Tokyo Tanshi	Active	Inactive	Active	Active	Inactive
Nippon Discount	Active	Inactive	Active	Active	Active
Nagoya Tanshi	Active	Inactive	Active	Active	Active
Ueda Tanshi	Active	Inactive	Active	Active	Active
Yagi Tanshi	Active	Inactive	Active	Active	Active

Note: Information above valid as of January 1983.

lished, since the early 1970s. In this sense Japan's present-day money market is relatively young.

Not all of Japan's financial institutions engage in active transactions with the money market. This is especially true for governmental financial institutions, such as the Japan Development Bank, or governmental financial units, such as the Postal Savings System. However, most of Japan's other financial institutions do participate in money-market transactions.

Japan's money market is not, in general, as open a market as those in the United States or the United Kingdom. Thus, transactions in the bill-discount, call-money, and NCD markets are restricted to financial institutions—nonfinancial institutions being excluded. In addition, Japan's money market, compared with the U.S. money market, has a more limited variety of money-market instruments, and is quantitatively much smaller. In the United States, money-market funds outstanding were equivalent to about 24 percent of GNP in 1980, but in Japan the proportion was only 6 percent.

The largest component in the money market through 1980 was the bill-discount market, but by 1982 its share of the market had slipped to 23 percent. On the other hand, the call-money market has increased in relative importance since 1980 and in 1982 accounted for about 27 percent of the market. The *gensaki* and NCD markets have each recently accounted for about one-fourth of the market.

In addition to the four major money-market components cited above, there are several other possible components of the money market. These are the Tokyo dollar call market, the market for interbank deposits, the market for short-term government securities, and the market for bank-guaranteed export and import bills. Except for the Tokyo dollar call market—which is now large enough to be an important part of the money market, but is a market in foreign rather than domestic currencies—the others are not really bona fide money markets. Consequently, this study concentrates on the four major domestic-money-market components listed earlier.

While they are not one of the money-market components, the Tanshi companies discussed earlier are an important element in the money market. They serve as intermediaries—usually as brokers rather than dealers—in most, if not all, of the components of the money market. In addition to playing a virtually indispensible role in the money market, they also act as brokers in the foreign-exchange market. During most of the postwar period there have been only six Tanshi companies and these six, since 1962, have organized themselves formally into a Call-Money Association (*Tanshi Kyokai*).

Notes

1. A complete listing of all the different types of financial institutions is published monthly on the last page of each issue of the Bank of Japan's *Economic Statistics Monthly*.

2. See, for example, *Economic Statistics Annual,* Bank of Japan, Tokyo, March 1982, pp. 3–6 in a special "Notes" section after p. 355.

3. As of 16 November 1982, there were 74 foreign banks operating 100 branches in Japan. Of these, 22 were U.S. banks and they had a total of 32 branches in Japan.

4. These markets are not bona fide in that true money markets involve many buyers and sellers, with relatively unrestricted entry and with the cost of funds being determined by the free interplay of demand and supply forces, rather than being negotiated or fixed by fiat.

5. Yusuke Kashiwagi, "The Yen's Future as a World Currency," *Euromoney,* London, September 1982, p. 175.

6. See, for example, Wilbur F. Monroe, *Japan: Financial Markets and the World Economy,* Praeger, New York, 1973, pp. 106–107.

7. The Tanshi companies do act as dealers in both the bill-discount market and the call-money market, but their dealer positions are very small.

8. *Money Market in Japan and Tanshi Companies,* Yamane Tanshi Co., Ltd., Tokyo, April 1977, p. 2.

9. Ibid., p. 1.

10. These are: (1) Yamane Tanshi Co., Ltd.; (2) The Tokyo Tanshi Co., Ltd.; (3) The Nippon Discount and Call Money Co., Ltd.; (4) The Nagoya Tanshi Co., Ltd.; (5) Ueda Tanshi Co., Ltd.; and (6) Yagi Tanshi Co., Ltd.

11. *Money Market in Japan and Tanshi Companies,* p. 3.

3 Important Money-Market Developments Since 1945

The Japanese money market has a long history, the call-money market having been established in 1902.[1] Japan's call market was patterned mainly after London's money market, though the U.S money market also served as a model. The desirability of having such a short-term market was reinforced by the financial panic of 1901 when the Japanese financial community realized their need for short-term liquid funds or reserves and a market to deal in such funds.[2]

This chapter deals with the main developments in the money market since the end of the Second World War, the rate of growth of the market in general, and its various components. Following a discussion of the main developments—which occurred mostly in the 1970s—a summary of these developments will be presented.

Money-Market Developments: 1945–1969

The first major development in the Japanese money market in the postwar period was the inauguration of the *gensaki* market. This market was started in approximately 1949, when the securities companies found that they needed cash funds on a short-term basis. Although operating in a gray legal area, the companies found that they could meet their needs for liquidity by selling bonds out of their portfolios on a conditional basis and repurchasing them later.

Another important development concerned interest rates in the call market. In the mid-1950s the authorities relaxed their control over call-loan rates. Earlier, from 1947 to August 1955, the maximum rate on overnight loans in the call-money market was regulated under the Temporary Interest Rates Adjustment Law—with the maximum level for other rates subject to administrative guidance by the Bank of Japan. But in August 1955 the guidance on the other rates was abolished, and twenty-one months later, in May 1957, legal control under the Temporary Interest Rates Adjustment Law was discontinued.[3] Thereafter, from July 1957 to September 1967, the maximum rates allowable were changed under a voluntary agreement among the member banks[4] whenever the Bank of Japan changed its basic discount rate. In September 1967 this voluntary agreement (which was not always observed), was discontinued because, according to the Bank of Japan, it was not suited to the existing circumstances.

During the late 1940s and the 1950s, the call-money market operated only in Tokyo and Osaka. In March 1961, however, the market was extended to Nagoya. Since then, neither the Osaka nor the Nagoya call market has been of major importance, the bulk of the transactions (about 85 percent) having been carried out in Tokyo.

Until 1969, call-money rates were generally quoted in terms of the old *hibu* system rather than in percent per year. Under the *hibu* system, the borrower paid a certain amount of yen per day for each 100 yen borrowed. On 1 September 1969, this system was discontinued for most financial transactions—though it is still used for call money with a half-day maturity—and it was replaced with the familiar occidental system of percent per year.

Money-Market Developments: 1970 to Present

Although it did not happen in a short period of time, one of the major developments in the money market in the early 1970s was the rise to prominence of the *gensaki* market. Rapid growth from a relatively small base began in the late 1960s, and by the end of 1971 the amount of repurchase agreements outstanding was ¥882 billion. This was equivalent to 44 percent of the loans outstanding in the call-money market. Except for two recession years, the *gensaki* market continued to grow rapidly during the 1970s.

The next major development occurred in May 1971 when the call-money market was, in effect, split into two parts. That part of the market with the shorter maturities continued and remains as the present-day call-money market. The other part, with maturities ranging from roughly two to four months, is the present-day bill-discount market. Further details on the bill-discount market are provided in chapter 4.

Passing mention should also be made of the market for interbank deposits which became prominent in 1972. While viewed by some authors as part of the Japanese money market,[5] it has largely been eclipsed by the other major components of the money market since the mid-1970s. Additional information on the interbank-deposit market is provided in chapter 8.

More important, in 1972, was the establishment of the Tokyo dollar call market (see chapter 7). This market, which is actually an extension to Japan of the Eurocurrency market, first began to operate on 17 April 1972. The Tokyo dollar call market has grown at a rapid rate in recent years and has the potential to become very important at some time in the future. However, certain administrative actions (which are described at the end of chapter 7) would first have to be taken before this could happen.

Another important development occurred 1 June 1972, when trading in over-month-end loans in the call-money market was discontinued, thereby assuring that the call-money market would remain a market in very short-term instruments.[6] At the same time, the authorities decided to make available to the bill-discount market those bills qualified for sale and purchase in dealing with the Bank of Japan, such bills having previously been used as security for call-money-market loans.[7] This step opened the way for a more rapid expansion of the bill-discount market, with much of this expansion reflecting Bank of Japan open-market operations in the market beginning in June 1972. Later, in August 1973, the Bank of Japan began to buy pre-screened bills directly from the large city banks without going through the bill-discount market.

It was also in 1973 that the Bank of Japan attempted to develop a market in yen-denominated export and import bills. For various reasons, an open market in such bills to finance international trade—as distinct from domestic trade—had never developed in Japan. Late in 1973 the foreign-exchange banks were granted the authority to guarantee such bills. Despite various actions taken by the Bank of Japan—including the sale by the bank for the first time in December 1975 of yen-denominated export bills and the introduction of a cover-bill system (*hyoshi tegata*) in May 1976—the Bank of Japan's efforts were unsuccessful and an open market in yen-denominated international bills failed to develop (see chapter 8).

Early in 1974 the *gensaki* market was accorded a more secure legal position when the Ministry of Finance issued several self-regulatory rules on securities companies' transactions in the market. Following a decline in activity in the *gensaki* market during the 1974–1975 recession, activity began to increase in early 1976. In October 1975, forward bond trading was introduced into the *gensaki* market, and in March 1976 the Ministry of Finance issued new, more formal, regulations for the *gensaki* market. These regulations tended to fully legitimize *gensaki* trading and encourage increased trading in the market.

Until March 1976 the *gensaki* market had been relatively free from official restraints. This began to change with the March 1976 regulations just mentioned and also with an action taken in December 1977. In that month the Ministry of Finance informed the securities companies—the intermediaries or principals in the market—that they would be subject to uniform quantitative restrictions on the amount of *gensaki* transactions they carried out using securities from their own inventory. However, in 1980 the Japanese authorities removed the ceilings that had been imposed on the amount of bond sales (that is, borrowings) that each financial institution could transact in the *gensaki* market.

Starting in June 1978, the Bank of Japan and the Ministry of Finance began to implement a series of measures aimed at eventually freeing the bill-discount and the call-money markets from administrative restraints. The first step was to liberalize part of the bill-discount market by allowing bills held for at least one month—but with more than one month to maturity—to be freely resold in the market at any time and at whatever rate dictated by demand and supply conditions. A second step was taken in October 1978 when seven-day call loans were introduced in the call-money market and the rate for these loans was allowed to fluctuate freely in response to demand and supply forces.

Although not a liberalizing action, the range of maturities available in the bill-discount market was broadened in November 1978. At that time the Tanshi companies introduced a new discount bill with a shorter maturity, that is, an over-month-end bill. Previously, the maturity for bills had to extend over a period covering the end of at least two consecutive months.

A month later, there was also some broadening of the types of bonds available for trading in the *gensaki* market. In December 1978 the government began to issue three-year-coupon bonds and authorized the trading of these bonds in the market. Previously, the only two national bonds available for trading in the *gensaki* market had been the five-year discount bonds and the ten-year interest-bearing bonds.

On 2 April 1979, several additional actions were taken to further liberalize trading in the bill-discount and call-money markets. An agreement was reached between the Bank of Japan and the Tanshi companies that the latter would discontinue the practice of predetermining the call rates a day in advance. The practical effect of this was that call-money transactions on a posted-rate basis were discontinued—the specific rates being determined by market forces. The rate on two-month bills, however, continued to be determined on a posted-rate basis. Also on April 2, there was a general liberalization of rates in the call-money market, especially for the unconditional call-money rate. The overnight-call-money category was discontinued and a new maturity range for call money introduced, namely, fixed maturities ranging from two to six days.

A major money-market development occurred 16 May 1979, when the NCD market was launched. The city banks had strongly argued for the right to issue NCDs, particularly since slower economic growth in the mid-1970s had decreased deposit growth, and also because the growing *gensaki* market had attracted funds away from the city banks. Operating in a manner similar to the United States' NCD market, the new market grew rapidly despite certain restraints placed on its rate of expansion by the authorities.

Also in mid-May 1979, the Ministry of Finance began to allow nonresidents to participate in the *gensaki* market without any restraints on the maturity of the issues purchased. Previously nonresidents were only allowed to purchase government securities with a maturity of thirteen months or more. As a result of this action, foreign participation in the *gensaki* market increased in relative importance.

By October 1979, all rates in the bill-discount market were, in principle, free to fluctuate in response to market conditions. Thus the full liberalization of the bill-discount market was accomplished when the Bank of Japan, on 16 October 1979, allowed the two-month bill rate to be determined by demand and supply conditions in the market. Up to that time, the two-month bill rate had remained subject to the posted-rate system.

In April 1980 a major step was taken to liberalize further the transactions in the *gensaki* market. The authorities removed the ceilings on the amount of bond sales that each participating financial institution could transact in the *gensaki* market. In an opposite move toward increased official control, however, the Bank of Japan in 1980 began to undertake direct intervention in the *gensaki* market.

In March 1980 there was a partial broadening of the NCD market in that intermediaries were introduced into the market. Prior to March 1980, NCDs were mainly purchased directly by enterprises from their principal, or main, bank. Late in March 1980, however, the Tanshi companies were allowed to act as intermediaries in the NCD market, bringing together the lenders (largely business enterprises) and the borrowers (the various financial institutions).

Lastly, a major action was taken on 1 December 1980, when the government liberalized the many foreign-exchange controls on capital movements. In principle, all external transactions from 1 December 1980, were freed from official control except for those explicitly cited in the new Foreign Exchange and Foreign Trade Control Law that became effective on that date. The basic law was thus changed from an orientation of prohibition in principle to one of freedom in principle. In the money market, the new law was mainly relevant for the *gensaki* market in that it provided a stronger legal basis for participation by nonresidents in the *gensaki* market. In this sense, it increased the attractiveness of the *gensaki* market.

Date	*Item*
About 1949	Inauguration of the *gensaki* market.
March 1961	Nagoya call-money market established.
Early 1970s	The rise to prominence of the *gensaki* market.
May 1971	Establishment of the bill-discount market.
April 1972	Operations begin in the Tokyo dollar call market.
June 1972	Bank of Japan begins open-market operations in the bill-discount market.
March 1976	Formal regulations for the *gensaki* market issued.

Date	*Item*
June 1978	First step taken to liberalize the bill-discount market.
October 1978	First action taken to liberalize the call-money market.
April 1979	Liberalization of various loan maturities in the bill-discount and call-money markets.
May 1979	Inauguration of the NCD market.

Rate of Growth of the Market

Until the late 1960s, the rate of growth of Japan's money market can be measured largely in terms of the growth of the call-money market. This is because two of the other money-market components (the bill-discount and the NCD markets) had not yet been established and because the *gensaki* market remained relatively unimportant until the late 1960s.

Between 1956 and 1966, the total amount of loans outstanding in the call-money market increased roughly tenfold. From a level of ¥100 billion at the end of 1956, total loans outstanding rose to approximately ¥1,000 billion at the end of 1966. Additional details, including data on the yearly amounts outstanding since 1956, are provided in chapter 5.

Because of the growing importance of the *gensaki* market in the late 1960s, it is appropriate to begin an examination of the growth of the money market with the period since 1967. Accordingly, table 3–1 presents data on the four main components of the money market, as well as the aggregate total outstanding, for the period from 1967 to 1982.

Measured in terms of the total amount outstanding for all components of the money market, the size of the market grew from ¥1.23 trillion at the end of 1967 to ¥17.0 trillion (about $72 billion) at the end of 1982. This growth in the size of the market reflected an average annual rate of increase during 1968–1982 of about 20 percent. However, there was considerable variation in the year-to-year rates of growth.

The period from 1969 to 1974 (except for 1972) was one of very rapid growth. Especially sharp was the 61 percent increase in the size of the market in 1973. Much of this reflected a favorable balance of international payments in the early 1970s, with banks and businesses flush with funds. At the other extreme, some of the lowest annual rates of growth were registered in 1976 (3 percent), 1981 (0.1 percent), and 1982 (5 percent).

Compared to the amount of credit provided by banks, Japan's money market more than doubled its relative size between 1967 and 1982. At the end of 1967 the total credit outstanding in the money market was equivalent

Table 3–1
Rates of Growth in the Money Market

Year	Call-Money Market Billions of Yen	Year to Year Percent Change	As a Percent of Total	Gensaki Market Billions of Yen	Year to Year Percent Change	As a Percent of Total	Bill-Discount Market Billions of Yen	Year to Year Percent Change	As a Percent of Total	NCD Market Billions of Yen	Year to Year Percent Change	As a Percent of Total	Total Billions of Yen	Year to Year Percent Change
1967	1,078		87.6	152		12.4							1,230	
1968	1,077	-0.1	78.7	291	91.4	21.3							1,368	11.2
1969	1,388	28.9	77.3	408	40.2	22.7							1,796	31.3
1970	1,693	22.0	73.2	619	51.7	26.8							2,312	28.7
1971	2,016	19.1	66.0	882	42.5	28.9	155		5.1				3,053	32.1
1972	1,542	-23.5	43.2	1,224	38.8	34.3	803	418.1	22.5				3,569	16.9
1973	1,546	0.3	27.0	1,738	42.0	30.3	2,448	204.9	42.7				5,732	60.6
1974	1,855	20.0	23.9	1,505	-13.4	19.4	4,400	79.7	56.7				7,760	35.4
1975	1,968	6.1	22.3	1,679	11.6	19.0	5,193	18.0	58.7				8,840	13.9
1976	2,417	22.8	26.5*	2,217	32.0	24.3	4,490	-13.5	49.2				9,124	3.2
1977	2,626	8.6	23.4	3,136	41.5	28.0	5,443	21.2	48.6				11,205	22.8
1978	2,809	7.0	22.2	4,207	34.2	33.3	5,615	3.2	44.5				12,631	12.7
1979	3,318	18.1	22.4	3,960	-5.9	26.7	5,684	1.2	38.4	1,853		12.5	14,815	17.3
1980	3,258	-1.8	20.1	4,507	13.8	27.8	6,120	7.7	37.8	2,323	25.4	14.3	16,208	9.4
1981	4,459	36.9	27.5	4,481	-0.6	27.6	3,989	-34.8	24.6	3,291	41.7	20.3	16,220	0.1
1982	4,528	1.5	26.6	4,304	-4.0	25.2	3,867	-3.1	22.7	4,342	31.9	25.5	17,041	5.1
Annual Average		11.1			27.7			63.9			33.0			20.0

Adapted from *Economic Statistics Annual* and *Economic Statistics Monthly* of the Bank of Japan.
Note: Yearly data for the call-money and bill-discount markets are averages of the twelve months of the year, with the monthly data also being averages for the days in the month; end-of-the-year data for the other two markets.

to only 4 percent of the holdings of loans, discounts, and securities of all banks.[8] By the end of 1982, however, this share had increased to slightly over 8 percent.

Growth Rates of the Four Money-Market Components Since 1967

Since this subject is covered in some detail later in the individual chapters on each of the components of the money market, only the highlights will be briefly presented here, and only for the period since 1967.

Although table 3-1 indicates that the bill-discount market has been the fastest-growing component (in terms of average annual increase) of the four main parts of the money market, this may be misleading since the percentage increases in 1972 and 1973 were from a small base and were therefore abnormally high. If a somewhat later period is selected, such as that after the maturing of the bill market—say 1975 to 1980—it is evident that the *gensaki* and the call-money markets grew faster than the bill market. During this period (1975-1980), the bill-discount market increased at an average annual rate of 6 percent, but the *gensaki* and call-money markets increased at average annual rates of 21 percent and 10 percent, respectively.

The NCD market is too new to have much of a growth record. But measured on a twelve-month basis, it appears to be growing rapidly. During 1980-1982, the average annual rate of increase was 33 percent.

Since 1967, not all of the money-market components have increased steadily from year to year. The call-money market, for example, dropped to lower levels in 1972-1975, partly because of recessionary conditions (1973-1975), but also because of competition from the new bill-discount market established in 1971. Similarly, the *gensaki* market experienced moderate declines in 1974 and 1979, as did the bill-discount market in 1976.

After slow growth in the early 1960s, the *gensaki* market grew rapidly from 1968 through 1973, averaging 51 percent per year during that period. After a pause, the market roughly doubled in 1977-1978 from the late-1976 level, and by the end of 1982 had reached ¥4.3 trillion—a roughly threefold increase over the depressed level in 1974.

Figure 3-1 indicates how the amounts outstanding in each of the four markets changed from 1967 through 1982. Overall there has been a substantial rate of growth, particularly after 1972. It is evident in the figure that the call-money market has not grown as rapidly as the other markets. From a level of ¥2.0 trillion in 1971, the market grew to only ¥3.3 trillion in 1980. For the entire period from 1967 through 1982, the average annual increase in the call-money market was 11 percent, although there was a spurt of growth (37 percent) in 1981.

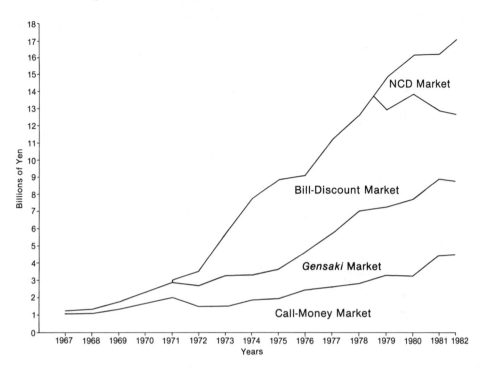

Adapted from table 3-1.

Figure 3-1. Money-Market Components: Amounts Outstanding

On the other hand, the *gensaki* market expanded from ¥ 0.9 trillion in 1971 to ¥4.3 trillion in 1982. In recent years, however, its average annual rate of growth has slowed substantially—reaching only 0.8 percent from 1978 through 1982. Its average annual rate of increase for 1967 to 1982 was 28 percent.

The bill-discount market grew rapidly through 1977. After rising moderately in 1978–1980, the amount outstanding declined sharply from ¥6.1 trillion to ¥3.9 trillion in 1981–1982. This sharp decline was mainly due to the rapid rise in the NCD market, which absorbed funds from the bill-discount market.

A comparison can also be made of the market shares of the four components of the money market over the same time period from 1967 through 1982 (see figure 3-2). One of the most dramatic changes during this period was the sharp drop in the call-money-market share—particularly between 1970 and 1973. This is primarily because of the establishment in 1971 of the bill-discount market, which absorbed a large part of the call-money market. Even after the sharp drop in 1971–1973, the share of the call-money market

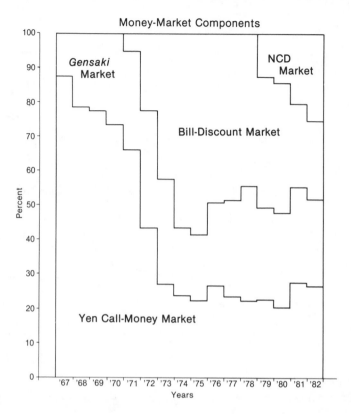

Adapted from table 3-1.

Figure 3-2. Market Shares of the Four Money-Market Components

continued to decline moderately through 1980. Thus, from the relatively high figure of 88 percent in 1967, the share of the call-money market dropped to only 27 percent in 1982.

The *gensaki* market, on the other hand, has roughly maintained its share of the total money market, at about one-fourth since 1970. During 1974–1975 there was a dip to the 20 percent level, but by 1982 the share had increased to 25 percent.

The bill-discount market accounted for the largest share of the total money market during 1973–1980, ranging between 38 and 59 percent. Since 1976, however, its share of the market has been steadily declining from the peak level of 59 percent in 1975. By 1982 it had fallen to 23 percent. This decline in the bill-discount market's share of the total money market, particularly since 1979, has been due largely to the growth of the NCD market—as indicated earlier.

The newest component—the NCD market—has increased its share of the total market steadily since its introduction in 1979. By the end of 1982 its share had increased to one-fourth of the entire market, this increase largely being at the expense of the bill-discount market.

Measured from largest to smallest, the respective shares in 1982 were: call money (27 percent), NCD market (25 percent), *gensaki* (25 percent), and bill discount (23 percent) (see table 3–1). Future trends are not easy to predict with confidence, but it would appear likely that the market may settle for a period of time at the roughly equal shares that prevailed for each component of the market in 1982.

Notes

1. During that year the first broker (Fujimoto Bill Broker) was established and started a brokerage business.

2. *Money Market in Japan and Tanshi Companies,* Yamane Tanshi Co., Ltd., Tokyo, April 1977, p. 6.

3. *The Japanese Financial System,* The Bank of Japan, Tokyo, 1972, p. 70.

4. That is, members of the Federation of Bankers' Associations of Japan.

5. See Wilbur F. Monroe, *Japan: Financial Markets and the World Economy,* Praeger, New York, 1973, pp. 106–107.

6. Fixed-maturity loans were also discontinued in the call-money market in June of 1972, but later—in October 1978—seven-day call money was introduced.

7. *Banking System in Japan,* Federation of Bankers' Associations of Japan, Tokyo, 1976, p. 70.

8. The all banks group in Japan includes the city, regional, trust, and long-term-credit banks.

4 The Bill-Discount Market

Until May 1971 the short-term money market in Japan consisted mainly of the yen call-money market and the *gensaki* market, which had begun to grow rapidly in the early 1970s. As early as 1919 various attempts had been made to develop a bill-discount market (that is, an open market in bills of exchange), but without success.

By 1971 certain developments had occurred that facilitated and prompted the establishment of a bill-discount market. One of these was that the average maturity of the yen call-money market was becoming less short-term and hence the market was not fulfilling one of its key functions of being a vehicle for the adjustment by participants of their very short-term financial positions. By early 1971, about 80 percent of the call loans outstanding consisted of over-month-end money, rather than loans for a few days or weeks. In addition, the Bank of Japan had almost exhausted its arsenal of instruments for carrying out open-market operations. It had been using mainly government and government-guaranteed bonds, and it was likely that these would be in short supply in the near future. There was therefore a need to develop new instruments, such as bills of exchange, which the Bank of Japan could use in its open-market operations.

What occurred in May 1971 was, in effect, a splitting of the call-money market into a relatively short-term market made up of the present-day yen call-money market, and a replacement of the previous over-month-end component of the market by the new bill-discount market. In essence, the bills traded in the bill-discount market took the place of the over-month-end call loans that were discontinued in the call-money market in June 1971.

The bill-discount market was formally established on 20 May 1971 by the money-market brokers who had long been active in operating the call-money market. The market was deliberately designed to include maturities over month end and up to a maximum of four months. Since its establishment, the market has operated in Tokyo, Osaka, and Nagoya. Of the three cities, Tokyo predominates, and during 1982 accounted for approximately 90 percent of the bills outstanding.

Japan's bill-discount market, when placed in the United States' context, is probably most closely related to the U.S. bankers' acceptance market. Although not exactly the same, it is similar both in function and operation.

29

Organization of the Market

The organization of the bill-discount market can perhaps best be understood by examining its main participants: (1) the borrowers in the market, (2) the six brokers who serve as intermediaries, and (3) the various lenders. As is the case with the yen call-money market, participation in the bill-discount market is restricted to financial institutions that are resident in Japan. Individuals and all nonfinancial enterprises are excluded from participation in the market, whether resident, or nonresident, entities.

The bill-discount market is closely related to the yen call-money market in that many of the participants in both markets are the same. Thus, transactions are conducted through the six call-money brokers; the city banks are the main issuers (or sellers) of bills; and roughly the same institutions are the buyers (that is, lenders) in both the bill-discount and the call-money markets. (This rather large group of lenders is described in more detail later.) The two markets differ, however, in the types of financial instruments utilized and the maturities of these instruments.

There is no single place—such as the floor of a stock exchange—where all market transactions are concentrated. Rather, the business offices of the Tanshi companies constitute the actual market place for transactions in the bill-discount market. In these offices bids and offers for funds are received, adjusted, and consummated.

Each of the Tanshi companies that operates in the bill-discount market maintains a deposit account with the Bank of Japan which it uses for carrying out market transactions. The Tanshi companies also have borrowing privileges at the Bank of Japan which they use, at times, on a very short-term basis to finance their inventory of bills.

In addition to their brokerage business in the bill-discount market, the Tanshi companies also serve as intermediaries in the yen call-money market, as brokers for the purchase and sale of national bonds, and as intermediaries in the handling of foreign drafts.[1] Although the Tanshi companies can act as dealers in both the bill-discount market and the call-money market, in practice their positions as dealers are very small in order to minimize any possible losses.

Frequently the Bank of Japan itself is an active purchaser in the bill-discount market. This is an indirect method that the bank can utilize to relieve the city banks from a shortage of funds. The bank began to operate in the market in June 1972 in order to increase the number of instruments of monetary control at its disposal. It also sold its own bills, at times, in order to soak up excess liquidity. Starting in August 1973, the bank also began to buy prescreened bills directly from the city banks without using the Tanshi companies as brokers for the transaction.

Occasionally some banks, as a result of special circumstances, will also bypass the Tanshi companies and conduct interbank-money-market trans-actions directly. This is, of course, with the approval of the authorities, par-ticularly the Director of the Banking Bureau in the Ministry of Finance.

Main Borrowers and Lenders

The main types of *borrowers* (that is, sellers of bills) in the bill-discount market are relatively few. The bulk of the borrowing is done by the thirteen large city banks, which at the end of 1982 accounted for approximately 92 percent of the total amount of borrowing in the market. Foreign banks accounted for roughly 8 percent of the total borrowing, and the small amount remaining chiefly represented borrowing by the securities finance companies.

The main *lenders* (that is, buyers of bills) in the market are the credit associations, various financial institutions for agriculture, and the trust banks. These three categories accounted for about 53 percent of the total lending at the end of 1982, with the balance being divided among a large number of other lenders.[2] Thus, unlike the borrowing side of the market, there are many different types of lenders in the market.

Since the mid-1970s, the city banks have tended to increase their reli-ance for funds on the bill-discount market—as opposed to the yen call-money market. This is mainly because the longer maturities in the bill-discount market (that is, two to four months) provide the city banks with a more-stable source of funds.

Nature of the Instruments

There are two basic categories of bills that are transacted in the bill-discount market. These are the *original bills* and *accommodation bills*.[3]

The *original bills* are bills of exchange that the banks have obtained from their most-creditworthy borrowers, such as trading and industrial companies, and have tacitly guaranteed. They include high-grade com-mercial bills, industrial bills, trade bills, and one-name bills.[4] The bills eli-gible for transaction in the market are limited to those issued by companies that are listed on the Tokyo stock exchange, which is generally an indication of the high creditworthiness of a company.

The *accommodation bills* are bills of exchange that have been drawn by a financial institution on itself and that it has also accepted, but has made payable to a Tanshi company (or to the order of a Tanshi company), with the original bills serving as collateral. Thus, with accommodation bills, several bills are put together into one bill of exchange. This device is used

because the original bills are seldom large enough for normal-size transactions and because they have odd sums. These accommodation bills
reportedly account for almost all market dealings in the bill-discount
market.[5] In either case—whether original or accommodation bills are being
traded in the market—the accepting bank continues to remain liable for the
bills after they are sold to a third party.

According to Monroe,[6] the bills of exchange transacted in the bill-
discount market must be related to a specific trade transaction. Thus,
purely financial paper is not permitted. In addition, the authorities have
restricted the paper eligible for transaction in the market to domestic paper,
with the result that export and import bills are excluded.

Lending Terms

The *maturities* for the bills traded in the bill-discount market range roughly
between two months and four months. The very shortest maturity possible
would be slightly more than one month, since at least two end-of-month
dates must be included in the minimum maturity period.[7]

There is no formal maximum maturity for the bills traded in the market, but as a matter of convention the participants have adhered to a maximum period of four months. Thus, a bank with a six-month bill will normally let it run at least two months before selling it in the discount market.

Most of the bills traded in the market have maturities ranging between
two and four months. Borrowers or lenders desiring shorter maturities
could utilize the yen call-money market or other components of the money
market. In November 1978, it was decided that the bills would be broadly
designated as either one-month, two-month, three-month, or four-month
items.[8]

Once the bills are purchased in the bill-discount market, there is some
restraint on their ready liquidation. This is because purchased bills are
resaleable only after they have been held for a period extending from the
date on which they were purchased to the day after the same date in the following month.

The smallest allowable transaction in the bill-discount market—as with
the yen call-money market—is ¥10 million, or the equivalent of $40,000 at
an exchange rate of 250 yen to the U.S. dollar. The bulk of the individual
transactions are in amounts of ¥100 million, or higher.

The interest rates in the bill-discount market, as well as those in the call-
money market, have generally not been pure market rates in the sense that
they are determined freely by market forces. Until 1978–1979, the brokers
decided upon changes in the rates, acting in close consultation with the
Bank of Japan, as warranted by changes in market conditions. Thus, the
brokers, in quoting rates, had to take into account not only the demand and

supply situation, but also the ". . . intention of the Bank of Japan's Policy Board."[9] There is also a lack of uniformity in that the rates at which the individual banks discount bills of exchange, are not uniform.

As is the case in the yen call-money market, the Tanshi companies quote the bill-discount rate on an annual basis in terms of the buyer's (that is, lender's) rate. The seller's (that is, borrower's) rate is 0.125 percentage point higher. The minimum change in rate quotations is .0625 percentage point.

In the yen call-money market, the interest on call loans is paid when the loan matures, but in the bill market the bills are discounted, with the discount charges being deducted from the proceeds in advance. The result is that the actual interest rate in the bill-discount market—for any given quoted rate—is higher than for the same quoted rate in the yen call-money market. In addition, in calculating the discount charges, the total number of days included in the calculation excludes the very last day.

Buyers (that is, lenders) of a bill will usually pay for the bill by transmitting to the Tanshi company a check on the Bank of Japan in exchange for the bill purchased. Sellers (that is, borrowers) receive their proceeds by delivering the sold bill to the Tanshi company against a Bank of Japan check. The Tanshi companies charge the sellers of bills—as well as the buyers—a brokerage fee of 0.125 percentage point.

Normally the amount of difference between the rate in the bill-discount market and in the yen call-money market is fairly stable, but the differential does tend to widen or narrow as a result of seasonal developments. Typically the rate in the bill-discount market will range roughly between 0.25 and 1.25 percentage points above the conditional call-money rate.

There are definite seasonal patterns in the degree of tightness or ease in Japan's money market. Although there are exceptions, the following would be fairly representative of the usual pattern during the year: January and February, adequate funds; March, possible shortage; April and May, easier conditions; June through August, tight; September through November, easy; and December, very tight.

Starting approximately in October each year, two basic rates are quoted in the bill-discount market. One is for bills maturing during the year and the other is for bills maturing the following year. The rates for the latter tend to be higher. Thus in October 1978, the quoted rate for bills maturing in 1978 was 4 3/8 percent, while for over-year-end bills the rate was 4 5/8 percent.

Liberalization of the Market in 1978–1979

In June 1978 a step was taken by the authorities that resulted in a moderate decrease in the degree of official restraint on the rates quoted in the market. Before June 1978, changes in the bill-discount rate were established after consultation with the Bank of Japan. However, beginning 5 June 1978, a new arrangement was introduced into the market whereby bills that had been held by the purchaser for at least one month, and that still had a period before maturity of more than one month, could be freely resold in the market at whatever rate market conditions dictated. But two-month-end bills continued to be traded at rates prefixed by the Tanshi through consultations with the Bank of Japan.[10]

A further action aimed at market liberalization was taken 27 November 1978, when the Tanshi companies introduced a new discount bill with a shorter maturity than existing bills. The new bill carried a maturity that extended over one month-end, whereas other bills had to have maturities that extended over at least two month-ends. The Tanshi companies stated at the time that the discount rate on this new one-month-end bill would be determined freely according to demand and supply conditions in the market. But the rates for the other two-month-end, or more, bills would continue to be set on a posted-rate basis and thus would not fluctuate during the business day.

This moderate liberalization of the market in June 1978 was carried a step further 2 April 1979, when the Tanshi companies and the Bank of Japan agreed in principle to let market demand and supply conditions freely determine most of the interest rates in the bill-discount and yen call-money markets. With the exception of the June and November 1978 liberalizations described above, other rates in both markets before 2 April 1979 had continued to be set on a posted-rate basis with no intraday fluctuations permitted. Thus, transactions on a posted-rate basis beginning 2 April 1979 were eliminated except for discount bills with a maturity of roughly two months. Later, on 16 October 1979, the Bank of Japan also decided to let market conditions determine the rate on two-month discount bills, which by then were the only remaining bills with a posted rate. The effect of their moves on the market will be discussed later in the chapter.

Growth of the Market

After its establishment in 1971, the bill-discount market grew rapidly through 1975, but then, following a dip in 1976, increased at a much slower pace through 1982. During this period, the bill-discount market in Tokyo accounted for at least 78 percent of the amount outstanding. The data in table 4–1 indicate the average yearly amounts outstanding since 1971 with a breakdown for the Tokyo and Osaka-Nagoya markets.

Borrowing in the bill-discount market increased rapidly in the early 1970s, and by 1973 the amount of bills outstanding exceeded the amount of loans outstanding in the yen call-money market. During 1973–1980, the bill-

Table 4–1
Bill-Discount Market: Average Yearly Balance
(billions of yen)

	Total	Tokyo	Osaka & Nagoya
1971[a]	155	126	29
1972	803	675	128
1973	2,448	1,927	521
1974	4,400	3,456	944
1975	5,193	4,188	1,005
1976	4,490	3,736	754
1977	5,443	4,612	831
1978	5,615	4,914	701
1979	5,684	4,993	692
1980	6,120	5,056	1,065
1981	3,989	3,500	490
1982	3,867	3,503	364

Adapted from *Economic Statistics Annual,* Bank of Japan.
[a]Average for May-December period.

discount market exceeded in size the call-money market, but in 1981–1982 it dropped substantially to lower levels.

As mentioned earlier, the bulk of the trading in the bill-discount market occurs in Tokyo. Trading in Osaka and Nagoya combined accounted for 13 percent of the bills outstanding at the end of 1982. The respective proportions of the market for the three cities have not changed greatly since the establishment of the market.

The Bank of Japan plays a major role in the bill-discount market through its purchases of bills. At the end of 1978, for example, of the ¥6,671 billion borrowed by financial institutions in the market, the Bank of Japan held ¥2,850 billion, or 43 percent, with the remaining bills being held by other financial institutions.[11]

The Bank of Japan's Role in the Market

Since June 1972—or approximately a year after the bill-discount market was established—the Bank of Japan has conducted open-market operations in the bill-discount market in order to influence credit conditions. Similar operations are carried out in the yen call-money market, with both markets serving as a base for the Bank of Japan's control of credit and monetary conditions.[12]

The Bank of Japan exercises its control of the market primarily through the volume of its purchases of bills in the market. An increase above normal in the volume of its purchases would tend to ease credit conditions, while a reduction below normal in the volume of purchases would tend to tighten credit conditions. Since it is not unusual for the Bank of Japan to account for as much as half of the total transactions in the market, it is evident that the bank's actions play a predominant role in influencing market conditions.

In order to increase its control of the bill-discount and yen call-money markets, the Bank of Japan also restricts commercial bank access to the *gensaki* market. Otherwise, the banks could circumvent Bank of Japan restraint measures by borrowing heavily in the *gensaki* market.

In addition, the Bank of Japan also controls foreign-branch banks' access to the bill-discount market. Some foreign banks, such as Citibank of New York, appear to have generous limits on their access to the market, but other banks—especially the more recently established ones—appear to be much more restricted in their ability to borrow in the market.

Regulation of the Market

Official regulation of the bill-discount market primarily involves regulating and supervising the activities of the Tanshi companies. Although the Tanshi companies act mainly as brokers, they are treated legally as a moneylending business. Thus they are subject to a 1954 law that deals with the receipt of deposits and the payment of interest on deposits.[13]

Normally the supervision of moneylenders is assigned by ordinance to the governor of each prefecture, but in view of the importance of the Tanshi companies, they have been placed under the direct supervision of the Ministry of Finance. The actual supervision is carried out by the Ministry's Banking Bureau. Representatives from the Tanshi companies visit the Banking Bureau once a month to report on their activities.

Actual examination of the Tanshi companies' financial records is carried out by the Bank of Japan rather than the Ministry of Finance. As indicated earlier, if the Tanshi companies want to change the interest rate in the bill-discount market, they have traditionally consulted with the Bank of Japan, rather than the Ministry of Finance.

A Brief Analysis of the Market

Of the four major components of the Japanese money market, the call-money market was the most important in 1982 in terms of the amount of credit supplied. The average balance outstanding in that market in 1982 was ¥4.5 trillion, as compared with ¥4.3 trillion in the *gensaki* market, and ¥3.9 trillion in the bill-discount market (see table 3–1).

In recent years, the amount of credit outstanding in the call-money market has increased, while in the *gensaki* market and the bill-discount market, it has declined. In 1981, for example, there was a 35 percent decline in the amount of credit outstanding in the bill-discount market, while the amount of credit outstanding in the call-money market increased 37 percent. Thus, in the period from 1980 through 1982, the bill-discount market dropped from constituting 38 percent of the market to only 23 percent, while the call-money market rose from 20 percent in 1980 to 27 percent in 1982. Part of the relative decline of the bill-discount market has been due to competition from the NCD market, which—like the bill-discount market—has some of the longer money-market maturities.

On the whole, the bill-discount market has performed the role that its originators envisaged in 1971. The yen call-money market has been restored to a shorter-term market and the establishment of the bill-discount market with maturities of up to four months has provided the city banks with a more-stable source of funds. In addition, the Bank of Japan has obtained—with its preponderant position in the bill-discount market—an instrument for carrying out open-market operations that it can use to influence the liquidity of the banking system.

The bill-discount market is heavily one-sided in that most of the borrowing is done by the large city banks. Thus the market is really not one where all the participants are either borrowing or lending at alternate times and adjusting their liquidity, but one where a variety of lenders of two- to four-month funds provide credit mainly to the large city banks who are perennially in need of these funds.

Although the bill-discount market bears a close resemblance to the U.S. bankers' acceptance market, it is technically different.[14] This is primarily because the lending banks have not normally accepted (that is, guaranteed) the bill of exchange, although there is a tacit understanding that the bank will ultimately stand behind the obligation in the event of a default.[15]

Japanese bankers have cited several factors in explaining the absence of a bankers' acceptance market in Japan. One is that the present system works well and hence there is no real need to establish such a market. In addition, banks and their customers like to perserve the confidentiality of their relationships, which would become less confidential if such a market were established. Lastly, the bankers have said that such a market has not developed because the Bank of Japan's eligibility requirements for bankers' acceptances would be so severe that only a limited number of companies would qualify.

Despite some of the bankers disinterest in establishing a Western-style bankers' acceptance market, it is possible that such a market will be established during the 1980s—particularly if Japan abolishes most of its exchange controls and moves toward making Tokyo a free and important international financial center.

On the whole, the bill-discount market appears to have performed its narrowly construed role efficiently and effectively. The large city banks know that they can usually meet their short-term-liquidity needs by borrowing in the bill-discount, or the call-money, market. In the rather infrequent cases where the funds are not available overnight, they will go to the Bank of Japan for credit accommodation.

However, there are several serious criticisms that can be made of the bill-discount market. One of these is that the market has not been open to a large number of borrowers and lenders. As stated earlier, the only entities allowed to participate in the market are financial institutions. Thus all individuals and nonfinancial firms are excluded from the market. In this sense, the market is not a truly free and open market, and this helps to explain the popularity of the *gensaki* market, which does allow nonfinancial corporations to be direct participants in the market.

As noted earlier, the authorities have been liberalizing the market since June 1978 and freeing it from official restraints. An important question is whether the actions taken in June and November 1978, and April 1979, resulted in a real liberalization of the market. Based on the evidence through the end of 1982, it would appear that interest rates in the bill-discount market are now much freer than they were prior to 1978. Since October 1979—when the liberalization process was ostensibly completed—money-market rates have tended to move much more closely together, reflecting arbitrage operations and freedom to move between the various components of the market. It is likely, however, that the Bank of Japan still retains some control over the market through its influence on the six money-market brokers who operate in the market.

Additional measures would appear to be merited if the market is to be freed from various restraints. One of these would be to open up the market to all firms and individuals, instead of confining it to financial institutions. Even within this last group, some financial institutions—such as certain foreign-branch banks—are restrained in their access to the market. Another measure would be to eliminate the minimum holding period of one month for purchasers of bills. This feature certainly reduces the bill's liquidity. Third, the market could be broadened to include more than just trade bills of exchange. Financial paper, which among other things would finance services, could be permitted. Confining the market to the finance of actual trade transactions is unduly restrictive. What is important is the credit-worthiness of the borrower and not whether trade or service activities are being financed. Lastly, the market should not be confined to domestic bills, but should be broadened to include export and import bills.

Notes

1. T.F.M. Adams and I. Hoshii, *A Financial History of the New Japan*, Kodansha International Ltd., Tokyo, 1972, p. 414.

2. The following lists the main lenders in the market: regional (that is, local) banks, trust banks, long-term-credit banks, foreign banks, mutual-loan and savings banks, credit associations, the National Federation of Credit Associations, Banks for Commerce and Industrial Cooperatives (that is, Shoko Chukin Bank), Central Cooperative Bank for Agriculture and Forestry (that is, Norinchukin Bank), credit federations of agricultural cooperatives, National Mutual Insurance Federation of Agricultural Cooperatives, prefectoral mutual insurance federations of agricultural cooperatives, securities companies, life-insurance companies, and non-life-insurance companies. See *Money Market in Japan and Tanshi Companies*, Yamane Tanshi Company, Ltd., Tokyo, 1977, p. 9.

3. *Money Market in Japan and Tanshi Companies*, p. 14.

4. *Banking System in Japan*, Federation of Bankers' Associations of Japan, Tokyo, 1976, p. 70.

5. *Money Market in Japan and Tanshi Companies*, p. 15.

6. Wilbur F. Monroe, *Japan: Financial Markets and the World Economy*, New York, Praeger, 1973, p. 15.

7. According to the Yamane Tanshi Company, the minimum maturity period in the bill-discount market extends from the day of discount to the beginning of the month following the next month, that is, over two consecutive end-of-month dates. See *Money Market in Japan and Tanshi Companies*, p. 15.

8. For additional details, see *Money Market in Japan and Tanshi Companies*, Yamane Tanshi Co., Ltd., Tokyo, March 1980, p. 17.

9. Ibid., p. 8.

10. To distinguish between the two, the Bank of Japan, beginning in June 1978, listed rates for the bills freely resold under a column labeled "Resale of Bills," while the rates on bills subject to prefixed terms were listed under a column labeled "Usual of Bills." See *Economic Statistics Monthly*, Bank of Japan, Tokyo, November 1978, p. 50.

11. "Flow of Funds in the Japanese Economy," Special Paper No. 82, Bank of Japan, Tokyo, July 1979, p. 19.

12. *Money Market in Japan and Tanshi Companies*, p. 8.

13. Law No. 195 of 23 June 1954, "Law Concerning the Regulation of

Receiving of Capital Subscription, Deposits, and Interest on Deposits." See *Money Market in Japan and Tanshi Companies,* p. 3.

14. The Japanese do not consider that they have a bankers' acceptance market in Japan. "Bankers' acceptances and sales finance paper are not available in Japan as short-term financing." *Japan Banker,* Tokyo, July 1975, p. 25.

15. The usual practice is for Japanese banks to stamp their name on the back of the bill. This is a kind of guarantee for the bill holder, but it is not a bona fide guarantee.

5

The Yen
Call-Money Market

The yen call-money market is the oldest component of Japan's money market and until approximately 1961, it constituted the major money market in Japan. It was only in the early 1970s that the other main components of the money market began to grow and become important.

In principle, the main function of the call-money market is to provide a facility that the participating institutions can use to adjust their financial position. Thus, the market is used by those institutions desiring to invest surplus funds on a short-term basis and by those needing to borrow short-term funds.

In Japan, the terms *call loan* and *call money* are both used. The term *call loan* is used when the funds involved are viewed from the lender's side. When viewed from the borrower's side, the term *call money* is used. This distinction may well be unique to Japan.[1] At present, the market is generally referred to as the call-money market, and since lenders' rates are usually quoted, the call rate will be referred to in this book as the call-loan rate, rather than the call-money rate, or simply as the call rate. Since a dollar call market (see chapter 7) has developed in recent years, the term *yen call-money market,* or simply *call-money market,* will generally be used here in order to avoid confusion with the Tokyo dollar call market.

Some Historical Aspects

Japan's call-money market was established in 1902 and was patterned after the British and U.S. money markets.[2] During the 1950s and 1960s, the market became an increasingly important source of funds for the large city banks. Thus, at the end of 1951, the city banks obtained less than 1 percent of their funds from the call-money market. By 1964, however, the proportion had increased to 6 percent and in December 1970—just before the establishment of the bill-discount market—the proportion was still about 6 percent.

During the 1950s and 1960s, less use was made, as time passed, of very short-term funds—such as *overnight* and *unconditional* funds—and greater use was made of the longer-term funds—such as those with a *fixed maturity* and the *over-month-end* funds. The former (that is, the very short-term funds) accounted for about three-fourths of the market at the end of 1956, but by the end of 1964 the proportion had declined to three-eighths, and by December 1970 the proportion had declined even further to one-sixth.

During most of the period since the end of the Second World War, the city banks have depended on the call-money market as one of their more reliable sources of funds. Often facing a shortage of funds to finance their lending operations (in Japan, this situation is frequently referred to as being overloaned), the city banks tended to use the call-money market almost continuously and they have been the major net borrowers in the market. On the other hand, the many lenders in the call-money market do not view the market as a temporary outlet for surplus short-term funds, but rather as a regular and profitable outlet for their excess funds.

A major change occurred in June 1972 when fixed-maturity and over-month-end call loans were abolished, leaving only the two shorter maturities of overnight and unconditional call loans. This action tended to restore, to a large extent, the call-money market's true function as a very short-term money market.

Organization and Operation of the Market

The organization of the yen call-money market is very similar to that of the bill-discount market described in chapter 4. The market is basically composed of the borrowers, the brokers (who serve as intermediaries), and the lenders. The brokers in the call-money market are the same Tanshi companies described in chapter 4. As with the discount market, there is no single physical location for the call-money market, since the business offices of the six Tanshi companies constitute the actual market place for the call-money transactions which are carried out by telephone.

As is the case with the bill-discount market, most call-money transactions are carried out with the Tanshi companies acting as brokers rather than dealers. The Tanshi companies act as dealers (that is, taking title) rather than as brokers for only about 5 percent of the total call-money transactions.

Some transactions in the market are arranged directly between the borrowers and the lenders on a bilateral basis. However, such transactions—which bypass the Tanshi companies—only account for roughly 5 percent of total call-money transactions.

Transactions in the call-money market are carried out between 9:00 A.M. and 1:00 P.M. and between 1:00 P.M. and 3:00 P.M. Monday through Friday. The clearing of accounts normally occurs at 1:00 P.M. and 3:00 P.M. on weekdays and at 11:30 A.M. and 12:00 noon on Saturdays, when the market is open from 9:00 A.M. to 12:00 noon.

Main Participants in the Market

The large city banks are the main participants on the borrowing side of the yen call-money market. During the 1970s they accounted, on average, for approximately 84 percent of the outstanding amount of borrowing in the market. The other main borrowers in recent years have been the foreign banks and the regional banks. Since 1978 the securities companies have been allowed to borrow in the call market. Borrowing by the trust banks decreased in absolute terms during the latter half of the 1970s and long-term credit banks stopped borrowing altogether in the market after 1976. After the establishment of the bill-discount market in 1971, the city banks reduced their relative dependence on the call-money market since the two- to four-month money in the bill market provided them with a more-stable source of funds.

There are about half a dozen major lenders. In rough order of importance, these are the: (1) trust banks, (2) financial institutions for agriculture and forestry,[3] (3) regional banks, (4) mutual-loan and savings banks, (5) life- and non-life-insurance companies, and (6) long-term-credit banks. The relative importance of these respective institutions has varied over time, but the trust banks have generally tended to remain the predominant lender. More detailed information is provided later in this chapter in the section on the size and growth of the market.

The role of the foreign banks in the market has been changing. The foreign banks increased the amount of their lending to the market through 1975, but then the outstanding amount generally declined until March 1979. Then, since the Bank of Japan increased its basic discount rate three times during April through November, the foreign banks again found it profitable to lend in the market. During 1979–1982, foreign-bank lending in the call-money market generally increased. On the other hand, the amount of borrowing by the foreign banks in the market generally increased from 1975[4] through March 1979. Beginning in April 1979, foreign-bank borrowing dropped sharply due to the rise in interest rates. Later, in 1980–1982, foreign-bank borrowing resumed its general uptrend.

While the foreign banks were, on the average, net lenders to the market in 1975–1976, they were net borrowers in 1977–1981. Some of the U.S. banks, such as Citibank, Chase Manhattan, and Bank of America, have been particularly heavy borrowers in the market in recent years.

The call-money intermediaries, generally known as the Tanshi companies, were described earlier in chapters 2 and 4. As is the case with the bill-discount market, the Tanshi companies are primarily brokers in the call-money market—their own financial position being relatively small. The main assets of the Tanshi companies are call loans and bills, the holdings of bank debentures being negligible.

There are six call-money brokers in Japan, at least four[5] of which are located in Tokyo. A fifth, Yagi Tanshi, is located in Osaka and the sixth, Nagoya Tanshi, is located in Nagoya. All six companies are active in Tokyo and all except Nagoya Tanshi are active in Osaka. Only Nagoya Tanshi does business in Nagoya.

The main source of income for the Tanshi companies operating in the call-money market is their brokerage fee. Since the fee has remained relatively fixed over time, their earnings have depended primarily on the volume of transactions.

Nature of the Instruments

Call-money transactions in Japan basically involve an exchange of promissory notes secured by acceptable collateral. More specifically, in the yen call-money market the lender delivers funds to the Tanshi company in exchange for the Tanshi company's at-sight promissory note secured by appropriate collateral. The borrower in turn delivers an at-sight promissory note together with appropriate collateral to the Tanshi company in exchange for the funds.

All call funds except the half-day funds,[6] are fully secured. The assets provided as collateral must be readily marketable and, in principle, should be the same as those accepted as collateral by the Bank of Japan in its lending operations.

In general, the type of collateral that is acceptable consists of government bonds, other prime securities, and commercial bills. More specifically, it usually includes bank debentures, national-government-guaranteed bonds, prime local-government bonds, prime bonds of public corporations, and commercial bills issued by companies of the highest standing.

For the exchange of funds, each Tanshi company utilizes its account at the Bank of Japan. This simplifies the operation and also facilitates Bank of Japan monitoring of transactions in the call-money market.

The Terms in the Call-Money Market

There are five main aspects of the terms that prevail in the call-money market. These are maturity, the traditional minimum amount for a loan, brokerage, interest rates, and acceptable collateral. The maturity aspects are the more involved of these five and they have tended to change over time.

At the end of 1982 there were three different types of maturities available in the call-money market. These were: (1) half-day loans, (2) unconditional loans, and (3) term, or fixed-date, loans. Through May 1971, borrowers could also obtain over-month-end loans (that is, loans to be repaid on a fixed day in the following month), but as indicated in chapter 4, these were phased out from May 1971 to May 1972 and abolished altogether in June 1972. Such loans were absorbed in the bill-discount market.

There are two types of *half-day loans,* often referred to as the morning half (*asahan*) and the afternoon half (*gogohan*). The morning type must be repaid before the bill-clearing settlement on the same day; the other type is settled during the period extending from the bill-clearing settlement to the close of business. The time border line between the morning half and the afternoon half is set, in principle, at the settlement time for clearing balances at the Bank of Japan.

Unlike other maturities, such as unconditional or fixed date, half-day money does not require collateral or promissory notes, since both parties merely deliver to each other their checks on the Bank of Japan at the same time. The parties thus complete in one process both the releasing and collecting of funds.

Since the half-day transactions are completed the same day they are initiated, and there is therefore no loan amount outstanding at the close of the business day, data are not available on the volume of half-day funds. However, the use of half-day funds is reportedly light during most of the month and then heavy at the end of the month.

Unconditional call loans are those that are made for at least two days[7] and can be repaid or called with one day's notice to the broker. It is not always necessary to give a formal notice one day before repaying or recalling the loan. Notice can also be given on a tentative basis and this notice must be observed by the respective parties just as if it were a formal notice. This is known as the Rule of Unconfirmed Notice.[8]

Term, or fixed-date, loans in the present call-money market are those with maturity dates fixed within the same month as the original transaction. Since October 1978, the main type of term loan has been seven-day call money. When the authorities introduced seven-day money in October 1978, they indicated that the interest rate for funds with this maturity would reflect freely the demand and supply forces in the market. Later, on 2 April 1979, a new call-loan maturity was introduced with fixed maturities ranging from two to six days. The interest rate for these funds was also supposed to fluctuate freely in response to market forces.

There is no legal minimum or maximum size for individual loan transactions in the call-money market. However, the minimum amount for an individual transaction has customarily been ¥1 million (equivalent to $4,000 at an exchange rate of 250 yen to the U.S. dollar).[9] At the other end, individual loans of ¥100 million are not uncommon, but most loans range between these extremes.

The brokerage fee, or margin, for the call-money brokers is usually

0.0625 percent per annum. The call-loan rate that the brokers quote is the lending rate and the charge to the borrower is the lending rate plus the brokerage fee. The Tanshi companies earn their income from the difference between the bid and offer rates, which is 0.125 percentage points.

Until 2 April 1979, changes in the call-loan rate occurred in minimum amounts of 0.125 percentage points, with one exception which will be noted later in the chapter. Since that date, however, changes in call-loan rates have been in smaller units of at least 0.0625 percentage points. The one exception to this is the half-day call loan, where, as a matter of convenience, the old *hibu* system of charging interest is used. Under this system, the borrower pays a certain amount of yen per day as interest for each 100 yen borrowed.

In call-money transactions, the interest is not paid by the borrower until the end of the transaction (unlike the bill-discount market) and it is paid at the same time that the principal is repaid. This system of deferring the interest payment to the end is referred to by the Japanese as *atobarai*.

In calculating the amount of interest to be charged for call loans, the borrower is not charged for the very last day. Thus, under a method of computation called *kataochi,* interest is based on the number of days for the loan, excluding the last day.[10]

In December 1982, the following were the average interest rates that prevailed for the main types of call loans:

1. Unconditional   6.9 percent

2. Seven days   7.0 percent

As mentioned earlier, borrowers in the call-money market must provide acceptable collateral. In roughly 90 percent of the transactions, national bonds are used as collateral. Since the foreign banks' holdings of national bonds are either nil or very small, they tend to provide bills as their collateral in borrowing in the call-money market.

Size and Growth of the Market

During the postwar period, the total amount of borrowing in the call-money market has generally increased over the years. However, while the general trend has been up, there have been some recessionary periods (such as in 1966–1968 and 1972–1975) when the total amount outstanding dropped. The data in table 5–1 indicate the year-to-year trends in the market, both for the total average yearly balance outstanding and the individual balances according to the type of maturity.

During the period from 1956 through 1982, the average annual rate of

Table 5-1
Call-Money Market: Average Yearly Balance by Terms
(billions of yen)

	Total	Overnight	Unconditional	Fixed Maturity Dates	Over-Month-End
1956	100	13	63	10	14
1957	158	13	126	9	10
1958	186	9	124	20	33
1959	314	12	234	33	35
1960	369	24	257	53	35
1961	432	20	296	55	62
1962	514	17	331	73	93
1963	683	7	367	137	171
1964	1,008	5	453	232	318
1965	1,232	3	644	236	349
1966	998	2	329	317	350
1967	1,078	3	274	406	395
1968	1,077	2	289	397	389
1969	1,388	1	276	586	524
1970	1,693	1	284	741	667
1971	2,016	1	894	518	604
1972	1,542	—	1,153	(abolished in June 1972)	
1973	1,546	—	1,546		
1974	1,855	2	1,853		
1975	1,968	1	1,967		
1976	2,417	1	2,416		
1977	2,626	1	2,625		
1978	2,809	3	2,689	467[a]	
1979	3,318	1[b]	2,127	1,826	
1980	3,258		2,082	1,175	
1981	4,459		2,822	1,638	
1982	4,528		2,772	1,756	

Adapted from *Economic Statistics Monthly* and *Economic Statistics Annual,* Bank of Japan.
Note: Data for 1956–1960 are end-of-year data; otherwise, average balance for the year based on monthly averages.
[a]Seven-days; in October 1978, a seven-day term was started.
[b]January–March, abolished in April 1979.

growth in the market was 17.5 percent. During the last four years (1979–1982), the average annual rate of growth was 13 percent, indicating a moderate deceleration in the rate of growth of the market.

Throughout this period of roughly three decades from the mid-1950s, *overnight money*—the first of the four maturities listed in table 5-1—constituted a relatively small proportion of the total and has been close to negligible since the mid-1960s. In April 1979, the category was abolished altogether. The most important category has generally been *unconditional call money*. Except for one five-year period (1966–1970), unconditional money has constituted the largest component of the call-money market. During 1982, unconditional call money accounted for 61 percent of the total borrowing in the call-money market.

The two remaining components of the call-money market—money with a *fixed maturity* and *over-month-end money*—increased rapidly during the first half of the 1960s. With the city banks anxious to acquire a more stable source of funds, these two types of funds became increasingly popular in the latter half of the 1960s and generally overshadowed unconditional call funds. This trend was broken in 1971 when the bill-discount market was established, and the over-month-end loans were eventually phased out by June 1972. In October 1978 the authorities inaugurated seven-day call money, and in 1979 this was changed to call money with fixed maturity dates (namely, two to seven days). During 1982 call money with a fixed maturity date accounted for 3.9 percent of the total borrowing in the call-money market.

In order to put in perspective the relative importance of the call-money market, the total amount of credit outstanding in the call-money market can be compared to the total credit outstanding of the deposit-money banks in Japan.[11] This ratio increased from 2.2 percent in 1956 to 3.3 percent in 1960. By 1970 the ratio had eased to 2.8 percent and in 1980 it was down to 1.4 percent. Overall, the total amount of call-loan credit outstanding increased 45 times between 1956 and 1982, while the total credit outstanding of the deposit-money banks increased 62 times during the same period.

Since the city banks are the major borrowers in the call-money market, some idea of the relative importance of the market can also be gained by relating the amount of deposits of the city banks to the market. In 1971 the average amount of credit outstanding in the market (¥2,016 billion) was equivalent to about 8 percent of the average amount of city-bank deposits. By 1982 this proportion had declined to 4.5 percent, with this drop mainly reflecting the splitting up of the old call-money market into two parts, that is, the new bill-discount market and the present-day call-money market.

The major lenders in the call-money market were discussed earlier. To provide an idea of the relative importance of these different lenders, as well as how the various lenders' shares have changed in the postwar period, data are presented in table 5–2 on the situation in 1955 and every five years thereafter through 1980.

In general, the trust banks have remained the most important source of funds since 1960, although they were heavily overshadowed by the regional banks in the 1950s. The regional banks have also been important suppliers

Table 5–2
Call-Money Market: Market Shares of Major Lenders
(percent)

	Trust Banks	Regional Banks	Agriculture and Forestry Financial Institutions[a]	Long-term-Credit Banks	Mutual-Loan and Savings Banks	Other[b]
1955[c]	5.6	22.4	n.a.	15.8	n.a.	n.a.
1960	30.7	20.2	n.a.	6.8	n.a.	n.a.
1965	24.1	12.4	25.4	3.9	3.4	30.8
1970	23.0	15.3	20.3	2.9	4.7	33.8
1975	19.5	17.9	9.4	6.3	10.3	36.6
1980	26.7	12.5	13.5	4.9	8.9	33.5

Adapted from: *Economic Statistics Annual,* Bank of Japan, Tokyo, March 1981 and earlier issues.

Note: The total for any year is 100 percent. Market shares are based on the average balance for the year.

[a]Includes Norinchukin Bank, National Mutual Insurance Federation of Agricultural Cooperatives, prefectural mutual-insurance federations of agricultural cooperatives, and credit federations of agricultural cooperatives.

[b]Includes, among other things, foreign banks, credit associations, National Federation of Credit Associations, securities companies, life- and non-life-insurance companies, and city banks.

[c]Data for 1955 cover only the Tokyo call-money market, hence the Osaka and Nagoya markets are excluded.

of funds to the call-money market in the postwar period, but with a moderately decreasing share of the total. Both the long-term-credit banks and agricultural institutions have become less important over time, while the relative importance of mutual-loan and savings banks has increased.

The Bank of Japan's Role in the Market

As in the bill-discount market, the Bank of Japan plays a crucial role in influencing developments in the yen call-money market—particularly the cost of funds in the market. There is fairly widespread agreement that in most of the postwar period, interest rates in the call-money and bill-discount markets have been held down by the Bank of Japan to levels lower than what would have occurred under completely free-market conditions.[12] During the latter half of the 1960s, for example, the Bank of Japan controlled the interest rate in the call-money market by being both a taker of excess funds (to prevent the rate from falling below some desired level) and a net supplier of funds (to prevent an excessive increase in the rate).

After the establishment of the bill-discount market, the Bank of Japan frequently intervened directly in that market to influence the level of the bill rate. In the late 1970s, the bank tended to concentrate its intervention in the bill market and intervened only indirectly, if at all, in the call-money market. This usually occurred during a liquidity squeeze. However, the bank has continued to remain in very frequent contact (via telephone) with the call-money brokers. The large city banks also report daily to the Bank of Japan on their transactions in the money market.

During most of the period since the early 1950s, the Bank of Japan has kept the call-loan rate at a level higher than the bank's basic discount rate. In the early 1970s, for example, the differential was roughly one-fourth percentage point, but during tight-money periods, the difference tended to increase substantially. Thus, while the level of the discount rate has influenced the level of the call-loan rate, it cannot always be said to determine it.[13] During the rest of the 1970s and early 1980s, the call-loan rate remained above the Bank of Japan's discount rate. Also, in the 1970s the call-loan rate generally remained below the bill-discount rate. However, by summer 1979 the differential between the two rates had narrowed substantially and since then the two rates have moved fairly close to each other.

Regulation of the Call-Money Market

Much of what was stated in chapter 4 about regulation of the Tanshi companies and the bill-discount brokers also applies to the call-money brokers, since they are part of the same Tanshi companies, if they are not the same person. The Tanshi companies are licensed by the authorities in perpetuity, that is, once they have been licensed, they do not have to renew their licenses periodically. The articles of each of the major Tanshi companies allow them to conduct transactions in the call-money market, the bill-discount market, the foreign-exchange market, and also to purchase and sell securities.[14]

According to Ezekiel, particular types of call-money transactions during the 1951–1964 period[15] were subject from time to time to interest-rate ceilings. These ceilings were ones to which the banks agreed mutually. In the period through 1956, overnight-call-loan rates were subject to ceilings that were set at unreasonably low levels. Because of this, the level of the overnight rates did not really reflect the underlying conditions in the market. During roughly 1960–1964, the unconditional-call-loan rates were also subject to ceilings.[16]

While the reported interest rates during 1951–1964 were frequently at the ceiling level, actual transactions were at times carried out at higher rates. This was particularly the case when the Bank of Japan was pursuing a tight money policy.[17] The role of the Bank of Japan in influencing interest rates and money-market developments is explored more extensively in chapter 9.

Liberalization of the Call-Money Market

Significant steps were taken in 1978 and 1979 to permit call-loan rates to more closely reflect actual market forces. In October 1978, seven-day call money for trading at freely moving rates was introduced into the call-money market. Then later, on 2 April 1979, agreement was reached between the Bank of Japan and the Tanshi companies that the latter would discontinue the practice of predetermining the call rates a day in advance.[18] The practical effect of this was that call-loan transactins on a posted-rate basis were discontinued, with the specific rates being left to negotiation. Despite this action, subsequent changes in the rates were relatively moderate. For example, the average seven-day rate in March 1979 was 4.7 percent, but increased to only 5.0 percent in April and to 5.2 percent in May.

Also on 2 April 1979, the overnight-call-money category was discontinued and replaced by a new unconditional call money, with the rate for this money reportedly being determined by free-market forces. Included in the new unconditional call money was two- to six-day call money.[19] It was also agreed at this time, as mentioned earlier, that the minimum change that could occur in call-loan rates would no longer be 0.125 percentage points, but 0.0625 percentage points.

In a further move to liberalize transactions and interest rates in the call-money market, the Bank of Japan, on 19 November 1980, allowed the four major securities companies (Nomura, Nikko, Daiwa, and Yamaichi) to borrow up to ¥20 billion per company in the call-money market. Since 1965, securities companies had not been allowed to participate in the market as a result of one major company facing a financial crisis. This move was followed in December 1981 by another Bank of Japan action to allow the second-tier securities companies to borrow in the call market. However, the amount of borrowing was limited to a maximum of ¥5 billion per company. Both moves tended to increase interest arbitrage. The actual extent to which these actions have created a truly free—rather than administered—call-money market, is discussed in the following section.

The November 1980 action to allow securities companies to borrow in the call-money market was followed by a further liberalization in April 1981. At that time the city banks were allowed to lend again to the call-money market. This was reportedly permitted by the Bank of Japan[20] and it constituted the first lending, as opposed to borrowing, by the city banks in the call-money market since 1973.

A Brief Analysis of the Market

Past trends in the call-money market indicate that it is not primarily a market for financial institutions to adjust their short-term liquidity surpluses or deficits—whether on a random or a seasonal basis. Rather, the city banks view the market as a perennial source of funds through which they can finance their continuing liquidity deficits. Similarly, the lenders do not see the market as a temporary outlet for surplus funds, but rather as a near-permanent vehicle for them to employ their excess funds profitably. Thus, the market actually reflects a basic imbalance among the various intermediaries in their sources and uses of funds.

It should not be concluded from this, however, that relationships in the market remain fixed or static. When money-market yields fall to relatively low levels—as, for example, in January 1976—major suppliers of funds have shifted to purchasing public and industrial bonds, rather than supplying funds to the market. Similarly, the relative importance of the market participants can change. Thus, the foreign banks after 1976 shifted to being net borrowers—rather than net lenders—in the market (except for 1979–1980). Even the maturity structure of the market can shift greatly. Thus, unconditional-call-money funds, which accounted for 70 percent of the market in 1960, accounted for only 17 percent in 1970, while the longer-term funds increased their relative share substantially over this period.

It is difficult to determine precisely to what extent the interest rates recorded in the call-money market in the postwar period have truly reflected free-market forces rather than administered or managed rates. Wilbur Monroe, writing in 1973, and impressed by the large fluctuations in the call-loan rate in the 1950s and late 1960s, concluded that: "In spite of all intervention and administrative guidance, it is probably true that the call-money market has been one of the more 'freely determined' of all Japanese credit markets."[21] Yet even this view implies that it is a matter of degree, and that the market has been—except for some tight-money periods—an administered market.

The actions taken since 1978 to liberalize both the call-money and bill-discount markets provide further evidence that the Japanese authorities themselves did not consider these markets to be really free markets up through 1977. Otherwise there would have been no need to introduce so-called free rates.[22] It is therefore probably fair to conclude that the call-money market, at least through September 1978, was not a truly free market and that the interest rates prevailing in the market were—to a greater or lesser degree—administered rates. This does not mean that the rates were set independently of market forces, but that the rates did not fully reflect actual market forces.

There are various reasons why the government was reluctant to allow a completely free call-money market in the postwar period. One of these was that a free market would have resulted in a higher level of interest rates, including the yields on government securities, and the government did not want to be faced with an increase in the cost of financing the national debt. In addition, the government had gotten used to controlling, or strongly influencing, the level of interest rates during the postwar period and was reluctant to change the financial structure (a major task in itself) and thereby subject itself to the vicissitudes of the market. It is also likely that a sharp increase in yields on short-term government securities would have created problems of disintermediation, with depositors shifting funds out of savings and time deposits, and into short-term government securities.

Of these three reasons, it can be said that the government is still reluctant to allow the yields on short-term government securities to rise to free-market levels. Thus the potential problem mentioned above of disintermediation has not occurred. However, short-term money-market rates are now less artificial or administered than they were prior to 1978, and this has forced the monetary authorities to accommodate their policies more closely to actual market conditions than had been the case in earlier years.

Notes

1. *Money Market in Japan and Tanshi Companies,* Yamane Tanshi Company, Ltd., Tokyo, 1977, p. 11.

2. "Japan's Short-Term Money Market," *Monthly Review,* Mitsui Bank, Tokyo, October 1977, p. 4.

3. Includes the Norinchukin Bank, credit federations of agricultural cooperatives, National Mutual Insurance Federation of Agricultural Cooperatives, and the prefectural mutual-insurance federations of agricultural cooperatives.

4. Separate data on foreign-bank borrowing in the call-money market were first published in 1975.

5. These are Ueda Tanshi, Tokyo Tanshi, Yamane Tanshi, and Nippon Discount. All four of these reportedly maintain branch offices in Osaka. See Wilbur F. Monroe, *Japan: Financial Markets and the World Economy,* Praeger, New York, 1973, p. 102.

6. These merely involve an exchange of checks with different clearing times.

7. Actually, the day of the original transaction plus the following day.

8. *Money Market in Japan and Tanshi Companies,* p. 12.

9. Ibid., p. 11.

10. Ibid., p. 13.

11. The data used in calculating this ratio are taken from table 5–1 and the annual issues of *International Financial Statistics* published by the International Monetary Fund.

12. See, for example, *The Japan Banker,* Tokyo, July 1975, p. 25.

13. A study by H. Ezekiel of the relationship between the discount rate and the call-loan rate on the basis of a regression analysis for the period from August 1955 to December 1964, concluded that the relationship was ". . . not very close." See Hannan Ezekiel, "The Call Money Market in Japan," *IMF Staff Papers,* International Monetary Fund, Washington, D.C., March 1966, p. 48.

14. *The Japanese Financial System,* The Bank of Japan, Tokyo, 1972, p. 70.

15. The cut-off year of 1964 is cited here since Ezekiel's article was written in 1965.

16. *The Japanese Financial System,* The Bank of Japan, Tokyo, 1972, p. 70.

17. *Money and Banking in Japan,* Bank of Japan, Tokyo, 1961, p. 27.

18. As explained by the Bank of Japan, the ". . . money dealers discontinued their conventional quoting of the standard rate on unconditional call loans . . . ". *Monthly Economic Review,* Bank of Japan, Tokyo, April 1979, p. 3.

19. *Tokyo Financial Review,* Bank of Tokyo, April 1979, p. 5.

20. *Japanese Banking,* The Financial Times Business Publishing, Ltd., London, 1981, p. 45.

21. Wilbur F. Monroe, *Japan: Financial Markets and the World Economy,* Praeger, New York, 1973, p. 102.

22. One of the Bank of Japan's footnotes to its table on bill-discount rates states that "Since October 1979, discount rates have been free rates." Similar language is used in describing the call-loan rates. See *Economics Statistics Annual,* Bank of Japan, Tokyo, 1982, p. 187.

6 The *Gensaki* Market

The *gensaki* market in Japan is basically a bond-repurchase market in that it involves bond trading coupled with a repurchase agreement. More specifically, a *gensaki* transaction is the conditional sale (or purchase) of an authorized bond for a fixed period, with an agreement that the bond be repurchased (or resold) later at a specific price. The difference between the selling and repurchase price is the main determinant of the yield on the transaction. All *gensaki* transactions—which normally have a maturity of six months or less—are carried out in Japan's over-the-counter bond market.

The name *gensaki* derives from the fact that both a present and a future transaction must occur in carrying out a complete transaction in this market. Thus, the word *gensaki* comes from two Chinese characters meaning "present" (*gen*) and "future" (*saki*).

Establishment of the Market

Gensaki transactions first developed in the late 1940s when the securities companies found that they needed cash funds on a short-term basis.[1] To meet these needs, they sold bonds out of their portfolio on a conditional basis and then repurchased them later.

At first they sold the bonds to agricultural financial institutions—particularly those that experienced seasonal inflows of cash funds. Later, in the last half of the 1960s, the commercial banks began to participate in the market during periods of monetary restraint. To avoid capital losses—with interest rates rising—the banks sold bonds in the *gensaki* market to raise needed funds, thus buying time until market conditions improved.

The volume, and the amount outstanding, of *gensaki* transactions remained relatively low, compared with other components of the money market, until about 1970. Since then, the amount of funds provided by the market has increased substantially to the point where it has, at times, exceeded in size both the call-money and the bill-discount markets. During 1982 the average balances outstanding for the bill-discount, *gensaki,* and call-money markets were ¥3.9 trillion, ¥4.4 trillion[2] and ¥4.5 trillion respectively.

Market Participants

The participants in the *gensaki* market can be classified as follows: (1) the borrowers, (2) the securities companies, and, (3) the lenders. While this three-part division is valid in those cases where the securities companies act as brokers, it should be noted that the securities companies can—and frequently do—participate in the market as borrowers. But regardless of whether the securities companies serve as brokers or principals, all transactions in the market must be arranged through the securities companies. *Gensaki* transactions are conducted over the counter twenty-four hours a day, with most transactions occurring between 7:30 A.M. and 8:00 P.M. when the computer facilities are operational.

Before discussing in detail the particular institutions that participate in the market, it should be noted that there are three basic types of *gensaki* transactions. The first is a one-sided trade (*jiko gensaki*) which usually involves the securities companies selling securities from their portfolio to a customer. The second is a matched trade (*itaku gensaki*) where the transaction is between two customers with the securities company acting simultaneously as buyer and as seller of the securities being transacted. The third is a transaction between, say, Customer A and Customer B, with the securities company merely acting as a broker. The securities companies reportedly have the responsibility of screening the creditworthiness of potential corporate borrowers.[3]

Although their relative positions change from time to time, the major borrowers in recent years in the *gensaki* market have been the securities companies, the city banks, business corporations, financial institutions for agriculture and forestry, life- and non-life-insurance companies, trust and long-term-credit banks, and various thrift institutions such as the credit associations and mutual-loan and savings banks.

The major lenders have been predominantly the nonfinancial industrial corporations and other nonfinancial enterprises, including foreign companies. In 1982, foreigners were the second largest purchasers (that is, lenders) after enterprises. The amount of lending in the market by the securities companies, unlike the amount of their borrowing, has generally been negligible. In general, the securities companies tend to dominate the market on the borrowing side and the nonfinancial business corporations tend to dominate it on the lending side.

For many years the Bank of Japan did not allow the city banks to lend funds in the *gensaki* and call-money markets. This was because the city banks were basically viewed as steady borrowers in the money market, and lending in the market was not thought to be compatible with borrowing from the Bank of Japan at interest rates below the market. (While Article 65 of Japan's Securities and Exchange Law prohibits banks from dealing in securities, they can participate in the *gensaki* market by going through the securities companies.) In spring 1981, however, this lending restraint was relaxed. In a move to further liberalize transactions and interest rates in the money market, the city banks with seasonally surplus funds were allowed to participate as lenders in both the *gensaki* and the call-money markets.

Not everyone is free to participate in the market. Thus, the nonfinancial business corporations that can participate in the market are restricted to those that would qualify to be listed on the First Section of the Tokyo Stock Exchange.[4] Individuals are not allowed to participate in the market. Until April 1979, only residents of Japan, including foreign banks operating in Japan, were allowed to participate in the market, but in mid-May 1979 the Ministry of Finance authorized the participation by nonresidents in the *gensaki* market.

Both cyclical and secular developments have affected the relative importance of the major participants in the market. Until roughly 1968, the main sellers of bonds in the market were the securities companies. But after 1968 the agricultural financial institutions also sold substantial amounts of bonds. As the market became increasingly popular in the 1970s, the number and variety of participants increased. During tight-money periods the nonfinancial business corporations tended to sell bonds (and thereby borrow funds) in the *gensaki* market due to the difficulty of borrowing funds from the usual sources. On the other hand, in spring 1976 when the industrial corporations had large amounts of excess working capital, due to the curtailment of their investment spending on plant and equipment during the recession, the amount of bond buying in the *gensaki* market by these corporations—particularly the automobile manufacturers and the home-electric-appliance makers—was relatively large.

There would appear to be at least four main reasons for participants in the *gensaki* market to sell bonds. The most common reason is probably to obtain liquid funds on a temporary basis. Another is to make a profit from arbitrage operations, for example, by borrowing in the *gensaki* market and investing the proceeds in the call-money or bill-discount market. A third reason would be to delay the final sale of bonds in the expectation that they could be sold later on a final basis at a higher price. And lastly, the bonds could be sold in the *gensaki* market in order to raise funds to buy additional bonds on a long-term basis, without having to engage in a final sale of the bonds currently held.

As for the main reasons why participants buy bonds in the *gensaki* market, one is because the *gensaki* market can, at times, provide higher yields than other segments of the money market or short-term time deposits. Another reason is to buy bonds only temporarily—that is, in the *gensaki* market—with the expectation of using the repurchase proceeds later to buy bonds on a long-term basis when the price, hopefully, is lower. A third reason is to hedge or balance a portfolio by selling long-term bonds with repurchase agreements and buying bonds short-term in the *gensaki* market.

Nature of the Instruments

There are two basic types of bonds that are traded in the *gensaki* market. These are discount bonds and coupon-bearing bonds. Some use is also made of bonds where interim interest payments are made, but transactions in this type of bond are relatively rare.[5]

Japanese law[6] restricts the types of bonds or debentures eligible for trading in the *gensaki* market to the following six types: (1) government, (2) government-guaranteed, (3) municipal, (4) public-corporation, (5) bank debentures, and (6) corporate bonds or debentures other than convertible bonds. All of these securities can be traded in the *gensaki* market, regardless of whether they have been issued privately or publicly, and whether they are in bearer or registered form.[7] As indicated earlier, all transactions in the *gensaki* market take place in the over-the-counter market (*tento shijo*) conducted by the securities houses. Formal bond transactions take place on the Tokyo, Osaka, and Nagoya exchanges, where prices are quoted for listed bonds. The volume on the official bond exchange is relatively small and in 1980 was about 3 percent of all secondary bond trading. In the over-the-counter market, *gensaki* transactions accounted for 57 percent of all transactions in the twelve months ending March 1981. By early 1982, however, this proportion had declined to about 35 percent.

Because of the short-term nature of *gensaki* transactions, as well as the detailed documentation involved, most of the bonds and debentures traded in the *gensaki* market are kept in the vaults of the securities companies. This is particularly true of registered bonds and short-term transactions of ten days or less. In lieu of actual transfer of the bond, *bond-custody certificates* or *letters of guarantee* are used.

For each *gensaki* transaction, written contracts must be exchanged between the parties. After all conditions are accepted by both parties, two contract notes are prepared, and each party signs both notes. Each party thus holds one original copy of the agreement. In those cases where the client of a securities company prefers to retain a document written in English, a letter of guarantee, rather than a bond-custody certificate, is provided.

The basic information contained in each contract note (with separate information for the purchaser and for the repurchaser) includes the following: (1) settlement date (that is, date of purchase and date for repurchase), (2) name of the issuer of the bond or debenture, (3) nominal or face value of the bond, (4) purchase and repurchase price per bond, (5) total amount of principal for purchase and repurchase, (6) interest accrued (if any) at time of purchase and repurchase, (7) amount of the transfer tax, (8) net amount (which is the principal amount plus accrued interest for the purchaser and the same less the transfer tax for the repurchaser), and (9) nominal yield (that is, coupon rate). From this information, it is possible to calculate the actual yield to the lender in the *gensaki* market.

Occasionally the customer of a securities company decides that the conditions or terms set forth in the contract note are not sufficiently detailed or complete. In such case, the securities company will offer to substitute an agreement for sale and purchase of bonds. This agreement, among other things: specifies the dates of sale and repurchase; states that the buyer shall make full payment to the seller immediately on delivery of the bond custody certificate or letter of guarantee; has the seller promise that each bond is a bearer bond, or registered certificate, with no defects or liens and that the seller has complete title; indicates that transfer or other taxes shall be borne by the seller; and specifies the various conditions under which a party to the contract can terminate the agreement.

Growth of the Market

Compared with the call-money market, the *gensaki* market remained relatively small until the late 1960s. At the end of 1967, for example, the outstanding balance in the *gensaki* market was equal to only 15 percent of the amount of loans outstanding in the call market. However, the annual rate of growth in the market increased significantly from 1968 to 1973, averaging 51 percent during that period.

As indicated in table 6-1, the outstanding balance in the *gensaki* market increased from ¥152 billion at the end of 1967 to ¥1,738 billion at the end of 1973. Due to the recession in Japan in 1974, activity in the market declined in 1974 and did not recover to the 1973 level until 1976. In 1977–1978 the size of the market roughly doubled from the end-of-1976 level, reaching ¥4.2 trillion at the end of 1978. During 1979–1982 the balance outstanding in the market—based on end-of-month figures—fluctuated between ¥3.9 and ¥5.7 trillion, ending the year of 1982 at ¥4.3 trillion. The market appears to have roughly leveled off in 1981–1982.

The resumption of the rapid growth of the market in spring 1976 was due mainly to the general economic recovery that was beginning at that time and to new regulations dealing with *gensaki* trading issued by the Ministry of Finance in March 1976. These regulations spelled out certain rules and reporting procedures for the brokers operating in the market and tended to legitimize *gensaki* trading, which had previously operated in an ambiguous

Table 6-1
Balance of Bond Trading with Repurchase Agreement
(billions of yen)

End of	Amount	Year-to-Year Change (percent)
1967	152	—
1968	291	+91
1969	408	+40
1970	619	+52
1971	882	+42
1972	1,224	+39
1973	1,738	+42
1974	1,505	−13
1975	1,679	+12
1976	2,804	+24
1977	3,136	+45
1978	4,207	+34
1979	3,960	−6
1980	4,507	+14
1981	4,481	−1
1982	4,304	−4

Adapted from *Economic Statistics Monthly,* Bank of Japan.

regulatory environment. The acceleration in market activity was also aided by the fact that the business corporations had ample, if not excess, liquid funds at the time. A major source of funds for the market has been the deposits held by business corporations, which would probably have been deposited with the large city banks in the absence of a *gensaki* market.

The volume of activity in the *gensaki* market is strongly influenced by the level of deposit rates and by the yields in other components of the money market. Thus, if the yields in the *gensaki* market are substantially above the yields on bank deposits, a relatively large volume of funds might flow into the gensaki market. When all short-term rates are at a similar level, there is much less activity by way of interest arbitrage.

Borrowing-Lending Terms

The contract period in the *gensaki* market can range from only a few days to up to one year. However, most contracts are arranged for a period of six months or less, with the majority contracted for one-, two-, and three-month periods. A very common period is three months.

The face value of a transaction can range from ¥30 million to ¥50 billion or more;[8] there is reportedly no upper limit.[9] The minimum trading amount has varied, at times, between ¥30 million and ¥100 million, but a minimum of ¥50 million is common. The bond prices in *gensaki* transactions are based on the prevailing prices for the same bonds in the over-the-counter market.

The yields in the *gensaki* market are based on the effective yield during the holding period. If one is borrowing (that is, selling bonds) in the *gensaki* market, the measured yield would be the interest a seller would pay to the buyer on the sales proceeds from the date of sale to the repurchase date. When the securities companies quote a yield to a buyer of a bond in the *gensaki* market, it is the effective yield on the purchase cost until the buyer (that is, lender) resells the bond.

The actual calculation of the repurchase price in a *gensaki* transaction is somewhat complex, but basically it involves five variables. These are: (1) purchase price, (2) time period involved, (3) net yield, (4) amount of accrued interest—if any, and, (5) amount of the transfer tax. Detailed examples of how to calculate the repurchase price are provided in Nomura's *Gensaki Manual*.[10]

Whether accrued interest is paid or not depends on the type of bond involved. If it is a coupon-bearing bond, accrued interest is included in the calculation since interest will eventually be paid on the bond. If a discount bond is involved, then no accrued interest is included in the calculation. As a result of this difference, there are at least two different formulas for calculating *gensaki* yields.[11]

It should be noted that the yield in *gensaki* trading does not vary according to the type of bond involved in the transaction (for example, coupon bearing versus discount). Thus *gensaki* rates do not reflect differences in the underlying securities being traded. However, the transfer tax on *gensaki* transactions, which is .03 percent of the principal amount,[12] does influence the yield and is included in yield calculations. The transfer tax is initially paid by the borrower when the bond is sold and by the investor when the bond is resold. There is no domestic withholding tax against any profit made from a *gensaki* transaction, and foreign investors are reportedly not subject to any domestic tax on their profit from a *gensaki* transaction.[13] On the other hand, interest payments on bonds registered in the name of both residents and nonresidents are considered taxable (though sovereign entities are tax exempt) and tax is withheld for both residents and nonresidents. However, if foreigners have their bonds registered under the name of a designated financial institution—securities companies included—then the interest receipts are exempt from the withholding tax.

The interest rates in the *gensaki* market are generally quoted on an annual basis; however, very short-term trades are frequently quoted on a *hibu,* or daily, basis. Yields commonly move in increments of five basis points. The *gensaki* rate that is quoted in the daily newspapers generally reflects the offered side of trades transacted in lots of ¥500 million. The actual spread between borrowing and lending rates in the *gensaki* market is usually narrow.

In 1973–1974, the *gensaki* rate often exceeded the call-loan and bill-discount rates. But since 1979, all of the money-market rates have been more bunched and have tended to move together as a group. The level of other short-term money rates exerts an important influence on the rate level in the *gensaki* market. Other important influences include the current stance of monetary policy and the expectations for future trends in the bond market.

Beginning in October 1975, *chakuchi,* or forward bond trading, was begun in the *gensaki* market. *Chakuchi* trading is generally stimulated during those periods when short-term interest rates remain lower than long-term rates.

Interest-Rate Trends

As indicated earlier, the *gensaki* market did not begin to assume a relatively important role in the Japanese money market until the early 1970s. It was only around the mid-1970s that the interest rates in the *gensaki* market began to be be published in periodicals such as the Bank of Japan's *Economic Statistics Monthly.* Consequently, data on the interest-rate trends in the *gensaki* market are only readily available beginning January 1975.

These data indicate that yields in the *gensaki* market generally declined in 1975—having reached high levels during the rapid inflation of 1974—and then roughly leveled off during 1976. Following a decline in 1977–1978, yields in the *gensaki* market rose sharply in 1979 and early 1980, reaching a high in March. By late 1982, however, yields for three-month transactions had declined from the March 1980 high of 12.7 percent to slightly below 7.0 percent. The data available on interest rates in the *gensaki* market since 1975 indicate that one-month and three-month *gensaki* yields have moved roughly together. Both rates have tended to fluctuate above and below the call-loan and bill-discount rates. These fluctuations tend to be greater during seasonally tight periods such as in March, June, September, and December.

The interest rates in the *gensaki* market are compiled by the twelve largest members of the Japan Securities Dealers' Association. In March 1977 the association began to publish *gensaki* yield quotations three times each week, namely, Monday, Wednesday, and Friday.[14]

Some Key Developments in the Market

The *gensaki* market was given a boost in 1971–1972 when the Bank of Japan's easy money policy left the business corporations—traditionally chronic borrowers—with temporarily uncommitted funds to invest. The corporations channeled these funds into the *gensaki* market, since the yields there were relatively attractive and—as nonfinancial institutions—they were prohibited from investing in the bill-discount and yen call-money market. Since that time the market has continued to grow, except during recessionary periods.

Later, in 1978, the government began to offer a new bond with a shorter maturity than the usual issues, and this added to the choices available to investors in the *gensaki* market. Up through late spring 1978, the government issued only five-year discount bonds and ten-year interest-bearing coupon bonds. Beginning June 1978, however, the government began to issue three-year coupon bonds and these began to be traded in the *gensaki* market. In 1981 the government also began to issue two-year interest-bearing bonds and four-year interest-bearing bonds.

In May 1979, the government began to allow foreigners to participate in the *gensaki* market without any restraints on the maturity of the issues purchased. Previously foreigners were allowed to purchase government securities with a maturity of thirteen months or more, and, prior to January 1979, the minimum maturity was sixty-one months.

With the unrestricted opening of the *gensaki* market to nonresidents, foreign participation in the market increased in relative importance. Reports indicate that private institutional investors in the United States and Europe favor trading in short-term *gensaki* market assets, while foreign central banks favor long-term government bonds.

Foreign trading in the *gensaki* market has tended to become an increasingly important element in contributing to international capital flows into, or out of, Japan. Thus, in April 1980, Japan experienced a large net long-term capital outflow of $2.3 billion in its balance of payments. This was reportedly due mainly to heavy net foreign sales of bonds in the *gensaki* market in the amount of approximately $1.9 billion. The liberalization of exchange controls on capital movements by the Japanese government 1 December 1980 further enhanced the attractiveness of the *gensaki* market.

Regulation of the *Gensaki* Market

Compared to other components of the money market, the *gensaki* market has been relatively free. While the bill-discount and call-money markets are subject to direct intervention by the Bank of Japan, interest rates in the *gensaki* market are relatively free to reflect demand and supply conditions, since there is normally no official intervention in the market. Because industrial and business corporations are allowed to participate in *gensaki* transactions, the market is also one of the few free markets available for short-term cash management by nonfinancial businesses in Japan.

Although the *gensaki* market is normally free from Bank of Japan open-market operations, the market is nevertheless regulated by the authorities—principally the Ministry of Finance. The government's authority to regulate the market is based on the Securities Exchange Law.[15] Ministry of Finance regulations are sent to the chairman of the Securities Dealers' Association of Japan for transmittal to the dealer companies.

There was very little, if any, regulation of the securities dealers' transactions in the *gensaki* market prior to 1974. In December 1973 the Ministry of Finance conducted a survey of the market and asked the securities companies to submit information on their *gensaki* activities. Then, early in 1974, the Ministry of Finance introduced several self-regulatory rules on *gensaki* transactions for the securities companies. This was followed by more formal regulations on *gensaki* transactions about two years later.

In March 1976 the Ministry of Finance issued a series of rules and reporting procedures for the securities companies. These were contained in the official notice of 10 March 1976 issued by the Securities Bureau of the Ministry of Finance. This notice requested the securities companies to voluntarily follow uniform principles and practices, such as having both parties to a *gensaki* transaction exchange and retain written contracts. This action by the Ministry of Finance tended to legitimize *gensaki* transactions that had previously occurred in an ambiguous regulatory environment.

Government regulations specify that only juridical persons can conduct *gensaki* transactions. In Japan, this means that *gensaki* transactions are mainly carried out by entities with high economic and community reputations, such as businesses listed on the stock exchange or regular government bodies.

Many of the participants in the *gensaki* market are subject to restrictions on the extent of their activity in the market. The Ministry of Finance, for example, has placed restrictions on the outstanding balances of the *gensaki* transactions on the part of securities companies.[16] In determining the volume of *gensaki* transactions, a company's financial position and distribution of ownership are considered.[17]

In December 1977, the Ministry of Finance notified the securities companies that henceforth they would be subject to uniform quantitative restrictions on the amount of *gensaki* transactions done from their own inventories. The intent of this new regulation was to control the dealer position of the securities companies in the *gensaki* market and to keep it within safe limits. This was done by linking the dealer position for each of the securities companies to the company's turnover in other types of bond trading, or to the company's net assets. In order to verify that the securities companies are observing these regulations, monthly reports are required. These are submitted to the Securities Bureau of the Ministry of Finance within no more than nine days after the end of the month for which the report is being submitted.

The securities companies are also subject to limits on the amount of *gensaki* bonds that they can take on a consignment basis. These limits have been increased from time to time. Thus on 1 June 1980 the amount was raised from ¥4.3 to ¥5.8 trillion in recognition of the continued growth of the *gensaki* market.

In addition to the quantitative restrictions on securities companies, bank borrowing in the *gensaki* market has also been restricted by the authorities. Since 1968 the Bank of Japan has regulated bank borrowing in the market by imposing limits on the outstanding borrowings—these limits differing depending on the group to which a bank belongs. Thus, in 1977 the maximum amount of bonds that each of the five largest city banks could sell in the *gensaki* market was limited to ¥5 billion. For each of the remaining city banks it was ¥4 billion, and for both local banks and mutual-loan and savings banks, it was ¥2.5 billion. [18] These ceilings were adjusted upward from time to time. Thus in October 1978 the ceiling for the large city banks was reportedly increased from ¥5 billion to ¥20 billion. Then in 1980 the ceilings on the amount of bond sales (that is, borrowings) that each financial institution could transact in the market were abolished altogether. Lastly, in April 1981 the city banks were permitted to supply funds to the *gensaki* market. This action eliminated the last form of direct control over the city banks in the *gensaki* market.

As indicated earlier, the authorities also regulate the type of bonds that can be traded in the *gensaki* market. For example, convertible bonds are not eligible for *gensaki* trading. Those that are eligible were listed earlier in the section on the nature of the instruments and are designated in Paragraph 1, Article 2, of the Securities Exchange Law. Ministry of Finance guidelines also state that the term for the *gensaki* transaction should be less than one year—thus reducing the risk involved. In actual practice, few, if any, maturities exceed six months.

Negotiated bond prices are also subject to some regulation. While the actual price of a bond is arranged at the discretion of the parties involved, Ministry of Finance regulations specify that the agreed price should not be greater than 2 percent above or below the prevailing market value for individual transactions involving more than ¥10 million. The purpose of this regulation is to prevent price manipulation. The phrase *market value* implies the market price for listed bonds, as well as the over-the counter price for unlisted bonds.

In 1979 the authorities changed the regulations for participation by nonresidents in the *gensaki* market. Prior to 1979, nonresident foreign investors were prohibited from participating in the *gensaki* market, although they were allowed after 22 January 1979, to engage in an outright purchase of government securities so long as the maturity was at least thirteen months. (The previous minimum maturity had been five years and one month.) Effective 21 May 1979, however, nonresidents were allowed to engage in *gensaki* transactions. For example, they could sell bonds with a repurchase clause upon application and approval by the Ministry of Finance. This change in the regulation coincided with a package of actions by the Japanese government at the time to relax restraints on the inflow of capital. Since May 1979 there has been substantial participation by nonresidents in the *gensaki* market.

An additional action was taken on 1 December 1980. In connection with the liberalization of international capital flows at that time, securities companies were allowed to make *gensaki* transaction offers in terms of U.S. dollars—rather than solely in yen- -using their own swap facilities to support the transaction.

In March 1981 there was a further expansion in the number of participants in the *gensaki* market when eight government financial institutions began to invest their excess funds in the market. Previously these institutions had invested excess funds solely in lower-yielding short-term government bills. In response to a suggestion from the government's Board of Audit, the eight institutions switched to the *gensaki* market in order to obtain a better yield on their investments and to thereby reduce somewhat the amount borrowed from the government's Trust Fund Bureau.

An additional liberalization of the bond market occurred in April 1981 when the Ministry of Finance reduced the minimum bond-holding period. Earlier, in April 1980, the minimum period had been reduced from one year to seven and one-half months. But on 4 April 1981 the minimum holding period before resale by financial institutions was reduced again—this time to approximately 100 days.

A Brief Analysis of the Market

Of the main components of the money market, the *gensaki* market is probably one of the least controlled, along with the NCD market. There is normally no direct Bank of Japan intervention in the market, nonfinancial businesses are allowed to participate in the market, and since May 1979 nonresidents can also participate in the market.

However, the market is not completely free since it is confined to juridical persons and there are restrictions on the amount of outstanding balances that the securities companies can maintain, as well as on the volume of activity that can be transacted from the companies' own inventories. There are also limits on the amount of bonds that the companies can take on a consignment basis. Finally, not all bonds are eligible for trading in the market and the bond prices that are negotiated in the market are subject to some regulation.

Because of the aforementioned factors, it is unlikely that the interest rate prevailing in the *gensaki* market is a true market-clearing rate. If the market were completely free, one would expect the interest rate in the market to be somewhat higher than the call-loan rate or the bill-discount rate—particularly in view of Bank of Japan intervention to those two markets—but such has generally not been true.

There are also indications that the *gensaki* market is not as dynamic or buoyant as it was at one time. As indicated in table 6-1, the market grew rapidly in 1968-1973 and in 1976-1978 even outpaced the call-money and bill-discount markets. Since 1979, however, the rate of growth in the market has slowed considerably, with most of the growth in the three markets since 1979 occurring in the call-money market. After rising further in 1980, the outstanding balance in the *gensaki* market generally leveled off in 1981-1982. Opening the market to nonresidents in May 1979 does not appear to have accelerated the market's growth rate. But the introduction of three-year government coupon bonds in December 1978 has helped to broaden the market by increasing the variety of securities available.

As noted earlier, participation in the call-money and bill-discount markets is restricted to financial institutions, but the *gensaki* market is open to participation by nonfinancial businesses. The extent to which these businesses have been active in the market depends heavily on whether lending or borrowing is involved. On the borrowing side, *enterprises*[19] (that is, private nonfinancial businesses) have constituted only a relatively small proportion of all borrowers. But on the lending side, enterprises have consistently been the largest group. Thus the *gensaki* market has been an important outlet for private businesses having surplus short-term funds.

The *gensaki* market should not be viewed as merely a vehicle for the securities companies to finance their inventories. While the market does serve that function, there are other important functions that it also meets. In addition to serving as a useful outlet for excess corporate liquidity, it also provides added flexibility for trading and investing in the bond market.

On the whole, the *gensaki* market has been generally successful in bringing together borrowers and lenders in the market. In this regard, the market has operated fairly efficiently—although there is still room for improvement. The securities companies have probably reached the point where they now regard the market as an important and permanent source of funds, rather than a minor or temporary source of funds. This could lead to problems if private nonfinancial enterprises are forced by tight money policies to sharply reduce their lending in the market.

Notes

1. Mark Borsuk, "How the Gensaki Market Works," *Euromoney,* London, May 1978, p. 86.

2. Average end-of-month data.

3. Mark Borsuk, "How the Gensaki Market Works," p. 89.

4. Ibid., p. 89.

5. Mark Borsuk, "How the Gensaki Market Works," p. 94.

6. Securities Exchange Law (No. 25 of 1948), Article II, Paragraph 1, Items 1 through 4.

7. *Gensaki Manual,* Nomura Securities Co., Ltd., Tokyo, May 1977, p. 35.

8. Assuming an exchange rate of ¥250 to the U.S. dollar, this range would be from $120,000 to $200 million or more.

9. *Gensaki Manual,* p. 15.

10. See *Gensaki Manual,* pp. 28–31.

11. For detailed examples, see *Euromoney,* London, May 1978, p. 90.

12. When the transfer tax is levied on the seller and securities that are issued by the national government are involved, the tax is 0.01 percent for brokers and 0.03 percent for others. For nonnational security issues, such as municipal bonds, the tax is 0.015 percent for securities companies and 0.045 percent for others.

13. "The Japanese Gensaki Market," Nomura Securities Co., Ltd., Tokyo, 1981, p. 2.

14. *Gensaki Manual,* p. 5.

15. Law No. 25 of 1948.

16. "Japan's Short-Term Money Market," *Monthly Review,* Mitsui Bank, Tokyo, October 1977, p. 5.

17. *Gensaki Manual,* p. 34.

18. *Gensaki Manual,* p. 10.

19. This is the term used by the Bank of Japan to indicate borrowing and lending by private nonfinancial institutions in the *gensaki* market.

7 The Tokyo Dollar Call Market

In 1972 a new, but small, market was added to the Japanese financial system. Known generally as the Tokyo dollar call market, this new facility provided a market in Tokyo for the borrowing and lending between the banks of unsecured short-term foreign currency. The name *dollar call market* is a slight misnomer in that the market is not confined to dollar transactions but also includes transactions in other foreign currencies—although the share of these currencies is relatively small.

The main reason the market was established was because many of the small local banks did not have ready access to the Eurocurrency market on a day-to-day basis. This was necessary if they were to clear their short-term foreign-exchange position by the close of each business day, as required by government regulations. This problem did not really exist in 1972 for most of the large city banks since they had ready access to the Eurocurrency markets and could place even extremely short-term funds in the Eurocurrency market or in New York. Although it was not impossible for banks in Japan to lend each other short-term foreign-currency funds, such transactions had to be licensed by the Ministry of Finance. As a result of this limiting regulation, a gap existed in Japan's money market in that there was no domestic market for interbank loans in foreign currency.

To fill this gap, the Ministry of Finance on 6 April 1972 granted a blanket licence to 41 foreign-exchange and foreign-branch banks in Japan authorizing them to execute short-term-loan transactions in foreign currencies with maturities not exceeding six months. Since 17 April 1972—when the dollar call market actually began to operate—the number of banks has increased substantially, reaching a total of 213 banks at the end of November 1982.

The Tokyo dollar call market is, in essence, an extension of the Eurocurrency market to Japan/Tokyo, particularly with regard to the level of interest rates that prevail in the market. However, the Tokyo dollar call market is not a bona fide Eurocurrency market in that it is not open to nonresidents or to nonbank financial institutions. In addition, interest earnings from dollar call loan transactions are not exempt from Japanese withholding taxes, whereas they are in the Eurocurrency market.

The Nature of the Market

The Tokyo dollar call market is basically a telephone market where seven different brokerage firms are active in arranging for the interbank lending or borrowing of short-term foreign-currency deposits by six different types of banks. The establishment of this market in 1972 was not particularly difficult. This was because the framework for such a market already existed in that all seven brokerage firms had been serving for many years as foreign-exchange brokers and it was relatively easy to add the brokerage business for foreign-currency borrowing and lending as part of their activities.

Some of the seven brokerage firms have more extensive activities than the others. Thus four[1] of the seven firms that are active in the dollar call market and the foreign-exchange market are also very active in the domestic call-money market. The remaining three,[2] which account for a relatively small proportion of the brokerage activity in the dollar call market, are not active in the yen call-money market, doing only foreign-exchange and dollar-call broking.

The six types of banks that participate in the market are the: (1) city banks, (2) regional banks, (3) trust banks, (4) long-term-credit banks, (5) mutual-loan and savings banks, and (6) foreign-branch banks. All of these are authorized foreign-exchange banks[3] and hold a license from the Ministry of Finance to engage in the borrowing and lending of short-term foreign-currency funds in Japan.

The number of banks participating in the market has increased substantially since April 1972, as indicated in table 7–1. Despite this substantial increase, there is still room for further growth in the number of participating banks, since not all regional banks and mutual-loan and savings banks have elected to participate in the market. However, the conditions that they had to meet for participation in the market were greatly relaxed late in 1980. Since 1 December 1980, when a new law was enacted liberalizing foreign-exchange transactions, all foreign-exchange banks have been automatically authorized to participate in the Tokyo dollar call market.

Each transaction of funds in the market is essentially a short-term foreign-currency loan (or borrowing) without collateral. The bulk of the transactions (90 percent or more) involve the U.S. dollar, but other major currencies such as the West German deutsche mark, the Swiss franc, and the British pound sterling are also transacted. The minimum amount that can be transacted is one hundred thousand U.S. dollars and the maximum maturity used to be six months. The new Foreign Exchange Control Law of 1 December 1980—previously cited—abolished the six-month maximum maturity.

Within the various maturities, there are six common maturities. These are: (1) overnight, (2) next-day (or tomorrow), (3) two-days, (4) three-days,

Table 7-1
Number of Banks Participating in the Dollar Call Market

Date	Japanese Banks	Foreign Banks	Total
17 April 1972	18	23	41
31 March 1973	46	35	81
31 March 1974	47	43	90
31 March 1975	53	50	103
31 March 1976	67	50	117
31 March 1977	81	53	134
31 March 1978	94	59	153
31 March 1979	97	61	158
31 March 1980	97	64	161
31 March 1981	113	64	177
31 March 1982	133	71	204

Data supplied by Bank of Tokyo and Bank of Japan.

(5) seven-days fix, and (6) term—which ranges from one month to any number of months. The bulk of the transactions (about 90 percent) carry maturities of seven days or less. Although a large number of transactions carry the common maturities just listed, the borrower does have the option to select any maturity between overnight and six or more months.

Major Borrowers and Lenders

Since its establishment, the major lenders in the dollar call market have generally been the large city banks and the foreign banks, while the major borrowers have been the trust banks, the regional (or local) banks, and the mutual-loan and savings banks. However, there have been deviations in the past from this pattern. For example, the foreign banks have occasionally been net borrowers rather than lenders, depending in part on the level of Eurocurrency rates and whether the U.S. dollar is at a premium or a discount in the forward foreign-exchange market. Similarly, some of the large city banks have been net borrowers, especially when they have experienced an unexpected need for import settlement funds. On the other hand, the trust banks have, at times, been net lenders, rather than borrowers, in the market.[4]

Not all of the banks that are eligible to participate in the dollar call market do so. Thus, in late 1977, only thirty-eight of Japan's sixty-three regional banks were participating in the market. Similarly, only twenty-four of Japan's seventy-one mutual-loan and savings banks were also participating in the market. But of the four remaining categories of banks, all the banks in each category were active in the market. In late 1977 this included thirteen city banks, seven trust banks, fifty-seven foreign banks, and four special-category banks.[5]

All transactions in the market must be closed by brokers. These intermediaries, who also serve as brokers in the Tokyo foreign-exchange market, function only as brokers and not as dealers, unlike the yen call-money market where they operate as both brokers and dealers.

All brokers in the dollar call market charge a fixed commission of .02 percent from both the borrower and lender, or a total commission of .04 percent of the sum transacted. All commissions must be paid by the banks no later than the end of the month during which the transaction occurred.

The dollar-call-market brokers are members of a formal association known as the Foreign Exchange and Money Brokers Association (*Gaikoku-kawase Gaikashikin Nakadachinin Kyokai*). However, the activities of the association with respect to the dollar call market are relatively minor due to the much greater importance of the volume and level of activities of the foreign-exchange market.

As indicated earlier, the main reason that participants in the market borrow foreign-currency funds is to clear their short-term foreign-exchange position. Borrowing also occurs to meet the foreign-exchange needs of the borrowing institution's customers or because of anticipated profit opportunities. Whether the participants meet their borrowing needs in the dollar call market, the Eurocurrency market (assuming they have access to this market), or from other available sources, depends on the respective borrowing costs in the different markets, the exchange-rate situation, and, at times, on policy guidance from the Bank of Japan.

Market Interest Rates

Since the dollar call market is essentially an extension of the Eurocurrency market to Japan, it follows that the interest rates in the Japanese market tend to parallel those in the Eurocurrency market. Because of the time difference, the Tokyo rates reflect the previous day's Eurocurrency rates except in the case of overnight items.

In general, the interest-rate quotations in the Tokyo dollar call market are .0625 to .125 percentage points above the rates for comparable maturities in the London Eurocurrency market. The larger spread of .125 percentage point tends to prevail for maturities ranging from about one week to one month, while even larger spreads can occur for overnight

Table 7–2
Dollar Call Market: Schedule of Rates
(percent)

	Offer	Bid
Overnight	19	18 15/16
7 days fix	6 5/8	6 1/2
1 month	6 3/8	6 1/4
2 months	6 3/4	6 11/16
3 months	7 1/16	7
6 months	7 1/2	7 3/8

Rates obtained from the week-day quotation sheet of the Tokyo Tanshi Co., Ltd., 28 October 1977.
Note: Rates are as of the close of business 27 October 1977.

funds. The minimum unit of fluctuation of these interest rates is .0625 percent.

A sample of the actual bid and offer rates at closing in the Tokyo dollar call market are cited in table 7-2. The very high rate for overnight funds reflects the fact that the borrower would have the effective use of these funds over a weekend. For the next day after October 27, the rates were much lower—2 1/2 to 2 7/16 percent.

Some idea of the trend in the level of the rates since April 1972 can be obtained from table 7-3.

Table 7–3
Dollar Call Market: Three-Month Rates
(percent)

Period	Highest	Lowest
1972[a]	6 3/4	4 13/16
1973	12	6 1/2
1974	16	8 1/2
1975	10 15/16	5 5/16
1976	7 1/16	4 15/16
1977	7 5/8	4 15/16
1978	12 3/4	7 1/8
1979	16 3/8	10 1/8
1980	22 7/8	8 11/16
1981	20 3/16	12
1982	17	9 5/16

Data supplied by Tokyo Tanshi Co., Ltd. and the Bank of Japan.
[a] April-December.

As is generally the case with interest rates in the Eurodollar market, the trend in the rates cited in table 7-3 tends to reflect developments in short-term money rates in the United States. The effect of economic fluctuations in the United States is also evident in the rate trends cited in table 7-3.

The Mechanics of a Market Transaction

Market transactions are carried out by telephone between brokers and prospective borrowers and lenders, and there is no central floor, or exchange, for the dollar call market. The minimum unit of interest that is permissible for market transactions is .0625 percentage point, which is the same as in the other Eurocurrency markets. No collateral is involved in market transactions, but there is an exchange of written statements of the transaction. Thus the borrower and lender each exchange contract slips that spell out the details of the transaction. In addition, the broker sends a confirmation memo to each of the parties.

The minimum amount of funds that can be transacted is one hundred thousand dollars and, as mentioned earlier, all transactions must be closed through brokers. While the lender can ask the broker the name of the borrower before undertaking the transaction, the borrower is not allowed to ask the name of the lender until the transaction is closed. The closing of a transaction in the dollar call market is handled in the same way as in the Tokyo foreign-exchange market.

In handling transactions, a distinction is made between the delivery date and the maturity date. Basically, the delivery date for funds is determined according to the terms and conditions of each deal, with the delivery date for a regular—or standard—deal being the business day following the date of the contract.[6] The banks that are involved in the transaction are responsible for the delivery of the funds—not the brokers, who disclaim any responsibility. It is up to the lender to arrange for a credit to the account designated by the borrower, often the account of a major U.S. bank in Tokyo.

The maturity date is also fixed according to the terms and conditions of each deal. This involves both the value date[7] and the due date. The value date for regular, or standard, transactions is the business day next to the day of dealings. The due date for one-month, or multiple-month, items is set on the corresponding date of each given month counting from the delivery date.[8]

For very short-term transactions, there in an inflexibility once the terms are set. Thus, in the case of so-called two-days-notice borrowings, neither the borrower nor the lender can change the terms and conditions or give notice of cancellation for at least two business days from the delivery date of funds.

The interest rate for call-loan transactions is calculated on the basis of a 360-day year. In calculating the number of days that the funds are borrowed, the maturity date (*kataochi*) is excluded. The interest and principle are to be paid to the lender on maturity.

The dollar call market is open weekdays from 9:00 A.M. to noon and from 1:30 to 3:30 P.M. It is closed all day Saturday and also on Sundays and national holidays.

Trends in the Size and Rate of Turnover of the Market

During the first four years of operation of the market (roughly through 1975), the amount of borrowing in the market, as measured by the balance outstanding, generally increased. From a level of $210 million at the end of 1972 (after approximately nine months of operation), the balance of funds outstanding rose to $1.08 billion at the end of 1975—as indicated by the data in table 7–4—and then declined slightly in 1976.

Since 1976, however, the amount of borrowing in the market—as reflected in the balance outstanding at the end of the year—has increased steadily. From slightly over $1 billion at the end of 1976 the amount outstanding rose to almost $5 billion by the end of 1979, then increased very rapidly to approximately $12 billion at the end of 1980 and to $24 billion

Table 7–4
Dollar-Call-Market Volume
(millions of U.S. dollars)

Period	Balance Outstanding (End of Period)	Average Monthly Turnover
1972	210	700 [a]
1973	560	1,750
1974	930	2,730
1975	1,080	3,480
1976	1,020	3,750
1977	1,350	4,473
1978	2,700	5,770
1979	4,490	10,490
1980	11,660	15,830
1981	23,830	23,010
1982 (September)	34,600	(not available)

Data supplied by the Bank of Japan and the Ministry of Finance.
[a] April-December.

at the end of 1981. By September 1982 the amount had increased further to $35 billion, surpassing in size the bill-discount and call-money markets combined.

There are several factors that contributed to this sharp increase and they all occurred as a result of liberalizing changes made in the new Foreign Exchange and Foreign Trade Law that became effective on 1 December 1980. One thing the new law did was to abolish the previous ceiling on the amount of holdings of foreign currency by Japanese citizens. Prior to 1 December 1980, both firms and individuals were subject to a ceiling of ¥3 million (approximately $12,000 at an exchange rate of 250 yen per U.S. dollar) on their holdings of foreign-currency deposits. Since December 1980, Japanese citizens have been free, in principle, to exchange yen for foreign currencies and to place the proceeds in foreign-exchange banks in Japan, or to invest in foreign assets such as land and securities. Secondly, the new law specified that any foreign-exchange bank in Japan could participate freely in the Tokyo dollar call market. Under the old law, permission had been granted only to the foreign-exchange banks that had received exclusive permission to carry out transactions in foreign currencies. Lastly, the period of lending in the Tokyo dollar call market was no longer limited to a maximum of six months, but was changed to an unlimited period. All of these have been important factors in the very sharp rise since 1980 in the size of the Tokyo dollar call market.

Average monthly turnover in the market has increased steadily since 1972, as indicated in table 7-4. From a level of $1.6 billion in 1973, it increased to $23.0 billion in 1981. A high proportion of the turnover represents very short-term maturities, ranging from overnight money to seven-day money.

There are few sources of data in Japan on developments in the dollar call market such as the rate of turnover, the amount of funds outstanding, and interest rates. The brokers, such as Tokyo Tanshi Co., Ltd., do issue one-page market reports giving closing interst-rate quotations for the latest two days of market activity. In addition, the interest rates are quoted in daily newspapers, such as the *Nihon Keizei.* But basic publications, such as the Bank of Japan's *Economic Statistics Monthly,* have not included data on the market—at least as of January 1983. One of the better descriptions in English of the dollar call market is contained in a booklet published in March 1980 by the Yamane Tanshi Co., Ltd.[9]

Official Regulation of the Market

The operations of the participants in the dollar call market are subject to regulation by the Ministry of Finance. As mentioned earlier, it was the Ministry of Finance that authorized the banks in April 1972 to engage in the borrowing and lending of short-term foreign-currency funds under Paragraph 2, Article 13 of the Foreign Exchange Control Law. In addition, the participants in the market are subject to the provisions of the 1949 Temporary Interest Rates Adjustment Law, which is also administered by the Ministry of Finance.

Unlike the yen call-money and the bill-discount markets, the Bank of Japan does not intervene in the dollar call market to influence the level of the rates. However, some control is exercised over the market by means of the regulations on banks' overall foreign-exchange positions and the imposition of dollar-to-yen swap quotas. In the case of the former, the foreign-exchange banks are required to balance their overall foreign-exchange assets and liabilities—both spot and forward—so as not to be exposed to possible losses on their holdings of foreign exchange due to unanticipated changes in exchange rates.

In the case of the swap quotas, foreign-branch banks in Japan have been subject since 1970 to ceilings on the amount of foreign exchange that they can swap (that is, convert) into yen. In June 1982 the overall limit for all foreign-branch banks was increased from $5.5 billion to $6.75 billion, with each bank being assigned its own individual limit by the authorities. The Japanese authorities have also allowed Japanese domestic banks similar conversion privileges, but only for relatively small amounts.

The brokers in the Tokyo dollar call market are not subject to examination by the authorities. Furthermore, they do not have to submit periodic reports to either the Ministry of Finance or the Bank of Japan.

A Brief Analysis of the Market

Japan's dollar call market is, in essence, a closely restricted extension of the Eurocurrency market. By limiting the market to banks in Japan and by excluding all nonresident transactions, the authorities have assured themselves a firm control over the market. There is, however, no doubt that the establishment of the market did meet a real need that the smaller banks had, namely, a facility to balance their foreign-exchange positions more easily.

The market has few interrelationships with other components of Japan's money market. This is partly because the transactions in other short-term markets are in yen—with only foreign currencies being transacted in the dollar call market—and because of the dollar call market's dependence on aggregate Eurocurrency-market developments. As mentioned earlier, the interest rates in the dollar call market are really a function of developments in the Eurocurrency market in Europe, which in turn is strongly influenced by developments in the U.S. money market.

It would not be too difficult, however, to convert Japan's dollar call market into a fully integrated component of the Eurocurrency market. This could be done: (1) by opening the market to nonresidents; (2) by allowing nonbanks, including individuals and business firms, to participate in the market; (3) by eliminating the 5 to 20 percent withholding taxes (which vary depending on the nationality of the lender) applied to the earnings on foreign-currency deposits; and (4) by removing the relatively low reserve requirement that the Bank of Japan applies against deposits held by nonresidents. In view of Japan's recent trend toward liberalizing international financial transactions, there is a definite possibility that some, or perhaps all, of the above steps might be taken in the future, if the authorities can agree among themselves.

During 1982, the growing interest in possibly establishing an international banking facility (IBF) in Japan—similar to the IBF in the United States—resulted in several specific actions. In April and May an Offshore Banking Survey Mission consisting of thirty-three officials from the government, banks, and securities companies visited New York, London, and other offshore banking centers to see what further steps Japan should take in order to establish an IBF. In its final report, the group was not able to reach a unanimous agreement on its specific recommendations, though it did provide information on what kind of IBF might be appropriate for Japan.

By August 1982 a conflict had surfaced between the Ministry of Finance and the Bank of Japan about the proposed IBF. The ministry indicated that it favored the establishment of an IBF in Japan—possibly as early as 1983—in view of the size of the Japanese economy and its volume of international capital transactions. In addition, the ministry believed that the operation of such a market in Japan would improve its surveillance of the Euro-yen market. However, the Bank of Japan stated that conditions were not yet ripe for the establishment of an IBF, its main concern being the possible adverse impact on the domestic financial market from the introduction of such a market. An additional point of controversy has been whether a Japanese IBF should incorporate yen transactions in addition to the usual transactions denominated in U.S. dollars and other major currencies.

Also in August 1982, the Ministry of Finance announced that it would undertake an official full-scale study of the proposal to establish an IBF in Japan. This decision was taken after the Foreign Exchange Council—an advisory body to the Ministry of Finance—recommended that a full study of the proposal be undertaken. It is therefore possible that an IBF will actually be established sometime during the 1980s.

Notes

1. These are the Tokyo Tanshi Company, Ueda Tanshi Company, Yamane Tanshi Company, and Nippon Discount and Call Money Company.

2. These are Hattori and Company, Minami and Company, and Kobayashi and Company. In recent years, two British firms (Astley & Pearce and M.W. Marshall) have also begun to serve as brokers in the foreign-exchange market.

3. Authorized foreign-exchange banks, other than the city banks and foreign banks, are also divided into two types of banks: Class A banks, which are permitted to conclude correspondent arrangements with banks abroad; and Class B banks, which are not permitted to do so.

4. *Money Market in Japan and Tanshi Companies,* Yamane Tanshi Company, Ltd., Tokyo, April 1977, p. 26.

5. These included two long-term-credit banks (Nippon Credit Bank and the Long-Term Credit Bank), a special bank for commerce and industrial cooperatives (Shoko Chukin Bank) and a central cooperative bank for agriculture and forestry (Norinchukin Bank).

6. If the following business day should fall on the day of a bank holiday in New York, the first business day after that in New York is regarded as the delivery date.

7. In banking, since the time needed for the collection of checks can vary, the value date is the date on which a deposit is recognized as being effective.

8. If the corresponding day should fall on a holiday either in Japan or in New York, the next business day in New York is treated as the maturity date.

9. See *Money Market in Japan and Tanshi Companies,* pp. 28–31.

8 Other Components of the Money Market

In addition to the more important components of the money market discussed in chapters 4 through 7, some authorities also include four other components in the Japanese money market. These are the markets for: (1) negotiable certificates of deposit (NCDs), (2) short-term government securities, (3) interbank deposits, and (4) bank-guaranteed export and import bills. Because the NCD market is still relatively new and information on the market rather limited, a separate chapter has not been devoted to that market.

While the relatively new NCD market can be considered as one of the recognized components of Japan's money market, the other three markets cited above are not really bona fide open markets. In the case of the short-term-government-securities market, the yields are fixed by the government at such artificially low levels that the bulk of the issues end up being purchased by the Bank of Japan and the various government trust funds. The interbank deposit system lacks most of the key features of an open money market; instead, it operates in a manner similar to the traditional bank-customer relationship. The on-again-off-again market in bank-guaranteed export and import bills remains extremely small and insignificant, hampered by the lack of well-defined trading arrangements and abnormally high interest rates in the market.

Of the last three markets just cited (short-term government securities, interbank deposits, and export-import bills), the short-term-government-securities market probably has the best prospect of eventually becoming a bona fide component of the money market. A major change in interest-rate policy could make the market attractive to nongovernment investors. While at least three of the markets discussed in this chapter fall far short of being bona fide money markets, it should be recognized that several of them are, at times, important outlets for the investment of short-term funds.

Negotiable Certificates of Deposit

The Japanese market for yen-denominated NCDs is comparatively new, having been established 16 May 1979. Although subject to official restraints on its maximum size, the market grew rapidly during its first half-month of operation, with total issues reaching ¥509 billion (about $2.3 billion) by 31 May 1979. Foreign banks accounted for approximately 6 percent of the total amount of NCDs issued.

Although Japanese banks had been allowed prior to May 1979 to issue NCDs overseas in such major money centers as London and New York, this was not the case in Japan. NCDs were a money-market instrument with which the Japanese authorities had not had much experience, and the Japanese banks apparently were able to mobilize sufficient funds without needing the assistance of this relatively new type of instrument.

However, during the 1960s and 1970s NCDs grew to be a very important component of the money market in New York and London, and it was only logical that a market for NCDs should be introduced in Japan to add breadth and flexibility to the existing money market. In addition, since the slower rate of economic growth in the mid-1970s had reduced the deposit growth of the large city banks, and the rapidly growing *gensaki* market had attracted funds to the security houses at the expense of the city banks, the latter lobbied aggressively for the right to issue NCDs.[1] Also, the foreign banks in Japan were anxious to obtain a new source of yen funds.

The subject was investigated carefully by the Financial System Research Committee, an advisory body to the Ministry of Finance, and late in 1978 it outlined its proposals for the establishment of such a market. These proposals became the basis for the Ministry of Finance's regulations (Kuragin, No. 653) that were issued 30 March 1979, to regulate issuance of NCDs by financial institutions. The key features of the regulations, as stated at the time, are summarized below:

1. Authority is granted to certain financial institutions to issue certificates of deposit that are negotiable. The authorized financial institutions include city banks, regional banks, trust banks, long-term-credit banks, foreign banks, mutual-loan and savings banks, and credit associations.

2. The total amount of NCD issues for an individual Japanese bank or financial institution is not to exceed 25 percent of its net worth.

3. The initial issue is not to exceed 10 percent of a Japanese institution's net worth, with the ceiling being raised each subsequent quarter to 15, 20, and 25 percent, respectively. This 10 percent ceiling (eventually 25 percent) applies to both the outstanding monthly average and the outstanding amount at the end of the business year.

4. For foreign-branch banks, the limit is 10 percent of a branch's loans and securities denominated in yen including yen credits to both residents and nonresidents.[2] So that the newer and/or smaller foreign branch banks are not put in a disadvantageous position, each foreign bank is allowed to issue at least ¥3 billion in NCDs. In May 1979 there were 60 foreign banks operating in Japan.

5. The maturities on the NCDs must be within the range of three to six months.[3]

6. The minimum amount for any one issue is ¥500 million. This high minimum was aimed at minimizing a shift of other deposits to the new NCDs, as well as avoiding competition with the *gensaki* market.

7. The amount of interest paid on the NCDs is free of government regulation.

8. All financial institutions are required to report before and after issuing NCDs to the Ministry of Finance.

For most of the small foreign-branch banks, the above restrictions have been rather confining. For example, with a minimum denomination of ¥500 million and a ceiling on issues of possibly ¥3 billion, a small foreign-branch bank could issue only six NCDs. In addition, the ¥500 million minimum is a hardship for those foreign banks that do not have large customers.

Some foreign banks have complained that the six-month maximum maturity is not sufficiently long to be attractive to the issuing banks.[4] However, the December 1978 report of the Foreign System Research Committee did suggest that at a later time the maximum maturity for NCDs might be extended to twelve months. Banks have also complained that the minimum maturity period of three months is too long. They would like to see it shortened considerably.

Data for approximately the first six and a half weeks indicated that the large city banks issued virtually their full authorization of NCDs, while other financial institutions were well below their ceilings. Thus in the period from May 16 to June 30, 1979, the thirteen city banks issued ¥433 billion in NCDs, which was 98 percent of their authorized second-quarter limit; the trust banks issued ¥73.2 billion (76 percent of their limit); and the long-term-credit banks ¥43.5 billion (43.5 percent of their limit). For these three institutions, the total amount issued was ¥550 billion. This compares with an eventual total limit (at the end of the first year of issuance) of ¥2 trillion.[5]

In general, the interest rates for the NCDs were slightly to moderately higher than the unconditional-call-money rate in 1979–1980. Thus the average monthly call-loan rate in June 1979 was 5.3 percent, while the rate on NCDs late in June ranged between 5.5 and 6.5 percent. NCD rates have also been higher than deposit rates of comparable maturity. In the first half of 1982, call rates tended to exceed average NCD rates.

The main investors in the market during its early months of operation were trading companies, motor-vehicle manufacturers, and manufacturers of machinery and electrical appliances. The oil-producing countries in the Middle East have also been substantial purchasers in the market and have been attracted to the market, in part, because the Japanese authorities have not imposed income taxes on the earnings by foreign central banks from their holdings of NCDs. Purchasers of CDs who resell before maturity are also not subject to withholding taxes—only the final holders at maturity of the yen CDs. Unlike the *gensaki* market, the secondary market in yen CDs is not subject to transaction taxes.

From May 1979 through late March 1980, most of the NCDs tended to be transacted between enterprises having the same principal—or main—bank. Late in March 1980, however, the brokers that normally operate in the call-money and bill-discount markets began to also act as intermediaries in the NCD market, thus helping to facilitate the development of a secondary market in CDs. This generally occurred where the parties involved had different main banks. This helped to make the market available to a wider group of investors. Securities dealers are prohibited from dealing in yen CDs.

In January 1981 the trading of CDs for short periods under repurchase agreements had begun on a modest scale. Active purchasers of the CDs in the secondary market have included automobile and electric-home-appliance enterprises. Since the summer of 1981, the secondary market for NCDs has expanded rapidly, with some of the expansion reflecting a shift of funds from the *gensaki* market. Trading volume on the secondary market rose from ¥0.2 trillion in December 1980, to ¥0.7 trillion in June 1981, and then to ¥2.5 trillion in December 1981. Most of this rise in volume represented *gensaki* trading of NCDs for short periods. A key factor stimulating the expansion was the fact that such trading was free from taxation, whereas each *gensaki* transaction is subject to a transaction tax based on the principal amount of the bond.

Also helping the growth of the market was an action taken by the government in the spring of 1980. On 1 April 1980, the Ministry of Finance authorized a doubling of the previous limit on the amount of NCDs that could be issued, by raising the limit from 25 percent of a bank's net worth to 50 percent. Foreign banks also had their ceilings increased from an amount equivalent to 10 percent of their loans and securities denominated in yen to 20 percent, with the increase being spread over a one-year period. This action had the effect of eventually raising the total overall ceiling from about ¥2.5 trillion to ¥5 trillion. By the end of December 1982, the balance outstanding of NCDs had reached ¥4.3 trillion.

In January 1983 the Ministry of Finance acted again to expand the size of the NCD market. Beginning with the first quarter of 1983, banks were authorized to increase their issue of NCDs by an amount equivalent to 5 percent of their net worth each quarter up through the first quarter of 1984, thus bringing the ceiling up to 75 percent of net worth. Foreign banks were also allowed, beginning in February 1983, to increase the amount of their NCD issues from a maximum of 20 percent of their total loans and securities, to 30 percent. In addition, each foreign bank was authorized on 1

February 1983 to issue at least ¥5 billion in NCDs; the previous minimum for the newer and/or smaller foreign banks was ¥3 billion.

Despite these actions, many banks still feel that the minimum size of ¥500 million per NCD issue is too high. They would like to see the minimum level lowered.

Table 8-1 below indicates the general growth pattern in the NCD market since May 1979. Since the establishment of the market, the amount of NCDs outstanding has generally increased. As indicated by the quarterly data in table 8-1, the total amount outstanding increased from ¥1.9 billion at the end of 1979 to ¥4.3 billion at the end of 1982. It is interesting to note, however, that every March there has been a dip in the amount outstanding—probably for seasonal reasons.

Foreign holdings of Japanese NCDs have been volatile recently. By April 1982, foreign holdings of CDs had reached ¥100 billion (about $400 million), but then declined by mid-year to about ¥57 billion ($230 million).

In August 1982 the CD market began to play an even more important financial role when a syndicated bank loan in yen to the French public housing authority (Credit Foncier de France) was approved by the Japanese authorities, with the floating rate on the ten-year loan tied to either the Japanese long-term prime-lending rate or the three-month-CD rate. Since then the rate on the ¥15 billion ($60 million equivalent) loan has been re-

Table 8-1
Negotiable Certificates of Deposit
(billions of yen)

Date		City Banks	Foreign Banks	Other	Total
1979	June	433	84	328	845
	September	662	200	594	1,456
	December	925	255	673	1,853
1980	March	883	216	454	1,553
	June	1,394	506	1,100	3,000
	September	1,041	227	859	2,127
	December	1,061	257	1,039	2,357
1981	March	775	175	721	1,671
	June	1,237	500	966	2,703
	September	1,666	454	921	3,041
	December	1,856	414	1,021	3,291
1982	March	1,565	307	791	2,663
	June	1,982	499	1,508	3,989
	September	2,289	363	1,452	4,104
	December	2,805	363	1,894	4,342

Adapted from *Economic Statistics Monthly,* Bank of Japan.

Note: Figures indicate the outstanding balance at the end of the period.

viewed every three months and has carried an interest rate equal to either the CD rate plus one percentage point, or the long-term prime-lending rate, whichever is higher.

The establishment of the NCD market reportedly marked a new epoch in the development of Japan's money market.[6] Although the market was established in May 1979—or approximately one year after the first steps toward freeing interest rates in the market—the planning for its establishment did help to encourage the official liberalization of the money market that occurred between June 1978 and October 1979. A brief assessment of the market is contained in chapter 11.

Short-Term-Government-Securities Market

Three types of bills are offered by the national government in the short-term-government-securities market in Japan. These are: (1) treasury bills, (2) food bills, and (3) foreign-exchange fund bills. The market does not normally include other government securities that have a remaining maturity of one year or less.

The treasury bills are issued by the government whenever the need arises to cover a temporary shortage of cash funds. Unlike the United States, where a relatively large amount of treasury bills always remains outstanding, the amount of treasury bills outstanding in Japan fluctuates sharply from month to month and, at times, all of the bills are redeemed, leaving none outstanding.

The other two types of bills relate to the Foodstuff Control Special Account, which is an account that the government uses in its agricultural-price-support program, and the Foreign Exchange Fund, which is an account that the government maintains for receiving and supplying foreign exchange to those authorized to conduct foreign-exchange operations. Both the food and the foreign-exchange-fund bills are issued by the government—or more specifically, the Ministry of Finance—to finance temporary fund shortages in the Foodstuff Account and the Foreign Exchange Fund. Large issues of the food bills occur in the autumn when the government is buying rice.

The usual maturity for all three types of bills is relatively short—sixty days. The minimum denomination is ¥1 million (about $4,000) and the largest ¥500 million ($2.0 million). The yield on the bills is rigidly controlled by the Ministry of Finance and is generally set at a level below other money-market rates, such as the rate on *gensaki* transactions. All three types of bills are offered on a discount basis. Usually the rate set for these bills is strongly influenced by the level of the Bank of Japan's basic discount rate.[7]

Japan's short-term government securities are placed three times a week through a tender system, with most of the bills acquired by the Bank of

Japan and various government trust funds—particularly the Ministry of Finance's Trust Fund Bureau. Although the bills are nominally offered to the general public, only a small portion of the total are purchased by private investors because of the relatively low yield on the bills. On 31 March 1981, for example, 44 percent of the short-term government securities were held by the government,[8] 44 percent by the Bank of Japan, 7 percent by government-related organizations, and 5 percent by others—primarily industrial corporations, smaller financial institutions, individuals, and foreigners. The purchases made by nonresidents are often undertaken when the yen is appreciating in the foreign-exchange markets, but the aggregate amount of such purchases has been relatively small.

Japan's securities companies, such as Nikko, Nomura, Yamaichi, and Daiwa, play a role in the sale of short-term government securities. The 1948 Securities Transactions Law (Number 65) stipulates that Japanese banks and foreign-branch banks, among others, should subscribe to short-term government securities through the securities companies and not directly from the government. The result is that the securities companies are involved in almost all of the sales of short-term government securities to the private sector. They serve mainly as brokers and charge a commission of 0.25 to 1 percent, but also serve as agents for foreign and other buyers.

As indicated earlier, the amount outstanding of any of the three kinds of bills can fluctuate sharply from month to month. For example, at the end of May 1978 there were no treasury bills outstanding, but at the end of the next month the amount outstanding was ¥2,012 billion ($9.8 billion).

Short-term government securities do not comprise a very large proportion of total national-government debt. On 31 March 1981, for example, the proportion was about 14 percent. Because of the large increase in the issue of medium- and long-term government debt in recent years, the ratio of short-term government securities to total national-government debt has actually declined from the 18 percent level in 1977 and 1978.

Since most of the purchasers of short-term government securities hold them to maturity, there is virtually no secondary market in these securities. Until the government permits the yields on these securities to rise to realistic (that is, free-market) levels, it is unlikely that much of a secondary market will develop in these securities.

The Interbank-Deposit System

Some observers of the Japanese money market have included as one component of that market the system of interbank deposits that became briefly prominent in 1972.[9] Most Japanese do not consider this system to be a bona fide component of the money market, and it is treated here only for the sake of completeness. The interbank-deposit system lacks most of the key features of an open market, such as the impersonal nature of market transactions, the presence of intermediaries such as brokers and dealers, and conditions close to perfect competition. Instead, it functions on a direct personal basis, without brokers or dealers, in a manner similar to the traditional bank-customer relationship.

The funds involved in the interbank-deposit system are the *term deposits* that banks deposit with each other, the bulk of which are usually for a fixed period of six months. The customary direction of flow of these funds is from the small- and medium-sized financial institutions that have excess funds to the large city banks. Unlike the United States, where interbank deposits frequently serve to compensate the city correspondent banks for services provided to the smaller banks, the interbank deposits in Japan appear to be motivated by profit considerations, in that the yield on fixed-term deposits during certain periods in the past has exceeded the yield on regular money-market instruments.

The system of interbank deposits first became quantitatively important in the first half of 1972 when certain financial institutions experienced substantial increases in their liquidity. This also occurred at a time when the yields in the call-money and bill-discount markets were at low to moderate levels due to the neutral monetary policy being pursued by the Bank of Japan. This combination of developments tended to greatly stimulate an increase in the level of interbank deposits. After remaining at a level of about ¥250 billion for some time, the amount of interbank deposits rose rapidly in the first seven months of 1972, reaching ¥1,570 billion by the end of July. This was more than the amount of credit outstanding in either the yen call-money market or the bill-discount market.

During the period from 1974 to early 1980, the amount of interbank deposits leveled off, fluctuating around roughly the ¥3,000 billion level. Beginning in the spring of 1980, however, the amount outstanding began to increase and even reached ¥6,025 billion by September 1982. At the end of 1982, however, the amount outstanding had dropped back to approximately ¥4,200 billion.

Under certain circumstances the interbank-deposit system can serve as a conduit of funds to the city banks that is outside the direct control of the Bank of Japan. Thus, if the smaller financial institutions have the liquidity, the interbank deposit system is a means whereby the city banks can circumvent the Bank of Japan's controls. This is essentially what happened in 1972 when the rapid expansion of interbank deposits helped to finance an increase in city-bank loans to customers, thus contributing to further increases in the prices of stocks and real estate. According to Monroe, the Bank of Japan partly offset this "conduit of liquidity" by maintaining relatively high rates of interest on bills eligible for the discount market.[10]

In recent years, the interbank-deposit system has not been of much consequence in Japan's financial system and therefore it is treated only briefly here. It bears very little similarity to the U.S.-federal-funds market, which is of major importance in the United States.

Bank-Guaranteed Export and Import Bills

Japan does not have, in a strict sense, a bankers' acceptance market similar to the one in the United States. Since 1973, however, the Bank of Japan has made some mild attempts to develop a market in yen-denominated export and import bills guaranteed by the foreign-exchange banks. The authority for the banks to guarantee such bills and to carry out direct bank-to-bank transactions in these bills was first granted by the government in late 1973. At roughly the same time, the Bank of Japan was authorized to carry out open-market operations in such bills. However, through May 1975, there was no trading in yen-denominated export and import bills in the bill-discount market.

In mid-June 1975, the Bank of Japan informed the foreign-exchange banks and the brokers in the bill-discount market that it would seek actively to develop a market in yen-denominated export and import bills. This would be an open market where the participating banks could discount such bills.

There were apparently several reasons why the Bank of Japan took this action in mid-June 1975. One was to encourage a wider use of the yen in financing international trade, thereby contributing to the so-called internationalization of the yen. Also, it was expected that greater reliance on yen-financed trade would help in reducing foreign-exchange risks. In addition, it was anticipated that the action would increase the amount of funds available for financing trade.

To further promote the development of the market, the Bank of Japan encouraged the foreign-exchange banks and the bill brokers to agree on simple, uniform standards for transactions in such bills. The Bank of Japan hoped that transactions in the bills could be limited to yen-denominated bills, with a fixed maturity, and with a Japanese foreign-exchange bank's guarantee.

Despite the June 1975 action by the Bank of Japan, market activity remained small, with relatively few transactions taking place. In December 1975, the Bank of Tokyo sold yen-denominated export bills for the first time. The total amount was ¥336 million at an interest rate of 9.125 percent and with maturities ranging from two to four months.[11] Despite these efforts, the amount of yen-denominated export bills outstanding by May

1976 was reported to be ¥1.6 billion, or only one-half of one percent of the ¥3,200 billion in domestic bills outstanding at that time.

The next action taken by the Bank of Japan occurred in the spring of 1976 when the bank approved the system of *hyoshi tegata,* or cover bills, for the market. The bank informed both the foreign-exchange banks and the bill brokers that, beginning 20 May 1976, they could group together many small yen-denominated export bills[12] into a single package to serve as collateral for one large, yen-denominated export parent bill. This device of a so-called cover bill has been used widely and for some time in Japan for domestic bills. The Bank of Japan indicated that if all of the collateral consisted of export bills, the maturity for the cover bill could be as long as five months. But if the collateral consisted of a combination of domestic bills and export bills, then the maturity had to be less than three months. The bank hoped that the availability of a longer maturity would prove sufficiently attractive to cause more yen-denominated export bills to be issued.

Despite the various actions taken by the Bank of Japan since 1973, the market for bank-guaranteed export bills has remained extremely small. There appear to be several reasons for this. One is the limited negotiability of the bills due to the lack of well-defined trading arrangements, which in turn has inhibited the banks and brokers from participating in the market. Another, and probably the most important, reason is that potential borrowers have not utilized the market because the interest rate has been too high. In late 1977, for example, the rate was roughly 5.875 percent, while the prime rate at the time was 4.5 percent. In addition, through 1982 the Bank of Japan had not taken any actions to provide interest-rate incentives to encourage greater use of the market.

In August 1979 it was reported that the Bank of Japan would terminate in December its import-bill-settlement system that had been established in May 1978. Outstanding credits extended under this program only totaled ¥150 billion ($700 million) at the end of June 1979, indicating that the facility had not been used as much as had been expected.

The prospects for the development of this market do not appear to be very good. In addition to the problems already cited, that is, the limited negotiability of the bills and their high cost to potential borrowers, the Bank of Japan appears to believe that there is actually little need—at least from a domestic viewpoint—to vigorously pursue the development of such a market. It has also been suggested that such a market would complicate the Bank of Japan's ability to control monetary conditions. For all of these reasons, plus the reluctance of some importers to reduce or cancel their dollar credit lines—which would be necessary if they were to switch to yen-denominated import bills—it seems unlikely that a market in bank-guaranteed export and import bills will flourish in the near future.

Notes

1. *New York Times,* New York, 5 January 1979, p. D 4.

2. Since the ratio of net worth to loans and securities is about 8 percent for Japanese banks, the 25 percent ceiling would limit the Japanese banks' issues of NCDs to about 2 percent of their portfolios. By comparison, the 10 percent ceiling for foreign branches would appear to be relatively generous.

3. Although NCDs cannot be cashed before maturity, they can be used as collateral for loans. *Asian Finance,* Hong Kong, 15 July 1979, p. 60.

4. See "Japan Plans Certificates of Deposit," *New York Times,* New York, 5 January 1979, p. D 4.

5. See the *Far Eastern Economic Review,* Hong Kong, 6 April 1979, p. 78.

6. See *Money Market in Japan and Tanshi Companies,* Yamane Tanshi Company, Ltd., Tokyo, March 1980, p. 32.

7. *Banking System in Japan,* Federation of Bankers' Associations of Japan, Tokyo, Japan, 1976, p. 68.

8. Primarily the Trust Fund Bureau, the Industrial Investment Special Account and the Postal Life Insurance and Postal Annuity funds.

9. See Wilbur F. Monroe, *Japan: Financial Markets and the World Economy,* Praeger, New York, 1973, pp. 106–107; and Henry C. Wallich and Mable I. Wallich, *Asia's New Giant,* The Brookings Institution, Washington, D.C., 1976, p. 314.

10. Monroe, *Japan: Financial Markets and the World Economy,* p. 107.

11. *Japan Economic Journal,* Tokyo, 25 May 1976.

12. Import bills were deliberately left out of the new parent-bill system.

9

Official Controls and the Money Market

Introduction

The two main official authorities that control Japan's money market are the Ministry of Finance and the Bank of Japan. The Finance Ministry is mainly responsible for drafting financial laws and issuing regulations, while the Bank of Japan both oversees the observance of these laws and intervenes actively in certain parts of the money market. Many of the interest rates in Japan's financial markets are fixed by these two official bodies on the basis of the authority extended to them under the 1947 Temporary Money Rates Adjustment Law. Despite its name, the law has not really been temporary, and was still in force in 1983.

As indicated earlier, Japan's domestic money market consists primarily of the following four markets: (1) yen call money, (2) bill discount, (3) *gensaki,* and (4) negotiable certificates of deposit. Of these four, the last two are relatively free, or open, markets. The first two, however, have not been truly free markets for much of their existence. Interest rates in the bill-discount market have been heavily influenced by Bank of Japan purchases (and sales) of bills in the market, while call-money rates have been set only after frequent and close consultation with the Bank of Japan throughout the business day.[1]

Both deposit and loan rates in Japan are controlled to a greater or lesser extent by the authorities, but there are exceptions. The maximum interest rates paid on deposits, for example, are subject to official control in most cases—one important exception being the interest rates on NCDs. For bank loans, the interest-rate controls depend on maturity and amount. Interest rates on bank loans with a maturity of more than one year are free from control, and this is also the case for short-term loans amounting to less than ¥1 million. Thus, interest rates on large (roughly, over $4,000), short-term loans are controlled. With many deposit and loan rates being set by administrative fiat, the bulk of the interest rates are not really determined freely by demand and supply forces in the market.[2] As noted above, however, the interest rates in the *gensaki* and NCD markets are relatively free.

During the last half of the 1970s, two important developments occurred. One involved a change in Japan's financial structure and the other a liberalization of the money market.

Starting roughly in the mid-1970s, the corporate sector began to experience a narrowing of its persistent financial deficit. For most of the postwar period up to the early 1970s, Japanese businesses seldom had excess liquidity for any extended period, and tended to depend heavily on the banking system for funds. This caused the city banks to constantly be in a so-called overloaned position, with their loans equivalent to a high proportion of their deposit liabilities. At the same time, the government sector began to experience persistent and substantial deficits. With more funds available, businesses began to diversify their financial assets—for example, by investing in the *gensaki* market—while the government continued to issue large amounts of bonds, a high proportion of which were purchased by financial institutions (including the Bank of Japan). With less demand for funds by businesses, the overloaned position of the city banks eased substantially.

The second important development consisted of official actions to liberalize segments of the money and bond markets, as well as the control over international capital movements into, and out of, Japan. The measures taken to liberalize Japan's financial markets will be discussed later in the chapter.

Controls on Interest Rates

The controls on interest rates in the money market by the Bank of Japan—whether directly through moral suasion in the yen call-money market, or indirectly in the discount market through large purchases and sales of bills—have been relaxed or removed on a piecemeal basis in recent years. In the case of the yen call-money market, this involved drawing a distinction between the so-called quoted rates and free rates.

Through the late 1970s, interest rates in the yen call-money market tended to be negotiated and determined by three groups. These were the call-money brokers, the *Sanmeikai* (a committee on which all city banks were represented), and the Bank of Japan.[3] The rates that were worked out had to be approved by the Bank of Japan, and usually the bank would keep the rate above the prime short-term-loan rate so as to encourage the regional banks to place funds in the call-money market.[4] The posted or quoted rates in the call market were determined by means of quotations based on an agreement between the borrower and the lender.[5] As mentioned in chapter 5, the posted or quoted rates in the call-money market were discontinued in April 1979, with the specific rates being left free for negotiation. Thus the interest rates on unconditional call money have, in principal, been free rates since April 1979. To delineate this change, the Bank of Japan since April 1979 has referred to the reported call-loan rates—both the unconditional and the seven-day rate—as the central rates.[6]

The interest rates in the bill-discount market were controlled until the late 1970s through Bank of Japan purchases and sales of bills in the market as well as by direct moral suasion by the bank in relation to the Tanshi companies. Prior to June 1978, all rates in the bill-discount market were prefixed, or posted, for the day's trading, after consultation with the Bank of Japan. As indicated in chapter 4, there was a piecemeal liberalization of the rates in this market during 1978–1979, with some rates being freed and other rates remaining on a posted basis. By October 1979, all bill-discount rates had, in principle, been freed.

While not directly involving the money market, recent changes in the interest-rate controls on freely convertible yen deposits are pertinent, particularly because of their possible implications for the Tokyo dollar call market. Until March 1980, interest rates on nonresident free-yen deposits[7] were subject to ceilings established under the authority granted by the 1947 Temporary Money Rates Adjustment Law. By February 1980, the ceiling set for free-yen deposits with a three-month maturity—namely, 4.5 percent—was considerably below the roughly 8 percent rate for three-month Euro-yen in the Eurocurrency market. Largely because of disadvantageous interest-rate differentials like this, nonresident free-yen deposits fell about 50 percent in 1979 from a high of $8.8 billion in February to $4.4 billion in December. In a move to strengthen the yen and to encourage capital inflow, the authorities, on 10 March 1980, removed the interest-rate ceilings on nonresident free-yen deposits held by foreign official institutions—such as central banks. Other holders continued to be subject to the ceilings. After rising to approximately $6 billion in early 1981, the nonresident free-yen deposits (measured in terms of U.S. dollars) did not change markedly during the balance of 1981 or in 1982.

Other Controls on Money-Market Transactions

In addition to the interest-rate controls discussed above, the Japanese authorities have also imposed other restraints on transactions in the money market. Most of these relate to controls on: (1) which entities can have access to the market, (2) the amount of access, and (3) the terms, particularly the minimum or maximum maturities.

With regard to the *gensaki* market, a ceiling was initially set by the Japanese authorities on the amount of bond sales (that is, borrowings) that each financial institution could transact in the market. These ceilings were subsequently raised on several occasions and were finally lifted in 1980.[8] In addition, nonresidents were not allowed to participate in the *gensaki* market, but as restraints were gradually relaxed on the Japanese bond maturities that nonresidents could buy (that is, shortening the maturities on bonds eligible for purchase), the short-term *gensaki* market was eventually opened up completely to foreigners (that is, nonresidents) in mid-May 1979. Since that time, foreign activity in the *gensaki* market has increased substantially, as discussed in chapter 6.

While not related directly to the money market, and only indirectly to the Tokyo dollar call market, the liberalization of the controls on foreign-currency lending is of some interest. For many years, existing laws, in principle, prohibited all foreign-currency lending among residents—one exception being the Tokyo dollar call market. This meant that Japanese domestic banks were excluded from extending impact loans[9] to Japanese businesses. Thus, except for a short period in 1974, the medium- and long-term-impact-loan business was a monopoly of the foreign banks and their branches in Japan. Early in 1979, however, the government began to consider a proposal that would allow Japanese domestic banks to make such loans. About a year later, in March 1980, Japanese banks were allowed to make impact loans, but within certain specific limits. Later, on 1 December 1980, foreign-currency impact loans were liberalized completely so that all banks had equivalent opportunities to engage in this business. During the first eleven months of 1980, medium- and long-term foreign-currency impact loans (on an approvals basis) totaled $3.9 billion.[10] Of this, about two-thirds was provided by foreign banks and their Japanese branches.

On 1 December 1980, a revised foreign-exchange- and foreign-trade-control law became effective. Among other things, this law removed all controls on monetary flows and capital transactions unless explicitly prohibited by the new law. One result of implementing the new law was the removal of ceilings on residents' holdings of foreign-currency (primarily dollar) deposits placed with banks in Japan. This action—along with the impact-loan liberalization mentioned above—appears to have had the effect of increasing the rate of growth of the Tokyo dollar call market. However, under the new law, nonresidents are still not permitted to participate in the Tokyo dollar call market.

Shortly before the new law was implemented on December 1, the Bank of Japan announced a liberalization of its controls in the yen call-money market. Since 1965 the securities companies had not been permitted to participate in the yen call-money market, largely as a result of one of the major companies being confronted with a management crisis at the time. On 18 November 1980, however, the Bank of Japan announced that four major securities companies[11] would be permitted to borrow funds in the yen call-money market, effective the next day. The maximum limit on borrowing was set at ¥20 billion per company. At the same time, the Bank of Japan also authorized regional and trust banks to act simultaneously as both lenders and borrowers in the market. These actions had the effect of increasing interest-arbitrage opportunities in the money market.

Despite the various measures taken by the authorities in recent years to liberalize the market, some restraints—especially those hindering freer interest arbitrage—remain. Three examples of this can be cited: (1) maturities in the *gensaki* market are limited to a period of three months or less, (2) maturities on NCDs are confined to a three- to six-month period, and, (3) the minimum denomination for an NCD continues to remain very large, namely, ¥500 million (or $2 million at an exchange rate of 250 yen to the U.S. dollar).

Bank of Japan Intervention

The Bank of Japan exercises its influence over the money market through open-market operations in bills and securities, and through changes in its basic discount rate and the reserve requirements for financial institutions. The bank maintains a careful day-to-day surveillance over the market and readily intervenes in order to obtain any desired adjustments in money-market conditions.

In addition to having influenced interest-rate levels in the money market, the Bank of Japan has also intervened in the past to change the level of bank reserves. Some past examples of bank intervention include the sale of short-term government securities to the call-money brokers in 1966, the sale of Bank of Japan bills to banks and call-money brokers in 1971, and, beginning in 1972, the sale and purchase of commercial bills with the banks and the call-money brokers—either directly or through the bill-discount market. By the end of 1973, the purchase of such bills constituted the single largest means by which the Bank of Japan provided reserves to the banking system.[12] One of the main reasons that the Bank of Japan began to actively purchase bills in June 1972 in the bill-discount market was to give itself a new intervention instrument, which helped to diversify further the bank's available monetary controls. Later, in August 1973, the Bank of Japan also introduced another method of market intervention. It was named *aitai ope* and involved bank-to-bank operations, with the Bank of Japan directly purchasing bills held by the commercial banks rather than going through the market.[13]

As indicated earlier, the Bank of Japan has generally adjusted demand and supply in the call-money market by giving its guidance on interest rates, and, in the case of the bill-discount market, by exercising open-market operations. The bank has operated on both the buying and selling side in the bill-discount market in order to adjust monetary conditions. Operations were especially heavy during 1973 when Bank of Japan holdings of bills bought increased by $11 billion.[14] At the end of 1974, the Bank of Japan held 82 percent of the bills outstanding.

From roughly 1972 to 1980, most of the Bank of Japan's direct money-market intervention occurred in the bill-discount market; thus it has been, and continues to be, the major market for Bank of Japan intervention. In general, the bank has tried to keep the call-loan and bill-discount rates above the Bank of Japan's basic discount rate. This aspect is explored in more detail in chapter 10, which deals with interest-rate trends.

Because of the authorities' desire to continue to use the bill-discount and call-money markets as vehicles for regulating monetary and credit conditions, they have discouraged any tying of these markets to other international transactions. In 1978 the Mitsubishi Bank made a loan to Mexico and tied the interest rate on the loan to the three-month rate in the bill-discount market. However, since then "the Government has expressly forbidden any subsequent efforts to tie overseas yen lending rates to domestic rates."[15]

Beginning in 1980, however, the Bank of Japan also began to undertake direct intervention in the *gensaki* market. The aim at the time was reportedly to lower money-market rates so as to eventually reduce the yield to subscribers of government bonds and hence reduce the cost to the government of raising funds.[16]

In 1981 the Bank of Japan conducted large-scale open-market operations in the money market. The bank sold ¥1.5 trillion in short-term government bills in May to the call-money brokers to reduce the excess seasonal liquidity in the market. The brokers resold the bills to banks, securities companies, and corporations at interest rates based on comparable bill-discount rates. The banks and securities companies, in turn, were allowed to sell the bills freely to trading companies and to other nonfinancial enterprises. At the time the bill-discount rate was roughly 7.3 percent, or 160 basis points higher than the yield on short-term government bills when first issued. In addition to the ¥1.5 trillion in short-term government bills, the Bank of Japan in April and May also sold a similar amount of bills drawn on itself. Later, in November, the Bank of Japan again sold ¥1.5 trillion in short-term government bills to money brokers to mop up seasonal excess liquidity in the market.

This operation was repeated again in 1982, except that the objectives of the Bank of Japan were expanded to include not only the absorption of excess seasonal liquidity, but also the firming of short-term interest rates in order to restrain the decline of the yen against the U.S. dollar in the foreign-exchange market. In March the bank reportedly sold about ¥1.8 trillion in bills drawn on itself and an additional ¥1 trillion of its holdings of commercial bills. From April through mid-August the bank also sold about ¥7 trillion (about $28 billion) in government bills to money brokers and they in turn resold the bills to banks and securities companies.

The Tanshi Companies and the Bank of Japan

The Tanshi companies, which serve as both brokers and dealers in the money market, are subject to the Bank of Japan's direct guidance and supervision. The bank carries out on-the-spot surveys of the companies—as is also the case with other institutions having relations with the Bank of Japan.

Two types of loans are provided to the Tanshi companies by the Bank of Japan—general loans and loans for relending to the securities companies. The general loans extended by the Bank of Japan to the Tanshi companies are made either by discounting bills, or by providing secured loans, depending on the money market situation. Such loans are also made to adjust money-market conditions in response to seasonal surpluses or deficits in the market.

The second type of loan involves the securities market. Loans are made by the Bank of Japan to the Tanshi companies, which in turn provide funds to the securities companies for financing margin transactions. These credits from the Bank of Japan are provided in the form of loans on bills.

Although the Bank of Japan extended credit to the Tanshi companies during much of the 1960s, it stopped doing so in August 1967. In July 1978, however, the Bank of Japan again began to extend credit to the Tanshi companies in order to smooth out the erratic movements in the call-loan rate following the June 1978 liberalization of the call-money market.

The Liberalization of Interest Rates

Serious and deliberate actions to liberalize the entire money market began as recently as 1978. However, the first signs of movement toward a relatively free market appeared in the late 1960s. This was when the *gensaki* market began to reflect the desire of the commercial banks to participate in that market during periods of monetary restraint. In this almost spontaneously created market, somewhat freer interest rates tended to prevail. During the last half of the 1970s, business firms participated in increasing numbers in the *gensaki* market, especially when they could get a better rate of return in the *gensaki* market than on bank deposits.

However, the *gensaki* market is only one part of the Japanese money market and, until the early 1970s, it was not a very important part. During Japan's high-growth period through 1973, interest rates were held artificially low in order to assure a cheap supply of funds to industry.[17] Since roughly the middle of 1978, however, there has been considerable progress in the liberalization of interest rates in the money market.

Most of this liberalization has occurred in the call-money and bill-discount markets—the two parts of the money market that had been most controlled by the authorities. The other main components of the money market, namely, the *gensaki* and NCD markets, have had less need for liberalization. However, even in the case of these two, some liberalization has occurred and additional liberalization in the future would appear to be appropriate.

In a 1980 publication, the Bank of Japan explains why the Japanese authorities finally decided to undertake liberalization measures in the money market and to do so on a gradual basis.

> let us give a brief retrospect to the measures for the liberalization of interest rates. . . Firstly, the call money and bill discount rates . . . had fluctuated markedly . . . However, these rates had not sufficiently well reflected the market conditions, as the quoted rates were traditionally based on a broad concensus between major borrowers (city banks) and the counterpart lenders (agricultural financial institutions, etc.). As a result, at a time when the demand and supply of funds in the market or the market participants' expectations for future rates shifted rapidly, the changes in the quotations could not follow the developments of market conditions, and occasionally the rates became rather nominal. For these reasons, the liberalization—the abolishment of the quotation—in the call money market and bill discount market was planned. But, in order to avoid a possible disorder arising from rapid liberalization, "free rate transactions" and "diversification of terms" were advanced gradually.[18]

The liberalization measures were primarily carried out between June 1978 and October 1979. Rather than discuss here the dozen or so measures undertaken, they are summarized in table 9-1. Most of these measures have already been detailed in earlier chapters and a table provides a means of listing them in abbreviated form.

Implicit in the Bank of Japan's explanation for the liberalization is the point that the liberalization measures were prompted by the growing distortion between rates in the call-money and bill-discount markets on the one hand, and the rates in the *gensaki* market on the other. Prior to June 1978, rates in the *gensaki* market tended to hover about 25 basis points above comparable rates in the bill market. Since the 1978–1979 liberalization measures, however, short-term rates in the money market for comparable maturities have differed by smaller margins.

Bond-Market Liberalization

Recent developments in bond-market liberalization are also of some importance, mainly because of their impact on the *gensaki* (bond-repurchase) market and the increased opportunities that liberalization has presented for interest arbitrage in Japan's money and capital markets.

During the last half of the 1970s, when the Japanese government issued bonds in very large amounts, a need developed for greater flexibility in bond yields—particularly in view of the more-liberalized rate structure in the money market. In addition, the large volume of government-bond issues had placed an increasingly heavy burden on the bond underwriters.

Beginning in January 1978, liberalization of the bond market got under way. At that time restrictions on bond sales began to be gradually relaxed.

Table 9-1
Money-Market-Liberalization Measures

Date	Market	Action Taken
June 1978	Bill Discount	Rate freed on bills already held for at least one month after issue; resale of bills before maturity permitted with no restriction on the selling rates.
June 1978	Call Money	Bank of Japan gives tacit approval to premium rates when they appear and to more frequent changes in rates.
October 1978	Call Money	One-week maturities introduced with rates to fluctuate freely.
October 1978	Bill Discount and Call Money	Partial abolition of interest-rate quotation system.
November 1978	Bill Discount	One-month free-rate bill newly introduced; interest rates liberalized for bills with a maturity over three months.
April 1979	Call Money	Maturity, within seven-day period, liberalized; quotation system for call-money rates abolished entirely.
May 1979	*Gensaki* and NCD	Access to both markets granted for foreign investors (that is, nonresidents).
October 1979	Bill Discount	Quotation system, especially for the over-two-month bill, abolished entirely.
1978-1979	*Gensaki*	Gradual easing in restrictions on financial institutions' (especially city banks') participation in market.
March 1980	Nonresident Free-Yen Deposits[a]	Interest rates freed for nonresident free-yen deposits held by foreign official institutions.

[a]Not a formal money-market component, but an important element in interest-rate arbitrage in the money market.

One action taken in May 1978 allowed financial institutions to sell their government bonds after they had been listed on the Tokyo Stock Exchange. Previously, financial institutions had been requested not to sell their bonds until at least one year after issuance. Since the listing of new bonds generally takes seven to nine months following issuance, this measure was not as much of a liberalization of the bond market as might be assumed.

In January 1978 the Bank of Japan also announced that it would adopt a public-tender system for its operations in securities, and in June 1978 the bank purchased securities under the new tender system for the first time. After January 1978 the Trust Fund Bureau and the National Debt Consolidation Fund also adopted the public-tender system for the buying and selling of government bonds. Utilizing a public-tender system marked a substantial change from the previous system wherein the issuing terms to subscribers were jointly determined by the Ministry of Finance, the Bank of Japan, and a syndicate of underwriters. This change in the system for the issuance of bonds helped to spur growth in the secondary market for government bonds.

These developments have helped to move the rates for government securities closer to market levels truly reflecting demand and supply conditions. This in turn has removed some of the impediments to increased interest-arbitrage activities between the capital and money market. Nevertheless, a problem still remains in that government-bond yields to subscribers continue to be determined by agreement between the government and the underwriters' syndicate. One result in the early 1980s was a widening spread between the yields to subscribers and the yields in the secondary market. The government has eased this problem somewhat by issuing medium-term bonds, with two-, three-, and four-year maturities—in addition to the standard ten-year bonds—and has utilized a public-tender-offering system for these new, shorter-maturity bonds. These actions have resulted in bond yields in the secondary market that are closer to the rates in the money market.

Conclusion

For many years the Japanese money market has been closely regulated by the government, the main exceptions being the *gensaki* market, and later the new NCD market. Since the middle of 1978, however, the authorities have liberalized operations in the money market, especially in the call-money and bill-discount markets. The new market in NCDs, which started in May 1979, has been a relatively uncontrolled market since its inception, except for certain quantitative restraints, such as the ceilings placed on the total amount of NCDs that can be issued and the rather large minimum amounts specified for individual certificates.

Some of the initial momentum for deregulation likely came from the rapid growth in the mid-1970s of the *gensaki* market. As a relatively free market offering attractive yields in 1973–1974, the size of the market expanded substantially. At the same time, the authorities recognized that this relatively free component of the money market did not pose any serious obstacles to their control of monetary and credit conditions. This provided some reassurance that liberalization of the call-money and bill-discount markets would not lead to disorder in Japan's financial markets.

In addition, the growing interest arbitrage between the various components of the money market made the desirability of freer money markets even more evident to the authorities. This view was reinforced with the introduction of the relatively free NCD market in May 1979. With freer markets, more realistic interest rates prevailed in all components of the money market, thereby lessening the likelihood of large disruptive shifts of funds within the financial markets.

By December 1980 it was already evident that the liberalization of interest rates in the money market had resulted in reduced rate disparities in the market. In one report, it is stated that the money-market rates had ". . . come to stand more closely in line with each other."[19]

It should not be concluded from the above, however, that the various components of the money market are truly free markets. Despite the liberalization measures that have been taken in recent years, there remain certain restraints and rigidities in the money market. Many of these, such as the official regulation of the market, have been discussed in earlier chapters. In addition, the cost of funds has played a role in influencing money-market rates, and yet, the financial institutions' deposit rates are largely fixed by the Bank of Japan. Also, the banks' prime lending rate is kept in harness with the Bank of Japan's basic discount rate. Further complicating matters is the fact that the rate paid on postal savings—a major outlet for funds in competition with bank deposits—is not fixed by the Bank of Japan, but by the independent postal authorities. Consequently, there is still substantial room for making further progress in achieving a truly free money market in Japan.

Notes

1. The Bankers' Association states that ". . . the call market and the bill discount market, while they are free markets on the surface, are virtually subjected to policy intervention by the Bank of Japan when they decide their rates." *Banking System in Japan,* Federation of Bankers' Associations of Japan, Tokyo, Japan, 1976, p. 71.

2. *Asian Finance,* Hong Kong, 15 July 1979, p. 56.

3. See T.F.M. Adams and I. Hoshii, *A Financial History of the New Japan,* Kodansha International Ltd., Tokyo, 1972, p. 414.

4. See Eric W. Hayden, "Internationalizing Japan's Financial System," Occasional Paper of the N.E. Asia-U.S. Forum on International Policy, Stanford University, December 1980, p. 4.

5. "The Liberalization of Interest Rates in Japan," *Tokyo Financial Review,* Bank of Tokyo, Tokyo, December 1980, p. 1.

6. See *Economic Statistics Annual,* Bank of Japan, Tokyo, 1980, p. 84, footnote 4.(c).

7. These are also referred to as "non-resident free yen accounts." Nonresidents are allowed to convert readily these yen-denominated deposits into foreign currency without any administrative restraint.

8. "The Liberalization of Interest Rates in Japan," p. 2.

9. Impact loans are general-purpose-noncollateralized-foreign-currency bank loans extended to Japanese corporations.

10. With the 1 December 1980 liberalization of these loans, there was no longer any formal requirement that data on these loans be collected, so the government stopped publishing the data.

11. Nomura, Nikko, Daiwa, and Yamaichi.

12. Henry C. Wallich and Mable I. Wallich, *Asia's New Giant,* The Brookings Institution, Washington, D.C., 1976, p. 199.

13. *Money Market in Japan and Tanshi Companies,* Yamane Tanshi Company, Ltd., Tokyo, 1977, p. 16.

14. Kanji Haitani, *The Japanese Economic System: An Institutional Overview,* Lexington Books, D.C. Heath and Co., Lexington, Mass., 1976, p. 159.

15. Hayden, "Internationalizing Japan's Financial System," p. 14.

16. "The Liberalization of Interest Rates in Japan," p. 2.

17. Ibid., p. 1.

18. "General Features of the Recent Interest Rate Changes," Special Paper No. 91, Bank of Japan, Tokyo, December 1980, pp. 2–3.

19. "The Liberalization of Interest Rates in Japan," p. 2.

10 Interest-Rate Structure and Trends

Although previous chapters have briefly discussed interest-rate developments in the various components of the money market, no overall examination of the structure of rates in the market has been presented. This chapter attempts to fill that gap by detailing the structure of short-term money-market rates, as well as the changes and trends in the rates over time. Some attention is also devoted to seasonal influences on the rates and to the amount of volatility in the rates for different parts of the market.

Much of the chapter focuses on the period beginning in 1971. Prior to 1971 the *gensaki* market had not yet become very important and the other components of the money-market—such as the bill-discount market and the NCD market—had not yet been established. Only the yen call-money market was really significant in the period prior to 1971, and thus there is some discussion of call-money rates in the 1950s and 1960s.

Other topics that will be discussed include the various problems with Japanese-interest-rate data, the structure of rates during 1971–1982, and the interest-rate trends in the four main components of the money market. I will characterize those rate levels that are relatively high or low and indicate the degree of volatility in short-term rates in recent years.

Interest-Rate-Data Problems

Before discussing interest-rate developments, it should be noted that there are various problems in utilizing the Japanese data on money-market rates. These mainly involve the unavailability of certain data, the lack of comparability in some of the data series—both over a period of time and between markets—and the artificiality of some data due to official controls or restraints on certain segments of the money market.

Data published by the Bank of Japan on the money-market rates are available for the four components of the market: (1) the call-money market, (2) the *gensaki* market, (3) the bill-discount market, and (4) the NCD market. Through January 1983 the Bank of Japan was still not publishing in its *Economic Statistics Monthly* any interest rates for the Tokyo dollar call market. Of these four interest-rate series, the longest running is for call money (from 1952) and the shortest is for NCDs (from May 1979).

Later in the chapter, specific monthly data on money-market rates will be presented in the form of graphs, but the time periods covered will vary since not all four components of the money market have been operating since the early 1950s. Consequently, the data series will include the following time periods:

1. Call-money market: 1952 to present.
2. *Gensaki* market: June 1961 to present.
3. Bill-discount market: August 1971 to present.
4. NCD market: May 1979 to present.

All four series are now published in the Bank of Japan's *Economic Statistics Monthly,* as well as the Bank's *Economic Statistics Annual.* Later, when the actual interest trends in the four markets are discussed, the reasons for selecting certain maturities will be indicated.

The problem of unavailable data is less serious than the comparability problem. This is because the gaps in the data are for relatively brief periods, or the absence of data coincides with a period—such as for the *gensaki* market in the late 1950s—when the particular money-market component was not very large or important. Thus, in the case of the bill-discount market, there is a period of three months in 1971 (May–July) where data are not available from the Bank of Japan, since this period was the first three months of the market's existence. Similarly, yield data on the *gensaki* market prior to 1961 do not appear to have been published by the authorities.

The problems of interest-rate comparability in the money market are more serious. These problems include both comparability between market components and comparability within the same series, such as the series for the two-month bill-discount rate.

Due to the basic nature of the Japanese money market, some components of the market have shorter average maturities than others. Hence, the interest-rate quotations for the shorter-term components of the market naturally relate to different maturities than the interest-rate quotations for the longer-term components of the market. The result is that the predominant maturities are different for the various parts of the market. Not very much can be done about this problem since the different maturity structure is mandated by the Japanese authorities.

Another problem relates to comparability of data within the same time series. In the case of the call-loan rate, for example, the monthly rates quoted by the Bank of Japan for the period 1955–1964 are really modes rather than arithmetic averages.[1] For the period after 1964, arithmetic averages are generally utilized. However, in some cases even the monthly average is dropped. For example, starting in October 1979, the Bank of

Japan stopped publishing the monthly average bill-discount rate and instead began to publish the range (that is, the high and low) of the rates during the month.

For some interest-rate data, it is necessary to rely on unofficial sources, which may affect the comparability of a series. For example, the Bank of Japan's call-loan rates on an unconditional over-month-end basis for the period up to March 1956 were based on survey data compiled by the Ueda Tanshi Company.[2] Similarly, the yields in the *gensaki* market cited in this chapter for the period before August 1973 were based on estimates compiled by the Nomura Securities Co., Ltd.

Another aspect affecting the comparability of market rates between different components of the money market is that some components of the market are freer than others. The result is artificially low rates in the markets that are heavily controlled, or influenced, by the Bank of Japan, and somewhat higher rates in the truly free markets. To the extent that the Bank of Japan tightens or relaxes its control of certain market components—such as the bill-discount market—the rates will be affected and hence problems of comparability created.

A further comparability problem has also been created as a result of the authorities' piecemeal liberalization of different parts of the money market. An example of this would be the bill-discount market, which was liberalized for different maturities in 1978–1979, the result being to make some of the post-1978 interest-rate data not strictly comparable to the pre-1978 data.

Lastly, changes in the method of measuring the interest rates has caused some incomparability in the money-market rates. Prior to 1 September 1969, most money-market rates were quoted as so many sen per 100 yen per diem. With 100 sen equal to one yen, this is the same as .01 yen per 100 yen per day. Thus a rate of 2.0 sen per 100 yen per diem would be equivalent to 7.3 percent per year.[3] Since the money rates usually changed by tenths of a sen, a certain degree of discontinuity in the rate data was created. Thus an increase from 2.1 sen per ¥100 per diem to 2.2 would be equivalent to an increase from 7.3 percent to 7.665 percent. There is consequently no provision, for example, for rates of 7.4 percent or 7.5 percent, since changes tend to be in multiples of 0.365. Although many Japanese reports in the postwar period reported money-market rates both ways, that is, in sen per ¥100 per diem and in percent, it was not until 1 September 1969 that Japan switched over on a fairly widespread basis to the percentage system.[4]

Call-Loan Rates prior to 1971

During the period from 1952 through 1970, there were several times when the call-loan rate exhibited a substantial degree of volatility. As shown in figure 10–1, the call rate rose sharply in 1957, 1961, and 1964. (See the appendix for information on the interest-rate data presented in figure 10–1.) All three of these sharp run-ups coincided with the peak periods in the Japanese business cycle, that is, June 1957, December 1961, and October 1964,[5] when loan demand tended to be at its strongest. In 1957 the run-up was extremely sharp, the rate jumping from 8.22 percent in April to 18.25 percent in June.

Abstracting from these brief, sharp run-ups, the call-loan rate generally moved in a range between about 5 percent and 11 percent. The Bank of Japan's basic discount rate moved in a narrower range during this period, namely, between 5.5 percent and 8.5 percent. With the sole exception of a fourteen-month period through November 1956, the call-loan rate remained higher than the basic discount rate.

There were also some periods in the 1950s and 1960s when the call rate remained unchanged for a long time. One of these occurred over a fourteen-month period between April 1954 and May 1955, and another over a fifteen-month period from October 1965 to December 1966. These periods of stability coincided with a period when there was no change in the Bank of Japan's discount rate.

During the period extending from 1952 to 1970, there does not appear to have been any tendency for call-loan rates to register either a general long-term uptrend or downtrend. In the early 1950s the rates were usually in the 7 to 8 percent range, and by 1968–1970 they were also in the same 7 to 8 percent range. The very high rates, such as those in 1957, were largely due to a combination of strong loan demand and a restrictive monetary policy.

In the case of the 1957 run-up in rates, the Bank of Japan used certain monetary instruments to create an acute fund stringency in the call-money market. Since the commercial banks wanted to maintain a normal relationship with their borrowers, they were willing to pay high rates for marginal funds in the call-money market.[6]

With the exception of the period during the 1954 recession in Japan, call-loan rates have generally declined during Japanese recessions. This was the case in 1957–1958, 1962, 1964–1965, and 1970–1971. In 1954 the decline came after the trough of the recession that year.

The effect of seasonal developments on monthly rates, particularly when measured in terms of monthly averages, does not appear to be very strong. As indicated by the monthly data in figure 10–1, the general stance of monetary policy tends to be a more important factor than seasonal developments. It usually overwhelms the brief periods of tightness in late March and late September when business accounts are closed.

Figure 10–1 also shows the trends in the *gensaki* rate from mid-1961 through 1971. Except for two volatile periods, the *gensaki* rate generally moved in rough tandem with the call-loan rate during this period. One exception, however, was from late 1961 through July 1962 when the *gensaki*

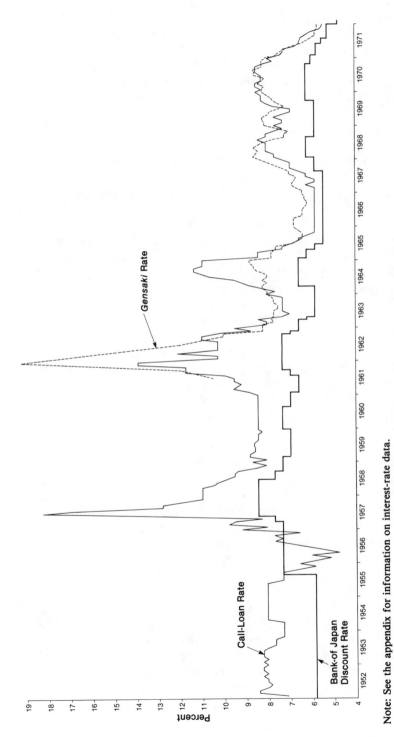

Note: See the appendix for information on interest-rate data.

Figure 10-1. Money-Market Rates, 1952–1971

rate spurted to a very high level (19.2 percent), which the call-loan rate failed to match (13.9 percent). The other exception was in 1964 when the call-loan rate (at about 11 percent) remained roughly 2 to 3 percentage points above the *gensaki* rate. By 1970 the rates were moving even more closely together, often in response to changes in the Bank of Japan's basic discount rate.

The Structure of Rates from 1971 to the Early 1980s

During the period from 1971 through 1982, there were two sharp run-ups in money-market rates. These occurred in 1973–1974 and in 1979–1980. (See figure 10–2, and see the appendix for information on the interest-rate data presented in figure 10–2.) The sharp increase in the first period reflected mainly the spurt in inflation due to a large rise in commodity prices in early 1973, and the inflationary impact from the major oil shock as a result of actions taken by the Organization of Petroleum Exporting Countries (OPEC), later in 1973. As the Japanese authorities gradually brought inflation under control after 1974, short-term money rates declined.

The second sharp advance in money-market rates in 1979–1980 also reflected the adverse impact from the second oil shock of 1979–1980, as OPEC more than doubled petroleum prices. The cost of other imported raw materials also rose at this time. In addition, a tight money policy, involving increases in the Bank of Japan's basic discount rate in order to reduce inflationary pressures, contributed to the sharp run-up in money-market rates in 1979–1980.

Characterizing the structure of the money-market rates has become increasingly difficult since the spring of 1979, since most of the rates have moved very close to each other due to a better integration of the market. However, it is possible to provide a rough characterization of the rate structure during the first half of the 1970s. During this period, the bill-discount rate generally exceeded the call-loan rate, and both rates tended to be higher than the Bank of Japan's basic discount rate. The *gensaki* rate, on the other hand, behaved like a maverick, sometimes being above the call-loan and bill-discount rates, sometimes below (see figure 10–2). Throughout the full period from 1971 through 1982, however, the Bank of Japan's basic discount rate—except for some very brief periods—was the lowest rate of all those plotted in figure 10–2. For that matter, during virtually all of the postwar period, money-market rates have exceeded the Bank of Japan's basic discount rate. A major factor contributing to this relationship has been a persistent shortage of financial capital, with the large city banks frequently experiencing a tight cash position.[7]

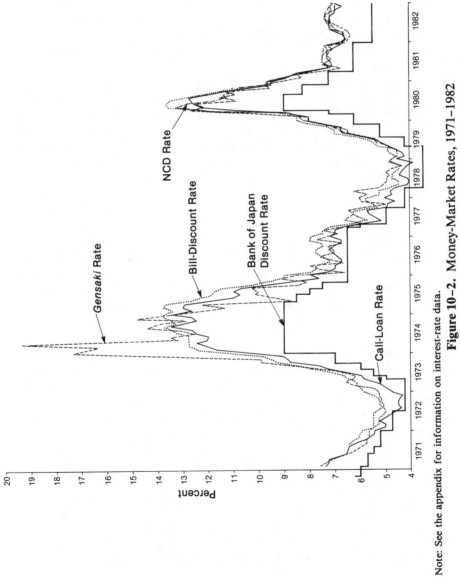

Note: See the appendix for information on interest-rate data.

Figure 10–2. Money-Market Rates, 1971–1982

Normally, the difference between the money-market rates and the basic discount rate is not very large. However, there have been two periods since 1971 when the money-market rates exceeded by a large margin the basic discount rate. These occurred during the sharp run-up in rates discussed earlier, that is, in 1974 and 1980 (see figure 10–2). In 1974 the Bank of Japan's basic discount rate remained at 9 percent, but most money-market rates fluctuated roughly at the 13 percent level. This large differential mainly reflected Bank of Japan reluctance to move its discount rate any higher than 9 percent—a historically high level in any event—even though market pressures and the virulent rate of inflation kept money-market rates at very high levels.

A similar situation occurred in 1980, except that the rate of inflation in Japan was considerably less than in 1974. Again, the Bank of Japan was reluctant to raise the discount rate above 9 percent, even though short-term money rates were at roughly the 12 percent level. Interest rates in short-term international markets and the United States were also at relatively high levels in the early part of the year and this influenced the level of Japanese short-term rates.

Throughout the postwar period there has been a rough relationship between the call-money rate and the Bank of Japan's basic discount rate. In a study published in 1966 on the Japanese money market, Hannan Ezekiel stated that ". . . the call money rate has shown a tendency to move in broadly the same direction as the discount rate."[8] However, he also concluded that the statistical relationship between the two series was weak since the correlation and regression results indicated that "the relationship between the discount rate and the call money rate is not very close." It is likely, however, that a much closer statistical relationship occurred during the 1970s, as is evident from an examination of the call-money and discount-rate trends in figures 10–1 and 10–2.

As indicated earlier, the bill-discount rate is generally higher than the call-loan rate. During the mid-1970s, the differential generally ranged between 0.6 and 0.9 percentage points. By 1980, however, the average differential had narrowed somewhat to approximately 0.5 percentage points, and in some months during 1980 the call rate exceeded the bill rate. With a closer integration of the different components of the money market in recent years, it appears likely that the rate differentials will continue to remain relatively small.

Seasonal influences on money-market rates appear to be relatively small. Money-market conditions tend to tighten at the end of March and September, as businesses dress up their balance sheets, and also at the end of the year when the demand for currency expands. Since the period of July and August is often one of surplus in the central government's treasury accounts, market conditions tighten at that time. But from September to

November, easier conditions prevail as treasury payments exceed receipts. At the beginning of the year there is a flow of currency from the nonbank public back to the financial institutions, and this tends to ease money-market conditions.

Several conclusions emerge from an examination of money-market rates during the postwar period. One is that since early 1979, the money market has been more closely integrated than earlier, as evidenced by the much closer and parallel movement of the rates. Even as recently as 1978 there was a greater spread between the money rates in the various components of the market.

Another conclusion is that in the 1970s and recently—if not prior to the 1970s—the changes in money rates paralleled changes in the Bank of Japan's basic discount rate, with one exception. This exception consisted of the periods of very tight money. In 1974, and again in 1980, for example, the money rates exceeded the basic discount rate by a substantial margin. A comparison of rates in figures 10–1 and 10–2 demonstrates that in the 1970s most money rates were generally closer to the discount rate (figure 10–2) than in the period prior to 1971 (figure 10–1).

A third and final conclusion is that the interest rates in the money market are still controlled to a certain extent by the Japanese authorities. Changes in the Bank of Japan's basic discount rate, as well as its particular level, strongly influence the level and trend of most money-market rates. In addition, indirect control is also exercised by the Japanese authorities through the ceilings set on foreign-bank-currency swaps.[9] In 1978 the authorities raised the total limit on outstanding swaps to $3.2 billion from $2.7 billion, and in March 1979 the swap ceiling was raised again to $3.8 billion.[10] Further increases occurred after that, and in June 1982 the swap ceiling was set at $6.75 billion. By restricting the amount of foreign-currency swaps for local currency, the authorities have distorted market forces and created a partly artificial situation in the financial market. Presumably one reason why the authorities have imposed an overall ceiling on swaps is to prevent the competitive position of indigenous banks from being eroded.

**Interest-Rate Features in Individual Components
of the Money Market**

The interest rates in the four components of the domestic money market merit attention. These are the call-loan rate, the *gensaki* rate, the bill-discount rate, and the NCD rate. Interest rates in the Tokyo dollar call market generally parallel the rates in the Eurocurrency market.

Call-Loan Rate

During the period from January 1952 to September 1955 the call-loan rate moved in a very narrow range (7.12 to 8.21 percent). In addition, there was no change in the monthly rate from April 1954 to May 1955, the rate remaining at 8.03 percent throughout. After September 1955, however, the call-loan rate became more volatile and eventually shot up to a very high level (18.25 percent) in 1957. In subsequent years, high rates were also reached in the call-money market at roughly the same time that each cyclical upswing peaked out.

During 1972, which was an easy-credit period, the call rate fell to almost the same low level as the Bank of Japan's basic discount rate. Then, with a powerful credit squeeze in 1973, the call rate rose very sharply, reaching 13.5 percent in 1974—a level well above the commercial banks' contracted-loan rates.

After the May 1978 liberalization of the call-money market, there were more-frequent changes in the call-loan rate. For example, in June 1978 the call rate changed six times, as compared with only three times in June 1977. In 1979–1980, call-loan rates again rose sharply to a high level, roughly in tandem with other short-term rates in Japan, as international-money rates rose to high levels.

Bill-Discount Rate

The bill-discount rate has generally moved in approximately the same trend as the call-loan rate, except that it has been a half percentage point or so above the call rate. Data on the bill-discount rate are only available from August 1971 (the market was established in May 1971), but as shown in figure 10–2, the bill rate has been less volatile than the *gensaki* rate. With few exceptions, the monthly rate has remained no more than one percentage point higher than the call-loan rate.

As was noted earlier, the data series for the bill-discount rate plotted in figure 10–2 is not a perfectly consistent series due to changes in maturities, among other things. Despite this aspect, however, the International Monetary Fund (IMF) has selected the so-called over-two-month bill rate as a representative short-term money rate in Japan for the purpose of calculating the interest rate paid by the IMF on the holdings by members of Special Drawing Rights (SDRs).[11]

From 1971 through 1982, the bill-discount rate ranged between 4.5 percent and 13.75 percent. This was a narrower range of fluctuation than for the call-loan rate or the *gensaki* rate. One possible explanation for this is that since its inception in 1971, the bill rate has been controlled to a greater or lesser extent on a continuing basis by the Bank of Japan, unlike the relatively uncontrolled *gensaki* rate. Presumably there has been much less influence on the bill rate since the liberalization actions of 1978–1979.

Gensaki Rate

During the early 1960s the rate in the *gensaki* market was very volatile, rising very sharply to 19.2 percent in December 1961. In contrast, the call-loan rate in the same month was 13.9 percent. This large differential was due partly to the thinness of the *gensaki* market, as well as its freedom from official control at the time.

By August-September 1964 the situation was roughly reversed, with the call-money rate more volatile, rising sharply to a high of 11.3 percent, while the *gensaki* rate never moved above 8.8 percent in 1964. This development was reportedly due to the attempts of the city banks to meet the credit needs of their important customers during a very tight money period. This period in the late summer of 1964 also marked the tail end of an economic upswing and the beginning of a mild recession which started in October 1964. Thereafter, the two rates moved more closely together.

From 1963 through 1972 the *gensaki* rate fluctuated within a much narrower range, that is, between 5.0 and 8.6 percent. This changed in 1973–1974, when the *gensaki* rate rose substantially above other money-market rates. For example, in March 1974 the *gensaki* rate peaked at 19.3 percent, while the call-loan and bill-discount rates moved up to only about 12.75 percent. Subsequently, the *gensaki* rate generally moved in tandem with the other money-market rates. In 1979–1980, when there was a sharp increase in money-market rates, the *gensaki* rate also rose rapidly along with the other rates.

An interesting feature of the *gensaki* market and the rate developments in that market is that, despite the relative freedom from official intervention the *gensaki* market purportedly enjoys, the *gensaki* rate—at least since mid-1974—has not differed greatly from other money-market rates. This would suggest that either the various components of the money market are freer from official intervention that one might assume, or that the official intervention and control extends also to the *gensaki* market. The truth would appear to be that the markets have become freer from official intervention and control, particularly since early 1979.

NCD Rate

Rate developments in the NCD market cover a relatively short period since the market was established as recently as May 1979. Rate quotations published in the Bank of Japan's *Economic Statistics Monthly* begin with that month.

From the very beginning, the NCD rate has moved closely with the other money-market rates (see figure 10–2). In general, it appears to have moved most closely with the *gensaki* rate, and to have deviated the most from the bill-discount rate. However, even the differences with the bill-discount rate have been relatively small.

As was the case with other money-market rates, the NCD rate rose sharply from the summer of 1979 through the spring of 1980. At the time of the market's inception the rate was about 5.33 percent, but by April 1980 it had increased to 13.25 percent. It then peaked out at a level slightly below the bill-discount rate, and generally declined to roughly the 7 percent level in 1981–1982.

Rate Levels and Volatility

Of the four major money markets in Japan, the NCD market has generally had the narrowest range of rate fluctuation. (Part of this is undoubtedly due to the relatively short life of the market to date.) Through the end of 1982, the highest level ever reached was 13.25 percent and the lowest level was 5.32 percent, or a differential of about 8 percentage points.

On the other hand, both the *gensaki* and the call-money markets have had the widest range of fluctuation, with as much as a 15 percentage point differential. The *gensaki* rate has ranged between 4.3 and 19.3 percent, while the call-loan rate has ranged between 3.9 and 18.3 percent. The range of fluctuation for the bill-discount market falls in between these two extremes at 9.25 percentage points, with a low of 4.5 percent and a high of 13.75 percent. It is likely that Bank of Japan control of the bill-discount rate prevented the bill rate from moving up to the high levels (18 to 19 percent) reached in the *gensaki* and call-money markets.

As mentioned earlier, money-market rates have frequently turned volatile near the end of an economic upswing, and have increased sharply. Then they have dropped rather steeply during the recessionary period. One exception to this was in mid-1970 when there was no sharp run-up in rates prior to the July 1970-December 1971 recession. During the recessionary period and well into 1972, however, money-market rates did decline.

A glance at figure 10–2 shows clearly that Japanese money-market rates can be volatile. In addition, the sharp run-up in rates in 1979-1980 indicates that there is approximately as much volatility in the rates in recent years as there was earlier. Compared to other major industrialized countries, there appears to be as much volatility in Japan's money-market rates as in other countries' short-term money rates.[12] Within Japan, money-market rates also tend to be more volatile than bank-loan rates.

During the postwar period the trend in money-market rates has roughly paralleled the typical business-cycle pattern. Thus, during the upswing phase of the business cycle, rates tend to rise, and during the downswing phase, rates eventually decline. Then there will be the usual so-called saucer-ing out before the next upswing in the rates. This is the general pattern, but no two cycles are precisely alike.

Is it possible to characterize certain interst-rate levels in the money market as being relatively high or relatively low? On the whole, it would appear that any rates at about the 5 percent, or lower, level could be characterized as being very low. More difficult is the top side, since monthly rates have been as high as 18 or 19 percent. But, in general, rates at about the 12 percent, or higher, level could be characterized as very high. This range, below 5 and above 12 percent for call-money rates, is used by Kanji Haitani as an approximate indicator of tight credit (above 12 percent) or excess liquidity (below 5 percent).[13] A glance at figure 10-2, covering the 1971-1982 period, provides further confirmation that the 5 percent and 12 percent levels are fairly good indicators of whether money-market rates have reached relatively high or low levels.

Whenever Japanese-money-market rates differ substantially from overseas rates, there is a tendency for interest arbitrage to occur. Thus, in the spring of 1980, when Eurodollar rates were relatively low and Japanese short-term rates were high (at about 12 percent), dollar funds were bor-rowed in the Eurodollar market for short-term lending by foreign-branch banks in the Japanese bill-discount market. Usually foreign-branch banks are net borrowers in the bill-discount market.

Conclusion

The structure of the money-market rates, as based on the data presented in this chapter, was relatively simple in the 1960s. It consisted of the call-loan rate and the *gensaki* rate, with the call-loan rate usually being at a level lower than the *gensaki* rate. With the introduction of the bill-discount market in May 1971, the money market increased to three main compo-nents. During the period from May 1971 to the spring of 1979, the bill-dis-count rate was usually higher than the call-loan rate, while the *gensaki* rate behaved like a maverick, moving erratically above and below the other rates.

By the spring of 1979—when the NCD market was established—the four money-market rates were clustering much closer together and, as time passed, it became increasingly difficult to discern a particular structure for the money-market rates. Over the entire period since 1952, however, the Bank of Japan's basic discount rate has usually been at a level below all of the money rates.

Volatility in the money-market rates has been present during all of the postwar period and as recently as 1980. During certain periods in the 1950s and 1960s, the call-loan rate was quite volatile. The sharp run-up in the rates (that is, the call rate and the *gensaki* rate) tended to coincide with the final stages of the upswing phase of the business cycle. During recessionary periods, the money-market rates generally declined. In general, money-market rates have been just as volatile in recent years as in the 1950s and 1960s.

Certain money-market rates have been more volatile than others. In terms of their range of fluctuation, the narrowest fluctuations have occurred in the NCD rate, and the widest in the *gensaki* and call-loan rates. The bill-discount rate has fallen somewhere in between these two extremes.

There has been only a rough relationship between the Bank of Japan's basic discount rate and the money-market rates. When there has been no change in the discount rate, the money-market rates have generally not evidenced any clear upward, or downward, tendency. In addition, changes in the discount rate have generally been followed by changes in the money-market rates in the same direction. During those periods when money-market rates are at their peak, the discount rate has been considerably lower.

Seasonal developments do not appear to play a very important role in influencing money-market rates, especially when measured in terms of monthly averages. There are, of course, influences at the end of the month, around the turn of the year, at the end of the semiannual business-accounting period and during times of government budgetary surplus or deficit, but these are often overwhelmed by the general upward or downward trend in the market. In short, the impact of seasonal developments on the market is weak.

Despite the piecemeal liberalization of the money market in 1978–1979, money-market rates are not completely free from influence by the authorities. One example indicating that the bill-discount rate may not be at truly free-market levels is the warning issued by the Ministry of Finance in September 1980. Earlier, on 10 March 1980, the Ministry of Finance eliminated the interest-rate ceilings on nonresident free-yen accounts held by foreign official institutions, such as central banks. After that, commercial banks began paying 13 to 14 percent on such foreign-official deposits. Then in September 1980 the Ministry of Finance urged the commercial banks to exercise restraint in offering such high rates, since they were often 0.5 to 0.75 percentage points above the bill-discount rate.

Following the piecemeal liberalization of money-market rates in 1978–1979, observers of the Japanese money and capital markets have drawn a distinction between administered and nonadministered interest rates. The former usually include commercial-bank savings rates, postal-deposit rates, dividend rates on loan trusts, five-year-bank-debentures rates, the ten-year-government-bond rate, the short-term prime-lending rate, and the long-term prime-lending rate. The nonadministered interest rates include, among others, the money-market rates. Since at least February 1981, negotiations have been proceeding within the government to improve and unify the government's administrative process for establishing the administered rates. It would appear highly unlikely, however, that the administered rates will be shifted to a nonadministered basis in the very near future.

Notes

1. See Hannan Ezekiel, "The Call Money Market in Japan," *IMF Staff Papers,* International Monetary Fund, Washington, D.C., March 1966, pp. 45–46.

2. *Economic Statistics of Japan: 1964,* Bank of Japan, Tokyo, March 1965, p. 171.

3. As based on: $\dfrac{\text{sen per ¥100 per diem x 365}}{100}$ = %/year.

4. T.F.M. Adams and I. Hoshii, *A Financial History of the New Japan,* Kodansha International Ltd., Tokyo, 1972, p. 417.

5. For a listing of the trough and peak months in the Japanese business cycle, see *Japanese Economic Indicators,* Economic Planning Agency, Tokyo, December 1980, p. 125.

6. See Ezekiel, "The Call Money Market in Japan," p. 46.

7. See Tomizo Takayamagi, "Recent Trends in the Short-Term Loan Market in Japan," *Quarterly Five Banks Review,* Tokyo, October 1975, p. 10.

8. Ezekiel, "The Call Money Market in Japan," p. 48.

9. Foreign banks in Japan are allowed to bring in foreign currency and swap it for yen, but only for specified amounts.

10. *Far Eastern Economic Review,* Hong Kong, 6 April 1979, p. 79.

11. Other short-term rates are based on the rates for three-month: (1) U.S. treasury bills, (2) interbank deposits in Germany, (3) U.K. treasury bills, and (4) interbank money against private papers in France.

12. An exception to this would be the rates for short-term (sixty day) government securities in Japan, which are maintained by the authorities at artificially low levels. However, the short-term-government-securities market is not a bona fide part of Japan's money market.

13. See Kanji Haitani, *The Japanese Economic System: An Institutional Overview,* Lexington Books, D.C. Heath and Co., Lexington, Mass., 1976, p. 159.

11 An Assessment of the Market

Japan's money market has developed significantly since the early 1970s; new instruments have been introduced and official control of the market has been relaxed. In this sense, the most important developments in the market since the end of World War II have occurred during the past decade. Consequently, much of the following assessment of the market concentrates on the period since the early 1970s.

In any assessment of the market, there are certain key questions that need to be answered. How does the rate of growth of the money market compare with the growth of other financial markets? Has there been an increase in the diversity of money-market instruments available? Has the market met the needs of short-term lenders and borrowers, or are there significant deficiencies in the market? How free has the market been in the past and how free is it now? What must be done for further development of the market? And what is likely to happen in the future in the Japanese money market?

The Growth of the Money Market—In Perspective

Measured in terms of the amount of loans outstanding, the call-money market grew fairly rapidly in the late 1950s and early 1960s. During the ten years through the end of 1966, the call-money market increased tenfold, from approximately ¥100 billion to ¥1 trillion. However, in the subsequent recessionary periods (1966–1968 and 1972–1975), the amounts outstanding declined.

The year-to-year growth rates of the entire money market have varied sharply—declining, for example, from a growth rate of 61 percent in 1973 to only 3 percent in 1976. The average rate of growth from 1968 to 1982 was 20 percent, with the 1969–1974 period being one of extremely rapid growth. In recent years the annual growth rate in the entire money market has slowed, registering only 9 percent in 1980, almost no change in 1981 and a 5 percent increase in 1982.

In general, the bill-discount and *gensaki* markets have declined in recent years while the call-money market has advanced. The new NCD

121

market has also grown rapidly, but this mainly reflects high percentage increases from a small base. The Tokyo dollar call market has also increased sharply, with the outstanding balance rising from $2.7 billion at the end of 1978 to $4.9 billion a year later and to $34.6 billion by September 1982.[1] There has also been a fairly steady and substantial increase in the number of banks participating in the Tokyo dollar call market.

There are several ways in which the actual size of the money market, as well as the changes in its relative size, can be put in perspective. One is to compare the amount of money-market funds outstanding to the claims on private business (loans, discounts, and securities) held by the deposit-money banks.[2] The ratio has more than doubled since 1967, when the proportion was 3.4 percent. By the end of 1982 the ratio had increased to 7.2 percent. In this sense, therefore, the money market has substantially increased its relative importance in relation to Japan's depository financial institutions.

Another way to assess the relative importance of the money market is to utilize the data in Japan's flow of funds accounts. In March 1967, when the bulk of the money market consisted of the call-money market, call money accounted for 2.1 percent of the total liabilities of financial institutions.[3] By March 1981 this proportion had increased to 2.7 percent.[4] However, this understates the actual ratio, since the flow-of-funds data exclude the *gensaki* market and measure only the call-money, bill-discount and NCD markets.

A third way to put the size of the money market in perspective is to compare it to Japan's gross national product (GNP) for different time periods, and also to examine the comparable ratios for the United States. At the end of 1972—by which time the *gensaki* market had become much more important and the bill-discount market had been established—total money-market funds outstanding were equivalent to 4 percent of Japan's GNP. The comparable figure in the United States at the time was 22 percent. By 1980 the money market in Japan had increased in relative size to where it was equivalent to 6 percent of the GNP, while the comparable ratio in the United States was 24 percent. These data indicate that while the money market has grown in relative importance in both countries since the early 1970s, the Japanese money market is still relatively small and underdeveloped.

An examination of the growth rates for the different components of the money market indicates that no single component has grown the fastest on a steady basis since the early 1970s. Rather, the component with the fastest rate of growth has tended to vary over different time periods, and it would appear likely that this will also be the case in the future.

In general, however, the money market has been increasing its relative share in the economy and this trend is expected to continue, at least in the near future. This increase in relative importance has occurred both with regard to other financial institutions and to the entire economy, as measured by GNP. In the *gensaki* market, for example, the amount of activity has been strongly influenced by the level of deposit rates and yields on other money-market instruments. When the *gensaki* yields are substantially above deposit rates, the amount of funds flowing into the *gensaki* market has increased substantially.

The Pace of Diversification of the Money-Market Instruments

Most of Japan's new money-market instruments have been introduced only since the early 1970s. Hence, the rate of diversification of these instruments has been fairly high since then with virtually no new money-market instruments (aside from the *gensaki*, that is bond-repurchase, instruments) having been introduced earlier in the postwar period.

The call-money instruments date from roughly the turn of the century and the bond repurchase instruments (that is, *gensaki*) from the late 1940s. But since the *gensaki* market was relatively small and unimportant in the 1950s and 1960s, virtually all of the diversification of the money-market instruments has occurred since the early 1970s.

The first market to compete significantly with the call-money market was the *gensaki* market in approximately 1970. Next was the bill-discount market in May 1971. (As indicated earlier, the call-money market was, in effect, split into two parts.) Then, in April 1972, the Tokyo dollar call market began to operate—the first interbank market in foreign currencies. Lastly, in May 1979, a market in NCDs was inaugurated.

The pace of diversification in the money market in the 1970s was definitely faster than in the preceding twenty-five postwar years. However, the Japanese money market is still short of its full potential and also is not as diversified as it could be, since there remain some important gaps in the market.

These gaps in the market—which will be discussed more fully later—include, among others, the absence of a commercial paper market, a bona fide market for short-term government securities, and a bankers' acceptance market. The market is also in need of appropriate instruments for nonfinancial businesses, especially on the borrowing side.

Has the Market Met the Needs of Borrowers and Lenders?

This question is perhaps best examined from the viewpoint of two groups—financial and nonfinancial businesses. Included in financial businesses are all of the financial institutions detailed in chapter 2. All others can be considered nonfinancial businesses.

For most financial institutions, especially the city banks, the money market has functioned satisfactorily and has met their short-term financial needs fairly well. The banks have had access to the bill-discount, call-money, NCD, and the Tokyo dollar call markets. With maturities ranging up to four months, the bill-discount market has provided a stable source of funds for the city banks. However, an exception to this, at times, has been the foreign-branch banks in Japan that have had to fund some of their local loans in Japan from their home offices, or other overseas offices, through foreign-currency advances which are then swapped into yen for local lending. The foreign-branch banks, at certain times in the past, have not always been completely free to borrow or lend in the various money-market components, including the *gensaki* market.[5] By the early 1980s, however, these restraints had largely, if not completely, disappeared.

Japan's nonfinancial enterprises have been less well served. The only market to which they have had access as borrowers has been the *gensaki* market, and even here their share of the market as borrowers has been relatively small. They have also been lenders in the *gensaki* and NCD markets. In short, access to the Japanese money market for nonfinancial businesses has been limited. Compared to the United States and the United Kingdom, the Japanese money market is much less open for nonfinancial businesses. Japan's nonfinancial businesses should have a market where the large, well-known firms can issue certain money-market instruments, such as short-term promissory notes.

The nonfinancial businesses could also benefit from a wider variety of investment instruments for their short-term funds. Although investment in the *gensaki* and NCD markets is possible, the choice of outlets is not as broad as it might be. For example, short-term government securities are unattractive and there is no bankers' acceptance or commercial-paper market. Thus, nonfinancial businesses with surplus short-term funds lack a wide, active, and attractive market in such money-market instruments.

One of the basic functions of a money market is to provide liquidity; banks and other financial institutions should be able to easily liquidate their short-term assets. However, the Japanese money market leaves a lot to be desired when it comes to market liquidity. Although the Bank of Japan is able to influence bank liquidity through its open-market operations in the bill-discount market, such actions only have a partial impact on the degree of liquidity. Aggravating the liquidity situation is the fact that many purchasers of money-market instruments in Japan tend to hold them to maturity.

In short, the present Japanese money market does not meet fully all the needs of the various borrowers and lenders. While certain financial institutions—such as the city banks—have most of their needs met, there is still substantial room for further development of the market, especially with regard to the nonfinancial enterprises. Japan needs to relax or eliminate the various rigidities that continue to prevail in the market, such as the artificially low interest rates set by the Ministry of Finance for short-term government securities.

Gaps in the Japanese Money Market

One of the major gaps in the market is the lack of an attractive and effective market for short-term government securities. In the United States, short-term government securities account for more than a third of the total money-market funds outstanding. These include not only short-term U.S. treasury securities, but also short-term municipal securities. None of these are traded in Japan's bona fide money market. Although short-term government securities are issued in Japan, their yields are set at such an artificially low level that there is no active market in these bills. (Other reasons for the absence of a bona fide market in short-term government securities are discussed in chapter 8 in the section on the short-term-government-securities market.) This gap in the market has deprived potential investors of a safe, highly liquid asset with a market-determined yield.

Another major gap is the absence in Japan of a commercial paper market, that is a market in short-term, unsecured promissory notes issued on a discount basis by large, well-known corporations in large denominations. Except for the *gensaki* market, there is no other component of the Japanese money market where nonfinancial businesses can borrow short-term funds. And even in the *gensaki* market, a nonfinancial enterprise desiring to borrow funds would have to have the appropriate type of government—or other securities—to sell. As indicated earlier, the Japanese call-money market is roughly similar to the U.S. Federal Funds market, and the bill-discount market is somewhat like the U.S. bankers' acceptance market. But there is nothing in the Japanese money market that is similar to the U.S. commercial-paper market. Thus nonfinancial businesses must rely heavily on the banks for their short-term funds.

In August 1982 the Ministry of Finance announced that, for the time being, it had decided not to authorize the introduction of commercial paper—and also dollar NCDs—into the Japanese money market. The new Japanese banking law passed in April 1982 had authorized the introduction of both types of instruments, but the appropriate rules and regulations to allow their actual introduction were not issued during the April through August period. The Ministry of Finance also announced in August that a study would be made whether to allow these instruments to be introduced into Japan, and the eventual decision by the authorities was likely to be strongly influenced by the results of that study.

A third gap is the absence of a true or bona fide bankers' acceptance market. Although Japan does have its bill-discount market, the bills traded in that market finance only domestic transactions. Attempts have been made by the Bank of Japan since 1973 to develop a market in yen-denominated export and import bills guaranteed by banks. (See the section in chapter 8 on bank-guaranteed export and import bills.) However, these efforts have generally been unsuccessful, partly because of the limited negotiability of the bills and also because of the higher cost of funds in this market to potential borrowers. It has also been suggested by one observer that, while importers are interested in financing their imports by means of yen-denominated import bills, they are reluctant to switch from dollar financing since they want to keep their dollar credit lines open. In addition, the Bank of Japan is reportedly opposed to the establishment of a bankers' acceptance market since it believes that this would complicate its ability to control monetary conditions.[6] While future prospects for developing a bona fide bankers' acceptance market appear poor, there do not appear to be any intractable obstacles to doing so, once appropriate measures are taken to make the market attractive.

Japan is also in need of more and better money-market instruments for nonfinancial businesses. The present selection of short-term domestic investments is actually rather limited. While the *gensaki* market is of some assistance for large, nonfinancial lenders, there is no well-established and attractive money market for nonfinancial borrowers. This results from the fact that the call-money and bill-discount markets are closed to nonfinancial businesses and the NCD market is for lending, not borrowing. Hence the strong need for some type of money-market instrument that nonfinancial businesses could issue to meet their short-term borrowing needs.

Although a good start has been made on developing an NCD market in Japan, the present market remains substantially below its full potential. Some of the factors tending to restrain the market are the large minimum denomination (namely, ¥500 million or about $2 million), the lack of flexible maturities—especially short maturities—and the absence of a truly bona fide secondary market. The last problem is mainly due to the requirement that the bank issuing an NCD must give its approval before the certificate holder can sell the certificate to another party. In addition, according to Andreas Prindl, Japanese NCDs are not, in actuality, freely transferable bearer instruments. Any changes in ownership must be physically recorded.[7] If there were to be a substantial liberalization of all these restraints, it is likely that the market would expand at a significantly faster pase.

Lastly, Japan lacks a bona fide market in offshore funds. While the

Tokyo dollar call market meets the needs of the smaller banks in Japan, the current restrictions on the market prevent Tokyo from becoming a major international money market. The key steps that would have to be taken to accomplish this include: (1) opening the market to nonresidents and allowing them completely free convertibility of any yen balances, (2) allowing both nonbank enterprises and individuals to participate in the market, (3) removing any reserve requirements on offshore deposits, and (4) eliminating any withholding taxes levied on interest earnings from holdings of foreign-currency deposits.

In conclusion, one of the main deficiencies in Japan's money market is that nonfinancial businesses cannot borrow very easily in the market. They do have access to the *gensaki* market, but this is mainly on the lending side. Thus, while the market serves the banks and other financial institutions reasonably well, it is still basically underdeveloped in terms of being an adequate market for nonfinancial businesses.

Freeing Up the Money Market

Until the late 1970s, the degree of control or freedom, of the Japanese money market was mixed. Until 1978, the call-money and bill-discount markets were not truly free markets. The Bank of Japan influenced brokers in the call-money market and intervened in the bill-discount market. On the other hand, the *gensaki* market—in relation to the call and bill markets—was freer, especially until 1974. Additional official regulation of the *gensaki* market was instituted in 1976, but despite this, the *gensaki* market still remained freer than the other two markets. The NCD market has remained relatively free since its establishment in May 1979. Official liberalization of the money market, mainly the call and bill-discount markets, began in mid-1978.

Although the Bank of Japan and Ministry of Finance did not admit it at the time (that is, from 1945–1977), it was stated when they began their liberalization program in 1978 that the money market had not been completely free. This can therefore be taken as after the fact proof that the call and bill-discount markets were not really free markets in much of the postwar period. Even when the authorities began the liberalization program, the introduction of free transactions was on a piecemeal basis—providing a clear indication of which part of the market was free and which part was not free.

No attempt will be made here to review the specific liberalization actions. Major aspects of the liberalization program are described in chapter 9, and for a summary of the key actions taken, see table 9–1.

By October 1979 all major components of the market had, ostensibly, been freed. As a consequence, interest rates in the money market were much freer to change than before the liberalization. A brief look at a chart of the interest rates in the market over time for the different market components shows that the rates have tended to move much closer together since early 1979, reflecting active arbitrage and freedom to move between different components of the market. In short, since 1978 Japan has clearly moved toward a market-oriented interest-rate system.

However, it should not be assumed that complete freedom exists in the money market, as there are still various types of restraints and impediments. In addition, there has been just as much volatility in the rates in recent years as earlier in the 1950s. One observer has noted that although controls were officially removed by 1979 in the call-money and the bill-discount market, the Bank of Japan still continued to exercise its influence over the market through the six money-market brokers. "Hence, while the rates are more flexible, . . . they are still not truly determined by the forces of supply and demand."[8]

In the *gensaki* market, there are limits on the bond prices negotiated, and individuals are excluded from the market. In addition, not all bonds are eligible for trading in the market, there are restrictions on the amount of outstanding balances that securities companies can maintain—as well as the volume of activity that can be transacted from the companies' own inventories—and there are limits on the amount of bonds that companies can take on a consignment basis. The nonfinancial business corporations participating in the *gensaki* market are restricted to those that would qualify to be listed on the First Section of the Tokyo Stock Exchange. Because of all these restraints, the interest rate prevailing in the *gensaki* market is probably not a true market-clearing rate, and at times the *gensaki* rate has been lower than the bill-discount rate.

Lastly, the Tokyo dollar call market remains subject to substantial restrictions. The market is closed to nonresidents and to nonbanks. In addition, the existence of a withholding tax on the interest earnings from these balances and lack of completely free convertibility of the yen have hindered the development of this market.

Despite all these restrictions, there has clearly been progress since 1978 in freeing up the transactions—and hence the rates—in the money market, as indicated earlier. One encouraging aspect of this trend is that the government has begun to use a tender system for its bond issues. There is consequently some hope that short-term government securities will eventually be issued at true market rates. Since 1979, various observers have tended increasingly to draw a distinction in Japan between administered and nonadministered interest rates.[9] It would appear unlikely that in the near future the authorities will be able to shift very many interest rates from the administered to the nonadministered (that is, relatively free) category.

The general trend in recent years has been one of decreasing intervention and control of the money market by the authorities. There has even been a partial liberalization of the bond market.[10] In some markets, such as the Tokyo dollar call market, there has not been any market intervention by the Bank of Japan. However, the Bank of Japan continues to exercise some control over the money market through its open-market operations in the bill-discount market. But compared to the situation in the early 1970s, the money market is now substantially freer than it was at that time.

**An Action Program for Further Development
of the Market**

There are a substantial number of actions that the Japanese authorities could take to further develop the money market. These include expanding the variety of instruments available, making the terms more flexible, developing appropriate secondary markets, opening up the money market to a wider group of participants, and establishing a bona fide offshore market in Eurocurrencies.

Nonfinancial businesses especially need access to additional types of money-market instruments. These could include commercial-paper, bankers' acceptance, and short-term government instruments yielding market rates of interest such as treasury bills, short-term municipals, and short-term agency-type securities. In addition, the bills of exchange traded in the bill-discount market should not be confined to trade bills, but should be expanded to include bills that finance services. Also, the bill-discount market should be broadened to include export and import bills and not just domestic bills.

Some of the terms for the various money-market instruments could be made more flexible, thereby improving their attractiveness to potential investors. For example, the maturities for the NCDs could be shortened so that they are similar to those in the money markets of other major industrial countries. In addition, the minimum NCD denomination could be reduced, particularly in view of the very high minimum now prevailing, namely, ¥500 million, or about $2 million. Also, in the bill-discount market, the minimum one-month holding period before purchasers can sell their bills could be substantially reduced or possibly eliminated.

Another area meriting attention is the development of secondary markets in Japan's money market. Many purchasers of money-market instruments tend to hold them to maturity, and this occurs, at times, because of the lack of a well-developed secondary market. In developing secondary markets, it is likely that the securities companies and Tanshi companies could play a useful role.

It would also help in developing the money market if more components of the market could be opened up to nonfinancial businesses and individuals, particularly if new money-market instruments are introduced. At present, the call-money and bill-discount markets are confined to domestic financial institutions, and the NCD market is not appropriate for nonfinancial businesses desiring to borrow short-term funds. Consequently, the borrowing and lending outlets in the money market for nonfinancial businesses and individuals are very limited.

Lastly, Japan could, without too much difficulty, take certain actions to establish a bona fide offshore market in Eurocurrencies, thereby complementing the other components of the money market. In actuality, it is not so much a question of whether Japan will ever establish such an offshore market, but when Japan will establish the market? The main actions that would be appropriate to take include: (1) abolishing any withholding taxes on the earnings from deposits placed in the offshore market, (2) eliminating any reserve requirement against such deposits, (3) opening the offshore market to nonresidents and nonfinancial entities, and (4) allowing completely free convertibility of the yen into other currencies.

The Japanese have been actively investigating the establishment of an offshore market and in the spring of 1982 sent an offshore banking mission to various countries to learn how such markets operate. One of the main problems for the Japanese will be to devise a regulatory framework that will adequately insulate the domestic market from offshore transactions. There is a good possibility that appropriate legislation will be passed sometime during the 1980s.

Likely Future Developments in the Money Market

Forecasting future developments is usually a risky business, but it seems appropriate to offer some educated guesses as to what is likely to happen in Japan's money market in the future.

In a continuation of recent developments, it would appear likely that the Japanese authorities in the future will move toward greater reliance on market forces. Thus, increased use of the tender system for the offering of government securities appears likely, in lieu of having terms dictated by administrative fiat.

It also appears likely that some existing restraints will be relaxed. This could include opening certain components of the money market to a wider group of participants and easing some of the terms. For example, there could be a lowering of the high minimum amount for the issue of individual NCDs and also some shortening of the long minimum maturity of three months for NCDs.

At some time during the 1980s, it is likely that a true offshore market will be established in Japan, the main question being when. As indicated earlier, an offshore banking mission from Japan has already studied other offshore markets and it issued a report in the fall of 1982.[11] Because of a difference of viewpoint, the mission could not agree unanimously on the establishment of a Tokyo offshore Eurocurrency center. The report of the mission therefore contains a statement summarizing the different views of the mission members, as well as a factual description of the offshore markets in New York, London, Singapore, Bahrain, and elsewhere. Should an offshore market be established in Japan, it is likely that this would stimulate the development of secondary markets in Japan's money market.

These, then, are some of the developments that would appear to have a high probability of occurring in the near future. Much less likely are two other developments. One is the establishment of a completely free market in short-term government securities, such as in food bills, foreign-exchange-fund bills, and treasury bills. The Ministry of Finance is very reluctant to pay true market rates on these bills; hence any change in this area would appear to be at least several years away, if not longer.

The second development that is also not likely to occur soon is the introduction of new money-market instruments, such as bankers' acceptances or commercial paper similar to that issued in the U.S. commercial-paper market. However, as the volume of consumer financing grows in Japan, pressures may well build to establish a commercial-paper market in order to tap nonbank sources of funds for financing expenditures by consumers.

In summary, Japan's money market, as measured by total funds outstanding, grew at a relatively rapid rate in the 1950s and 1960s. However, there was virtually no change in the types of money-market instruments available during this period. This situation changed in the 1970s when several new money-market instruments were introduced and official control of the market was relaxed in the late 1970s. Overall growth of the market was also relatively rapid in the 1970s.

At present, the market is freer and more diversified than in the 1950s and early 1960s. However, there is still ample room for further development—both by broadening the market to include the participation of more nonfinancial institutions and by introducing a wider variety of money-market instruments. While progress in these two areas appears unlikely in the very near future, some progress in the late 1980s and 1990s does appear likely.

Notes

1. See table 7–4.

2. See, for example, table 7 (3) of *Economic Statistics Annual,* Bank of Japan, Tokyo, March 1982, p. 17.

3. *Flow of Funds Accounts in Japan: 1964–71,* Bank of Japan, Tokyo, December 1972, p. 38.

4. *Economic Statistics Annual,* Bank of Japan, Tokyo, March 1982, p. 31.

5. According to a 1979 report, the Bank of Japan has discouraged foreign-branch banks from borrowing in the money market during periods of monetary restraint and has also imposed ceilings on interbank loans to foreign banks. See *Report to Congress on Foreign Government Treatment of United States Commercial Banking Organizations,* Department of the Treasury, Washington, D.C., 1979, p. 289.

6. Donal Curtin, "What the Rising Yen Means for Tokyo," *Euromoney,* London, September 1982, p. 186.

7. Andreas R. Prindl, *Japanese Finance: A Guide to Banking in Japan,* John Wiley and Sons, New York, 1981, p. 101.

8. Eric W. Hayden, "Internationalizing Japan's Financial System," Stanford University, December 1980, p. 6. See also Stephen Bronte, *Japanese Finance: Markets and Institutions,* Euromoney Publications, London, 1982, p. 144.

9. See chapter 10.

10. See chapter 9.

11. *World Financial Centres: Report of the Offshore Banking Survey Mission '82,* Institute for Financial Affairs, Inc., Tokyo, October 1982.

Appendix

Figure 10.1. Money-Market Rates, 1952–1971

1. *Call-Loan Rate:* The average of typical lenders' rates for unconditional (that is, repayable on one day's notice) loans as recorded on every business day in the month. From 1952 through 1968 the rate is for the mode; beginning in 1969 the rate is the average of the daily rates. Sources: Bank of Japan monthly and annual statistical publications; *Interest Rates: 1960–1974,* Organization for Economic Cooperation and Development, Paris, 1976.

2. *Bank of Japan Discount Rate:* The basic discount rate of the central bank. It is normally the discount rate for commercial bills and the rate to borrowers from the Bank of Japan on loans secured by government bonds, specially designated securities and bills corresponding to commercial bills. Source: *Economic Statistics Annual* of the Bank of Japan.

3. *Gensaki Rate:* The rate shown is the mid-point of the monthly trading range of *gensaki* rates. Source: Estimates made by the Nomura Securities Co., Ltd.

Figure 10–2. Money-Market Rates, 1971–1982

1. *Call-Loan Rate:* The average of lenders' unconditional, or central, rates. It is the simple arithmetic average rate of the business days (that is actual transaction days) during the month. Sources: *Economic Statistics Annual* and *Economic Statistics Monthly* of the Bank of Japan.

2. *Bank of Japan Discount Rate:* The same as in figure 10–1.

3. *Gensaki Rate:* Same as in figure 10–1 through January 1977. Beginning in February 1977, the rate is the average rate for three-month repurchase transactions. Sources: *Bond Review,* Nomura Securities Co., Ltd. and *Economic Statistics Monthly* of the Bank of Japan.

4. *Bill-Discount Rate:* The average rate shown is the simple arithmetic average rate for each of the business days during the month. Starting with the June 1978 figure, the rate shown is for *usual of bills* rather than *resale of bills.* Starting in December 1978, the rate shown is for an *over-two-months* maturity. Starting in October 1979, the rate is the midpoint between the month's low and high for bills on a *new-purchase basis.* Starting in October 1980, the rate shown is for a *two-month-period* and is an average.

5. *NCD Rate:* This rate is measured on the basis of new deposits. It is an average based on the weighted arithmetic average of new issues classified according to interest rates. Sources: *Economic Statistics Annual* and *Economic Statistics Monthly* of the Bank of Japan.

Bibliography

Adams, Thomas F.M., and Hoshii, Iwao. *A Financial History of the New Japan.* Tokyo: Kodansha International Ltd., 1972.

Banking System in Japan. Tokyo: Federation of Bankers' Associations of Japan, 1976 and 1982.

Borsuk, Mark. "How the Gensaki Market Works." London: *Euromoney,* May 1978, pp. 86–94.

Bronte, Stephen. *Japanese Finance: Markets and Institutions.* London: Euromoney Publications, Ltd., 1982.

Dufey, Gunter, and Giddy, Ian H. *The International Money Market.* Englewood Cliffs, N.J.: Prentice-Hall, 1978.

Ezekiel, Hannan. "The Call Money Market in Japan." Washington, D.C.: *IMF Staff Papers,* International Monetary Fund, March 1966, pp. 26–51.

"General Features of the Recent Interest Rate Changes." Tokyo: Bank of Japan, Special Paper No. 91, December 1980.

Gensaki Manual. Tokyo: Nomura Securities Co., Ltd., May 1977.

Haitani, Kanji. *The Japanese Economic System: An Institutional Overview.* Lexington, Mass.: Lexington Books, D.C. Heath & Co., 1976.

Hayden, Eric W. "Internationalizing Japan's Financial System." Palo Alto, Calif.: Stanford University, Occasional Paper of the N.E. Asia-U.S. Forum on International Policy, December 1980.

Ishida, Sadao. "The Tokyo Money Markets." London: *The Banker,* October 1972, pp. 1329–1333.

Japanese Banking. London: The Financial Times Business Publishing, Ltd., Banker Research Unit, 1981.

The Japanese Financial System. Tokyo: Bank of Japan, 1972 and 1978.

"The Japanese Gensaki Market." Tokyo: Nomura Securities Co., Ltd., 1981.

"Japan's Money Markets." Tokyo: *Tokyo Financial Review,* Bank of Tokyo, March 1977, pp. 1–2.

"Japan's Short-Term Money Market: Its Present State and Problems." Tokyo: *Monthly Review,* Mitsui Bank, October 1977.

Kemp, Lynette J. *A Guide to World Money and Capital Markets.* London: McGraw-Hill Book Company (U.K.) Ltd., 1981.

"The Liberalization of Interest Rates in Japan." Tokyo: *Tokyo Financial Review,* Bank of Tokyo, December 1980, pp. 1–3.

"Manual of the Tokyo Foreign Exchange Market and Tokyo Dollar Call Market." Tokyo: Tokyo Foreign Exchange Market Practice Committee, 10 January 1975.

Money Market in Japan and Tanshi Companies. Tokyo: Yamane Tanshi Co., Ltd., April 1977 and March 1980.

Monroe, Wilbur F. *Japan: Financial Markets and the World Economy.* New York: Praeger Publishers, 1973.

Monroe, Wilbur F. "The Rise of Tokyo as an International Financial Center." Twickenham, England: *Journal of World Trade Law,* November/December 1974, pp. 655–667.

Prindl, Andreas R. *Japanese Finance: A Guide to Banking in Japan.* New York: John Wiley & Sons, 1981.

Report to Congress on Foreign Government Treatment of United States Commercial Banking Organizations. Washington, D.C.: U.S. Treasury Department, 1979.

Takayamagi, Tomizo. "Recent Trends in the Short-Term Loan Market in Japan." Tokyo: *Quarterly Five Banks Review,* October 1975, pp. 6–14.

Wallich, Henry C., and Wallich, Mable I. "Banking and Finance." In *Asia's New Giant: How the Japanese Economy Works.* Washington, D.C.: The Brookings Institution, 1976.

World Financial Centres: Report of the Offshore Banking Survey Mission '82. Tokyo: Institute for Financial Affairs Inc., October 1982.

Index

137

About the Author

Robert F. Emery received the B.A. in economics from Oberlin College and the Ph.D. in economics from the University of Michigan. Since 1955 he has been an international economist with the Board of Governors of the Federal Reserve System, specializing in the economies of East Asia. He has also served since 1960 as adjunct professor of finance at Southeastern University in Washington, D.C. Dr. Emery is the author of more than a dozen articles—mostly on the economic and financial problems of the East Asian countries—and is also the author of *The Financial Institutions of Southeast Asia* (1971).